Foundations of Risk Management and Insurance

Foundations of Risk Management and Insurance

Edited by
Arthur L. Flitner, CPCU, ARM

1st Edition • 4th Printing

The Institutes
720 Providence Road, Suite 100
Malvern, Pennsylvania 19355-3433

Foreword

The Institutes are the trusted leader in delivering proven knowledge solutions that drive powerful business results for the risk management and property-casualty insurance industry. For more than 100 years, The Institutes have been meeting the industry's changing professional development needs with customer-driven products and services.

In conjunction with industry experts and members of the academic community, our Knowledge Resources Department develops our course and program content, including Institutes study materials. Practical and technical knowledge gained from Institutes courses enhances qualifications, improves performance, and contributes to professional growth—all of which drive results.

The Institutes' proven knowledge helps individuals and organizations achieve powerful results with a variety of flexible, customer-focused options:

Recognized Credentials—The Institutes offer an unmatched range of widely recognized and industry-respected specialty credentials. The Institutes' Chartered Property Casualty Underwriter (CPCU) professional designation is designed to provide a broad understanding of the property-casualty insurance industry. Depending on professional needs, CPCU students may select either a commercial insurance focus or a personal risk management and insurance focus and may choose from a variety of electives.

In addition, The Institutes offer certificate or designation programs in a variety of disciplines, including these:

- Claims
- Commercial underwriting
- Fidelity and surety bonding
- General insurance
- Insurance accounting and finance
- Insurance information technology
- Insurance production and agency management
- Insurance regulation and compliance

- Management
- Marine insurance
- Personal insurance
- Premium auditing
- Quality insurance services
- Reinsurance
- Risk management
- Surplus lines

Ethics—Ethical behavior is crucial to preserving not only the trust on which insurance transactions are based, but also the public's trust in our industry as a whole. All Institutes designations now have an ethics requirement, which is delivered online and free of charge. The ethics requirement content is designed specifically for insurance practitioners and uses insurance-based case studies to outline an ethical framework. More information is available in the Programs section of our Web site, www.TheInstitutes.org.

Flexible Online Learning—The Institutes have an unmatched variety of technical insurance content covering topics from accounting to underwriting, which we now deliver through hundreds of online courses. These cost-effective self-study courses are a convenient way to fill gaps in technical knowledge in a matter of hours without ever leaving the office.

Continuing Education—A majority of The Institutes' courses are filed for CE credit in most states. We also deliver quality, affordable, online CE courses quickly and conveniently through our newest business unit, CEU.com. Visit www.CEU.com to learn more.

College Credits—Most Institutes courses carry college credit recommendations from the American Council on Education. A variety of courses also qualify for credits toward certain associate, bachelor's, and master's degrees at several prestigious colleges and universities. More information is available in the Student Services section of our Web site, www.TheInstitutes.org.

Custom Applications—The Institutes collaborate with corporate customers to utilize our trusted course content and flexible delivery options in developing customized solutions that help them achieve their unique organizational goals.

Insightful Analysis—Our Insurance Research Council (IRC) division conducts public policy research on important contemporary issues in property-casualty insurance and risk management. Visit www.ircweb.org to learn more or purchase its most recent studies.

The Institutes look forward to serving the risk management and property-casualty insurance industry for another 100 years. We welcome comments from our students and course leaders; your feedback helps us continue to improve the quality of our study materials.

Peter L. Miller, CPCU
President and CEO
The Institutes

Preface

Foundations of Risk Management and Insurance is the assigned textbook for CPCU 500, designed to serve as the first course in the Chartered Property Casualty Underwriter (CPCU®) designation program.

The goals of CPCU 500 are to enable you to understand and apply basic concepts of risk management and insurance, to comprehend insurance within the larger context of risk management, and to learn a systematic approach for analyzing property-liability insurance policies. Each assignment of the text-book supports one or more of those goals.

Assignment 1, Introduction to Risk Management, provides an overview of risk and risk management, including the benefits of risk management, risk management goals, and the risk management process.

Assignment 2, Risk Assessment, explains how to use various methods for identifying and analyzing loss exposures, including probability and statistical analysis.

Assignment 3, Risk Control, examines risk control techniques (which reduce the frequency and/or severity of losses or make losses more predictable) and how to select risk control techniques that are appropriate for meeting an organization's risk control goals.

Assignment 4, Risk Financing, examines risk financing techniques (which generate the funds to pay for losses) and how to select risk financing techniques that are appropriate for meeting an organization's risk financing goals.

Assignment 5, Enterprise-Wide Risk Management, explains how the emerging discipline of enterprise-wide risk management (ERM) expands upon and enhances the traditional approach to risk management.

Assignment 6, Insurance as a Risk Management Technique, examines how pooling reduces risk, the benefits of insurance, the characteristics of insurable loss exposures, and the role of government insurance programs.

Assignment 7, Insurance Policy Analysis, considers the characteristics and structure of insurance policies, the different categories of policy provisions, and the primary methods of analyzing an insurance policy.

Assignment 8, Common Policy Concepts, explains basic concepts affecting property-casualty insurance policies, including insurable interest, insurance to value, valuation methods, the use of deductibles or retentions, and alternative sources of recovery.

The persons who participated in developing this edition of the text are acknowledged on the Contributors page.

For more information about The Institutes' programs, please call our Customer Service Department at (800) 644-2101, e-mail us at customerservice@TheInstitutes.org, or visit our Web site at www.TheInstitutes.org.

Arthur L. Flitner

Contributors

The Institutes acknowledge with deep appreciation the contributions made to the content of this text by the following persons:

Richard Berthelsen, JD, MBA, CPCU, AIC, AU, ARe, ARM

Pamela J. Brooks, MBA, CPCU, AAM, AIM, AIS

Jacqueline Lorince, AIM, AIS

Pamela Lyons, BA, FCIP, CRM

Ann E. Myhr, CPCU, ARM, AU, AIM, ASLI

Charles Nyce, PhD, CPCU, ARM

Contents

Direct Your Learning ▶▶

Introduction to Risk Management

Educational Objectives

After learning the content of this assignment, you should be able to:

▷ Describe each of the following in the context of risk:

- Uncertainty
- Possibility
- Possibility compared with probability

▷ Explain how the following classifications of risk apply and how they help in risk management:

- Pure and speculative risk
- Subjective and objective risk
- Diversifiable and nondiversifiable risk
- Quadrants of risk (hazard, operational, financial, and strategic)

▷ Describe the three financial consequences of risk.

▷ Describe the basic purpose and scope of risk management in terms of the following:

- How risk management is practiced by individuals and organizations
- The basic distinction between traditional risk management and enterprise-wide risk management

▷ Describe the following elements for property, liability, personnel, and net income loss exposures:

- Assets exposed to loss
- Causes of loss, including associated hazards
- Financial consequences of loss

▷ Describe the benefits of risk management and how it reduces the financial consequences of risk for individuals, organizations, and society.

▶▶

1

Educational Objectives, continued

▶ Summarize pre-loss and post-loss risk management program goals and the conflicts that can arise as they are implemented.

▶ Describe each of the steps in the risk management process.

Introduction to Risk Management

UNDERSTANDING AND QUANTIFYING RISK

Although risk may intuitively seem undesirable, it can yield both positive and negative outcomes. Opportunities cannot be pursued, and reward cannot be obtained, without incurring some risk. Because of this risk/reward relationship, individuals and organizations seek to maximize reward while minimizing the associated risk. Risk management helps individuals and organizations to avoid, prevent, reduce, or pay for the negative outcomes of risk so that opportunities for reward can be pursued. Understanding and quantifying risk are the logical starting point for learning how to use risk management.

Risk is a term regularly used by individuals in both their personal and professional lives and is generally understood in context. However, properly defining risk is often difficult because it can have many different meanings. As used in this discussion, risk is defined as the uncertainty about outcomes, with the possibility that some of the outcomes can be negative. Risk can be quantified by knowing the probability of the possible outcomes. See the exhibit "Industry Language—Risk."

Industry Language—Risk

Risk can be used in many contexts in risk management and insurance and can have any of the following meanings:

- The subject matter of an insurance policy, such as a structure, an auto fleet, or the possibility of a liability claim arising from an insured's activities

- The insurance applicant (the insured)

- The possibility of bodily injury or property damage

- A cause of loss (or peril), such as fire, lightning, or explosion

- The variability associated with a future outcome

[DA02845]

Uncertainty and Possibility

The two elements within the definition of risk are these:

- Uncertainty of outcome
- Possibility of a negative outcome

First, risk involves uncertainty about the type of outcome (what will actually occur), the timing of the outcome (when the outcome will occur), or both the type and timing of the outcome. Consider an individual who buys a share of stock in a publicly traded corporation. This individual may experience a positive outcome if the value of the stock increases or a negative outcome if the value of the stock decreases. The timing of either outcome is uncertain because the individual does not know if or when the stock price is going to change or what the new stock price will be. Whether uncertainty involves what will actually happen, when something will happen, or both, it results from the inability to accurately predict the future.

Second, risk involves the possibility of a negative outcome. Possibility means that an outcome or event may or may not occur. The fact that something may occur does not mean that it will occur. For example, it is possible that an individual may be injured while driving to or from work, loading a truck at work, moving some furniture at home, or falling in an icy parking lot at the mall. However, the possibility that these events may occur does not mean that they will occur. Nonetheless, because of the possibility of a negative outcome (injury), risk exists.

Possibility and Probability

The possibility that something may occur does not indicate its likelihood of occurring. Possibility does not quantify risk; it only verifies that risk is present. To quantify risk, one needs to know the **probability** of the outcome or event occurring.

Probability

The likelihood that an outcome or event will occur.

Unlike possibility, probability is measurable and has a value between zero and one. If an event is not possible, it has a probability of zero, whereas if an event is certain, it has a probability of one. If an event is possible, but not certain, its probability is some value between zero and one. Probabilities can be stated as a decimal figure (.4), a percentage (40 percent), or a fraction (four-tenths or two-fifths).

To help understand the difference between possibility and probability, consider the possibility that an individual will be injured in an auto accident while driving to or from work tomorrow. That person will not necessarily be injured in an auto accident tomorrow, and the fact that it is possible does not give any indication of its likelihood. The risk exists and has simply been identified.

Contrast this with there being a 5 percent probability that the same individual will be injured in an auto accident while driving to or from work tomorrow. This statement not only indicates that it is possible the individual will be injured tomorrow, it gives the likelihood. The risk has now been not only identified but also quantified.

Understanding the probability of various outcomes helps focus risk management attention on those risks that can be appropriately managed. Probability can also be used to help decide which activities (and associated risks) to undertake and which risk management techniques to use.

In the previous example:

- If the probability of injury while driving to or from work was 5 percent, and the probability of injury if the individual took the train to work was 1 percent, the individual may decide to take the train.
- However, if the risk of auto injury was reduced to 1 percent by driving a car with airbags and antilock brakes, and if it was more convenient and quicker to drive, then the individual may decide (cost permitting) to buy a new car with airbags and antilock brakes and then drive to work.

RISK CLASSIFICATIONS

Classifying the various types of risk can help an organization understand and manage its risks. The categories should align with an organization's objectives and risk management goals.

Classification can help with assessing risks, because many risks in the same classification have similar attributes. It also can help with managing risk, because many risks in the same classification can be managed with similar techniques. Finally, classification helps with the administrative function of risk management by helping to ensure that risks in the same classification are less likely to be overlooked.

These classifications of risk are some of the most commonly used:

- Pure and speculative risk
- Subjective and objective risk
- Diversifiable and nondiversifiable risk
- Quadrants of risk (hazard, operational, financial, and strategic)

These classifications are not mutually exclusive and can be applied to any given risk.

Pure and Speculative Risk

A **pure risk** is a chance of loss or no loss, but no chance of gain. For example, the owner of a commercial building faces the risk associated with a possible fire loss. The building will either burn or not burn. If the building burns, the owner suffers a financial loss. If the building does not burn, the owner's financial condition is unchanged. Neither of the possible outcomes would produce

Pure risk

A chance of loss or no loss, but no chance of gain.

a gain. Because there is no opportunity for financial gain, pure risks are always undesirable. See the exhibit "Classifications of Risk."

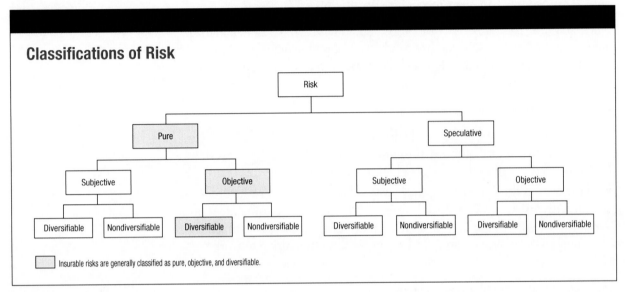

Classifications of Risk

Insurable risks are generally classified as pure, objective, and diversifiable.

[DA02396]

Speculative risk

A chance of loss, no loss, or gain.

In comparison, **speculative risk** involves a chance of gain. As a result, it can be desirable, as evidenced by the fact that every business venture involves speculative risks. For example, an investor who purchases an apartment building to rent to tenants expects to profit from this investment, so it is a desirable speculative risk. However, the venture could be unprofitable if rental price controls limit the amount of rent that can be charged.

Certain businesses involve speculative risks, such as these:

- Price risk—Uncertainty over the size of cash flows resulting from possible changes in the cost of raw materials and other inputs (such as lumber, gas, or electricity), as well as cost-related changes in the market for completed products and other outputs.

Credit risk

The risk that customers or other creditors will fail to make promised payments as they come due.

- **Credit risk**—Although a credit risk is particularly significant for banks and other financial institutions, it can be relevant to any organization with accounts receivable.

Financial investments, such as the purchase of stock shares, involve a distinct set of speculative risks. See the exhibit "Speculative Risks in Investments."

Insurance deals primarily with risks of loss, not risks of gain; that is, with pure risks rather than speculative risks. However, the distinction between these two classifications of risk is not always precise—many risks have both pure and speculative aspects.

Distinguishing between pure and speculative risks is important because those risks must often be managed differently. For example, although a commercial

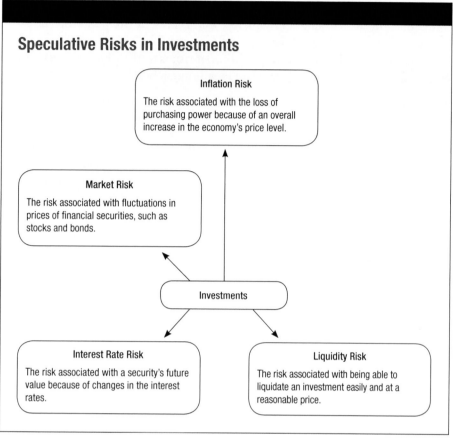

Speculative Risks in Investments

Inflation Risk
The risk associated with the loss of purchasing power because of an overall increase in the economy's price level.

Market Risk
The risk associated with fluctuations in prices of financial securities, such as stocks and bonds.

Investments

Interest Rate Risk
The risk associated with a security's future value because of changes in the interest rates.

Liquidity Risk
The risk associated with being able to liquidate an investment easily and at a reasonable price.

[DA02398]

building owner faces a pure risk from causes of loss such as fire, he or she also faces the speculative risk that the market value of the building will increase or decrease during any one year. Similarly, although an investor who purchases an apartment building to rent to tenants faces speculative risk because rental income may produce a profit or loss, the investor also faces a pure risk from causes of loss such as fire.

To properly manage these investments, the commercial building owner and the apartment owner must consider both the speculative and the pure risks. For example, they may choose to manage the pure risk by buying insurance or taking other measures to address property loss exposures. The speculative risk might be managed by obtaining a favorable mortgage and maintaining the property to enhance its resale value.

Subjective and Objective Risk

When individuals and organizations must make a decision that involves risk, they usually base it on the individual's or organization's assessment of the risk. The assessment can be based on opinions, which are subjective, or facts, which are objective.

Subjective risk
The perceived amount of risk based on an individual's or organization's opinion.

Objective risk
The measurable variation in uncertain outcomes based on facts and data.

Because it is based on opinion rather than fact, **subjective risk** may be quite different from the actual underlying risk that is present. In fact, subjective risk can exist even where **objective risk** does not. The closer an individual's or organization's subjective interpretation of risk is to the objective risk, the more effective its risk management plan will likely be.

The reasons that subjective and objective risk can differ substantially include these:

- Familiarity and control—For example, although many people consider air travel (over which they have no control) to carry a high degree of risk, they are much more likely to suffer a serious injury when driving their cars, where the perception of control is much greater.

- Consequences over likelihood—People often have two views of low-likelihood, high-consequence events. The first misconception is the "It can't happen to me" view, which assigns a probability of zero to low-likelihood events such as natural disasters, murder, fires, accidents, and so on. The second misconception is overstating the probability of a low-likelihood event, which is common for people who have personally been exposed to the event previously. If the effect of a particular event can be severe, such as the potentially destructive effects of a hurricane or earthquake, the perception of the likelihood of deaths resulting from such an event is heightened. This perception may be enhanced by the increased media coverage given to high-severity events.

- Risk awareness—Organizations differ in terms of their level of risk awareness and, therefore, perceive risks differently. An organization that is not aware of its risks would perceive the likelihood of something happening as very low.

Both risk management and insurance depend on the ability to objectively identify and analyze risks. However, subjectivity is also necessary because facts are often not available to objectively assess risk.

Diversifiable and Nondiversifiable Risk

Diversifiable risk
A risk that affects only some individuals, businesses, or small groups.

Diversifiable risk is not highly correlated and can be managed through diversification, or spread, of risk. An example of a diversifiable risk is a fire, which is likely to affect only one or a small number of businesses. For instance, an insurer can diversify the risks associated with fire insurance by insuring many buildings in several different locations. Similarly, business investors often diversify their holdings, as opposed to investing in only one business, hoping those that succeed will more than offset those that fail.

Examples of nondiversifiable risks include inflation, unemployment, and natural disasters such as hurricanes. Nondiversifiable risks are correlated—that is, their gains or losses tend to occur simultaneously rather than randomly. For example, under certain monetary conditions, interest rates increase for all firms at the same time. If an insurer were to insure firms against interest rate increases, it would not be able to diversify its portfolio of interest rate risks by underwriting a large number of insureds, because all of them would suffer losses at the same time.

Systemic risks are generally nondiversifiable. For example, if excess leverage by financial institutions causes systemic risk resulting in an event that disrupts the financial system, this risk will have an effect on the entire economy and, therefore, on all organizations. Because of the global interconnections in finance and industry, many risks that were once viewed as nonsystemic (affecting only one organization) are now viewed as systemic. For instance, many economists view the failure of Lehman Brothers in early 2008 as a trigger event: highlighting the systemic risk in the banking sector that resulted in the financial crisis. Not understanding the systemic nature of risk posed by the securitization of mortgage obligations was at the root of AIG's risk management failure in writing a large number of collateralized debt obligations to back the securitizations—the high correlation and systemic risk were not recognized or managed.

> **Systemic risk**
> The potential for a major disruption in the function of an entire market or financial system.

Quadrants of Risk: Hazard, Operational, Financial, and Strategic

Although no consensus exists about how an organization should categorize its risks, one approach involves dividing them into risk quadrants:

- Hazard risks arise from property, liability, or personnel loss exposures and are generally the subject of insurance.

- Operational risks fall outside the hazard risk category and arise from people or a failure in processes, systems, or controls, including those involving information technology.

- Financial risks arise from the effect of market forces on financial assets or liabilities and include **market risk**, credit risk, **liquidity risk**, and price risk.

- Strategic risks arise from trends in the economy and society, including changes in the economic, political, and competitive environments, as well as from demographic shifts.

Hazard and operational risks are classified as pure risks, and financial and strategic risks are classified as speculative risks.

The focus of the risk quadrants is different from the risk classifications previously discussed. Whereas the classifications of risk focus on some aspect of the risk itself, the four quadrants of risk focus on the **risk source** and who traditionally manages it. For example, the chief financial officer traditionally manages financial risk, and the risk manager traditionally manages hazard risk. Just as a particular risk can fall into more than one classification, a risk can also fall into multiple risk quadrants. For example, embezzlement of funds by an employee can be considered both a hazard risk, because it is an insurable

> **Market risk**
> Uncertainty about an investment's future value because of potential changes in the market for that type of investment.
>
> **Liquidity risk**
> The risk that an asset cannot be sold on short notice without incurring a loss.
>
> **Risk source (ISO 31000)**
> Element which alone or in combination has the intrinsic potential to give rise to risk.

pure risk, and an operational risk, because it involves a failure of controls. See the exhibit "Risk Quadrants."

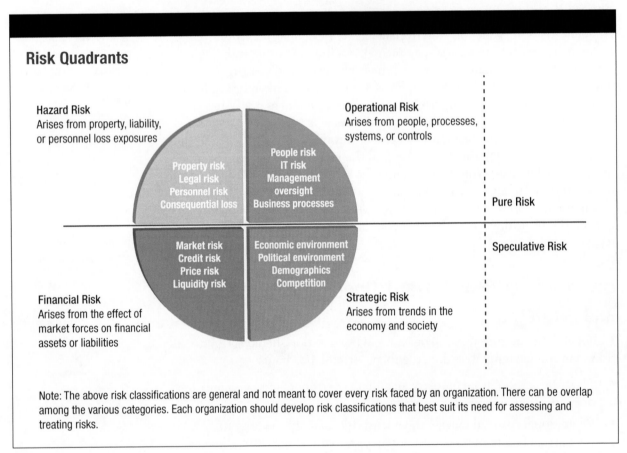

Risk Quadrants

Hazard Risk
Arises from property, liability, or personnel loss exposures

Property risk
Legal risk
Personnel risk
Consequential loss

Operational Risk
Arises from people, processes, systems, or controls

People risk
IT risk
Management oversight
Business processes

Pure Risk

Market risk
Credit risk
Price risk
Liquidity risk

Economic environment
Political environment
Demographics
Competition

Speculative Risk

Financial Risk
Arises from the effect of market forces on financial assets or liabilities

Strategic Risk
Arises from trends in the economy and society

Note: The above risk classifications are general and not meant to cover every risk faced by an organization. There can be overlap among the various categories. Each organization should develop risk classifications that best suit its need for assessing and treating risks.

[DA08677]

Organizations define types of risk differently. Some organizations consider legal risks as operational risk, and some may characterize certain hazard risks as operational risk. Financial institutions generally use the categories of market, credit, and operational risk (defined as all other risk, including hazard risk). Each organization should select categories that align with its objectives and processes.

Apply Your Knowledge

The New Company manufactures electronic consumer products. The company's manufacturing plant is highly automated and located in the United States. However, it purchases components from three companies in Asia. The majority of its sales are in the U.S., but European sales represent a growing percentage.

Describe the types of risk New Company would have in each of the four risk quadrants.

Feedback: In the hazard risk quadrant, New Company would have property damage risks to its plant and equipment resulting from fire, storms, or other events. It would also have risk of injury to its employees and liability risks associated with its products.

In the operational risk quadrant, New Company would have risks from employee turnover or the inability to find skilled employees. It would also have business process risk related to how it manages its supply chain and information technology risk related to its automated manufacturing process.

In the financial risk quadrant, New Company would have exchange rate risk related to its European sales. It would also have price risk for raw materials and supplies.

Strategic risks include competition, economic factors that could affect consumer demand, and the political risk arising from countries in which the company's component suppliers are located.

FINANCIAL CONSEQUENCES OF RISK

Although it may be difficult to precisely calculate the financial consequences of risk, by considering all of its components and at least estimating its financial consequences, an individual or organization is better able to determine where to focus risk management efforts.

The financial consequences of risk faced by individuals or organizations can be broken into three components:

- Expected cost of losses or gains
- Expenditures on risk management
- Cost of residual uncertainty

Expected Cost of Losses or Gains

The first financial consequence of risk is the expected cost of losses or gains. In his seminal work on calculating the expected cost of losses or gains, Herbert W. Heinrich discussed the cost of one specific risk, the cost of risk associated with industrial accidents (pure risk).[1] Industrial accidents can demonstrate the various costs that need to be accounted for when determining expected costs of losses.

Heinrich observed that not only do industrial accidents include the cost of the compensation paid to the injured employee, but they also include other, hidden costs, including these:

- Time lost by the injured employee
- Time lost by other employees who stop work

- Time lost by foremen, supervisors, or other executives
- Time spent on the case by first-aid attendants and hospital department staff (when not paid for by the insurer)
- Damage to the machine, tools, or other property or the spoilage of material
- Interference with production, failure to fill orders on time, loss of bonuses, payment of forfeits, and other similar causes of loss
- Continuation of the injured employee's wages in full after the employee's return to work—even though the employee's services may temporarily be worth less than normal value
- Loss of profit on the injured employee's productivity and on the idle machines
- Lost productivity because of employee excitement or weakened morale resulting from the accident
- Overhead per injured employee, that is, the expense of light, heat, rent, and other items that continue while the injured employee is not productive

Many of these hidden costs are indirect costs and are more difficult to measure than direct accident costs. Consequently, the overall effect of losses is much greater than the direct losses themselves. Therefore, it is important to identify and try to assign a value to hidden costs in order to get a reasonably accurate view of expected costs.

Calculating the expected cost of losses or gains for speculative risks is more complex than calculating pure risk. For example, suppose a manufacturer was considering adding a second plant to its production facilities. The manufacturer would have to consider all of the expected costs associated with all the pure risks of the new plant, including industrial accidents, as well as the costs or gains associated with the speculative risks. Those costs or gains may include the cost of raw materials, the financing costs for the capital to build the plant, the market price at which the manufacturer can sell its goods, or the expected demand for its products. All of these expected costs and/or gains need to be considered with speculative risks.

Expenditures on Risk Management

The second component of the financial consequences of risk is the individual's or organization's expenditures on risk management. The most widely known risk management technique used by individuals is risk financing by purchasing insurance. Homeowners insurance, auto insurance, health insurance, and life insurance are all risk financing measures used by individuals to manage some of the risks they face. Organizations tend to use a wider variety of risk control and risk financing techniques than do individuals. The expenditures on these activities are a financial consequence of risk.

Cost of Residual Uncertainty

The third component of the financial consequences of risk is the cost of residual uncertainty (cost of worry). Residual uncertainty is the level of risk that remains after individuals or organizations implement their risk management plans. This residual uncertainty is also influenced by an individual's or organization's subjective view of the risks to which they are exposed.

For example, if an individual is unduly concerned about a particular risk, he or she may overestimate the frequency or severity of it, resulting in a subjective interpretation of the true objective risk. Residual uncertainty can be minimized, but doing so is costly because more has to be spent on attempts to control or finance the risks involved.

The cost of residual uncertainty may be difficult to measure and is largely ignored in cost of risk studies. However, it may still have a significant effect on the ultimate financial consequences of risk for an individual or organization. For example, because it may be more costly to an employer to hire an employee who is perceived as presenting a high risk (for example, because he or she changes jobs frequently), the employer may not be willing to hire or will not be willing to pay a high salary for such an individual. This lost salary opportunity is the cost of residual uncertainty for the individual.

For organizations, the cost of residual uncertainty includes the effect that uncertainty has on consumers, investors, and suppliers. Consumers may not be willing to pay as much for products from organizations with a poor safety reputation, investors will require a larger rate of return on their investment from riskier organizations, and suppliers will be less willing to sell their supplies on credit to financially unstable organizations.

Individuals and organizations vary greatly as to how much residual uncertainty they are willing to accept. However, differences in willingness to accept uncertainty (risk) are beneficial to society and economic development. It allows different individuals and organizations to pursue a variety of risky activities that may offer substantial rewards, not just for the investors, but also for society as a whole.

BASIC PURPOSE AND SCOPE OF RISK MANAGEMENT

Risk management involves the efforts of individuals or organizations to efficiently and effectively assess, control, and finance risk in order to minimize the adverse effects of losses or missed opportunities.

Individuals practice risk management to protect their limited assets from losses and to help meet personal goals. For an organization, sound risk management adds value and helps to ensure that losses or missed opportunities do not prevent it from meeting its goals. While many organizations have traditionally focused their risk management efforts on pure risk, the emerging discipline of enterprise-wide risk management is focused on managing all of an organization's pure and speculative risks.

Risk Management for Individuals and Organizations

Risk management

The process of making and implementing decisions that will minimize the adverse effects of accidental losses on an organization.

In its simplest form, **risk management** includes any effort to economically deal with uncertainty of outcomes (risk). For individuals, risk management is usually an informal series of efforts, not a formalized process. Individual or personal risk management may be viewed as part of the financial planning process that encompasses broader matters such as capital accumulation, retirement planning, and estate planning.

Individuals and families often practice risk management informally without explicitly following a risk management process. For example, individuals purchase insurance policies to cover accidental or unexpected losses, or they contribute to savings plans so that they have money available to cover unforeseen events.

In smaller organizations, risk management is not usually a dedicated function, but one of many tasks carried out by the owner or senior manager. In many larger organizations, the risk management function is conducted as part of a formalized risk management program. A risk management program is a system for planning, organizing, leading, and controlling the resources and activities that an organization needs to protect itself from the adverse effects of accidental losses.

Most risk management programs are built around the risk management process. The risk management process is the method of making, implementing, and monitoring decisions that minimize the adverse effects of risk on an organization. Although the exact steps in an organization's risk management process may differ from the process discussed in this section, all risk management processes are designed to assess, control, and finance risk.

Traditional Risk Management and Enterprise-Wide Risk Management

Traditionally, the risk management professional's role has been associated with loss exposures related mainly to pure, as opposed to speculative, risks. This view excludes from the scope of risk management all loss exposures that arise from speculative risk, also referred to as business risk. Therefore, organizational risk management has focused on managing safety, purchasing insurance, and controlling financial recovery from losses generated by hazard risk.

Enterprise-wide risk management (ERM) is the term commonly used to describe the broader view of risk management that encompasses all types of risk. ERM is an approach to managing all of an organization's key risks and opportunities with the intent of maximizing the organization's value.

An ERM approach allows an organization to integrate all of its risk management activities so that the risk management process occurs at the enterprise level, rather than at the departmental or business unit level. How ERM is implemented in practice varies significantly among organizations, depending on their size, nature, and complexity.

LOSS EXPOSURES

Individuals and organizations incur losses when assets they own decrease in value. Situations or conditions that expose assets to loss are called loss exposures. In order to effectively manage risk, individuals and organizations must identify all the loss exposures they face.

Every **loss exposure** has three elements:

- An asset exposed to loss
- Cause of loss (also called a peril)
- Financial consequences of that loss

These three elements can be described for each of these four basic types of loss exposures: property loss exposures, liability loss exposures, personnel loss exposures, and net income loss exposures.

Loss exposure
Any condition or situation that presents a possibility of loss, whether or not an actual loss occurs.

Elements of Loss Exposures

The three elements are necessary to completely describe a loss exposure. For example, identifying a building (an asset exposed to loss) is not sufficient for describing that building as a loss exposure. It is also necessary to identify the causes of loss associated with that building (such as fire, flood, or hurricane) and the financial consequences of that loss (such as a decline in the market value of the building or in the income produced by the use of the building).

Asset Exposed to Loss

The first element of a loss exposure is an asset exposed to loss. This asset can be anything of value an individual or organization has that is exposed to loss. Assets owned by organizations can include property (such as buildings, automobiles, and office furniture), investments, money that is owed to them, and cash. In addition to these are assets that are often overlooked, including intangible assets (such as patents, copyrights, and trademarks) and human resources.

Individuals may have many of the same assets as organizations (property, money, investments, and so on). In addition, individuals may have intangible assets such as professional qualifications, a unique skill set, or valuable experience.

Cause of Loss

The second element of a loss exposure is cause of loss. Fire, windstorm, explosion, and theft are examples of causes of loss that present a possibility of loss to property.

Loss exposures and causes of loss that affect them can be influenced by **hazards**. For example, a fire hazard, such as storing oily rags next to a furnace, increases the frequency and/or severity of loss caused by fire. Insurers typically define hazards according to these four classifications:

Hazard

A condition that increases the frequency or severity of a loss.

- Moral hazard
- Morale hazard
- Physical hazard
- Legal hazard

Regardless of whether they are moral, morale, physical, or legal, hazards can have a compounding effect. For example, the loss frequency associated with a safe driver in a safe car is increased by either the physical hazard of an unsafe car or the moral hazard of an unsafe driver. The frequency is further increased by the compound effect of an unsafe driver in an unsafe car. Therefore, risk management and insurance professionals need to carefully monitor any situation that may involve multiple hazards.

Moral hazard

A condition that increases the likelihood that a person will intentionally cause or exaggerate a loss.

Examples of a **moral hazard** include intentionally causing, fabricating, or exaggerating a loss. For example, one moral hazard incentive is financial difficulty. Someone who is facing overwhelming debt might be tempted to intentionally cause a loss in an attempt to profit from the situation and thereby reduce or eliminate the debt.

Purchasing an insurance policy is another moral hazard incentive—some people might be inclined to behave differently once they enter into a contract that shifts the financial consequences of risk to another party. In insurance, this behavior can include filing false claims, inflating a claim on a loss that did occur, or intentionally causing a loss.

Morale hazard (attitudinal hazard)

A condition of carelessness or indifference that increases the frequency or severity of loss.

Driving carelessly, failing to lock an unattended building, or failing to clear an icy sidewalk to protect pedestrians are examples of **morale hazard**.

Both moral and morale hazards are behavior problems that can increase the frequency and/or severity of losses. The fundamental difference between these two types of hazard is intent. A moral hazard results from a deliberate act; a morale hazard results from carelessness or indifference.

Physical hazard

A tangible characteristic of property, persons, or operations that tends to increase the frequency or severity of loss.

A **physical hazard** is a condition of property, persons, or operations that increases the frequency and/or severity of loss. For example, a slip-and-fall accident is more likely to occur on an icy sidewalk, a fire is more likely to start in a building with defective wiring, and an explosion is more likely to occur in a painting area that has inadequate ventilation. Inadequate ventilation may also create environmental problems for workers and therefore increase the frequency and/or severity of workers compensation claims.

A **legal hazard** is a condition of the legal environment that increases the frequency and/or severity of loss. For example, courts in some geographic areas are much more likely to find in favor of the plaintiff or to grant large damages awards in liability cases than are courts in other areas. Various trends can also be legal hazards. For example, an increasing number of decisions against tobacco manufacturers would present a legal hazard for companies participating in the tobacco industry.

> **Legal hazard**
> A condition of the legal environment that increases loss frequency or severity.

Financial Consequences of Loss

The third element of loss exposures is the financial consequences of the loss. The financial consequences of a loss depend on the type of loss exposure, the cause of loss, and the loss frequency and severity. Some financial consequences can be established with a high degree of certainty; for example, the value of a building that has been damaged by fire.

Other financial consequences may be more difficult to determine, such as the value of business lost while the building damaged by fire is being restored. In addition, although some financial consequences are known as soon as a loss occurs, such as the value of property lost in a robbery, others may take months or years to determine, such as the ultimate value of liability claims regarding a defective product.

Types of Loss Exposures

For insurance and traditional risk management purposes, loss exposures are typically divided into these four types:

- Property loss exposures
- Liability loss exposures
- Personnel loss exposures
- Net income loss exposures

The three elements of loss exposures apply to each of these four types. However, each type is distinguished in relation to how it affects the first element of a loss exposure, that is, the asset exposed to loss.

> **Property loss exposure**
> A condition that presents the possibility that a person or an organization will sustain a loss resulting from damage (including destruction, taking, or loss of use) to property in which that person or organization has a financial interest.

Property Loss Exposures

A **property loss exposure** is a condition that presents the possibility that a person or an organization will sustain a loss resulting from damage (including destruction, taking, or loss of use) to property in which that person or organization has a financial interest. Property can be categorized as either tangible property or intangible property.

Tangible property
Property that has a physical form.

Real property (realty)
Tangible property consisting of land, all structures permanently attached to the land, and whatever is growing on the land.

Personal property
All tangible or intangible property that is not real property.

Intangible property
Property that has no physical form.

Tangible property is property that has a physical form, such as a piece of equipment. Tangible property can be further subdivided into **real property** and **personal property**. **Intangible property** is property that has no physical form, such as a patent or copyright. See the exhibit "Elements of Property Loss Exposures."

Elements of Property Loss Exposures

1. **Asset Exposed to Loss**

    - Tangible property

    - Real property, such as offices and warehouses

    - Personal property, such as office furniture and office equipment

    - Intangible property, such as patents, copyrights, trademarks, trade secrets, and customer goodwill

2. **Cause of Loss**

    Some of the more frequent causes of loss include the following:

    - Lightning or hail

    - Tornadoes or high wind

    - Water from failure of indoor appliances; heavy rain or flooding; or sewers or drains

    - Theft

    - Snow or ice

    - Fire

    - Mold

3. **Financial Consequences of Loss**

    The maximum financial consequence of a property loss is limited by the value of the property. However, a property loss may also have an effect on the financial consequences of liability, personnel, or net income losses.

[DA02384]

Damage to property can cause a reduction in that property's value, sometimes to zero. For example, when property is stolen, the owner suffers a total loss of that property because the owner no longer has use of it. In addition to these losses, property damage can result in a loss of income (net income loss exposure) because the property cannot be used to generate income or because extra expenses are incurred to continue operations.

Liability Loss Exposures

A **liability loss exposure** results from the claim itself, not necessarily the payment of damages. See the exhibit "Industry Language—Property and Liability Loss Exposures."

Liability loss exposure
Any condition or situation that presents the possibility of a claim alleging legal responsibility of a person or business for injury or damage suffered by another party.

Industry Language—Property and Liability Loss Exposures

Property

A property loss occurs when a person or an organization sustains a loss as the result of damage (including destruction, taking, or loss of use) to property in which that person or organization has a financial interest. The possibility that such a situation could occur is a property loss exposure.

Insurance professionals often use the term "loss" to mean the event itself. In addition, they often refer to the loss in terms of the applicable property, the cause of loss, the consequences, or the applicable policy.

- When focusing on the type of property, they often refer to a "building loss" or a "personal property loss," regardless of the peril involved.

- When focusing on causes of loss, they often refer to a "fire loss," a "smoke loss," or a "theft loss."

- When focusing on consequences, they often refer to a "business income loss," an "extra expense loss," or an "additional living expense loss," regardless of the type of property or causes of loss involved.

- When focusing on the applicable policy, they often use the policy name or type, such as a "homeowners loss," "auto loss," or "business interruption loss."

Similar language is used for loss exposures. Insurance practitioners often refer to a building loss exposure, a fire loss exposure, a homeowners loss exposure, or a business interruption loss exposure.

Liability

Insurance and risk management professionals often refer to specific types of liability losses in terms of the applicable coverage or the activity leading to the loss. For example, a claim for damages arising out of a product defect might be referred to as a "products liability loss," and the possibility of such a claim might be referred to as a "products liability loss exposure." Similarly, owning, operating, maintaining, or using an automobile might be referred to as "auto liability" or "auto liability loss exposures."

[DA02385]

Even if a claim is successfully defended, and therefore does not result in payment of damages, the party against whom the claim was made nonetheless incurs defense costs, other claim-related expenses, and potentially adverse publicity, all of which produce a financial loss. See the exhibit "Elements of Liability Loss Exposures."

Elements of Liability Loss Exposures

1. **Asset Exposed to Loss**

   The asset exposed to loss for a liability loss exposure is money. Payments that may be required include the following:

   - Damages to the plaintiff if the claim is not successfully defended

   - Settlement costs if the claim settles out of court

   - Legal fees

   - Court costs

2. **Cause of Loss**

   The cause of a liability loss is the making of a claim or suit against the particular organization by another party seeking damages or some other legal remedy. Even the threat of another party to make such a claim or suit can cause a liability loss in the form of costs the organization incurs to investigate and settle the threatened liability claim or suit.

3. **Financial Consequences of Loss**

   In theory, the financial consequences of a liability loss exposure are limitless. In practice, financial consequences are limited to the total wealth of the person or organization. Although some jurisdictions limit the amounts that can be taken in a claim, liability claims can result in the loss of most or all of a person's or an organization's assets, as well as in a claim on future income.

[DA02386]

Personnel Loss Exposures

Personnel loss exposure

A condition that presents the possibility of loss caused by a person's death, disability, retirement, or resignation that deprives an organization of the person's special skill or knowledge that the organization cannot readily replace.

Personal loss exposure

Any condition or situation that presents the possibility of a financial loss to an individual or a family by such causes as death, sickness, injury, or unemployment.

A **personnel loss exposure** is a condition that presents the possibility of loss caused by a key person's death, disability, retirement, or resignation that deprives an organization of that person's special skill or knowledge that the organization cannot readily replace. A key person can be an individual employee, an owner, an officer or manager of the organization, or a group of employees who possess special skills or knowledge that is valuable to the organization. See the exhibit "Elements of Personnel Loss Exposures."

For example, the possibility that the CEO of an organization can resign to take a position in a more prestigious organization is a personnel loss exposure. The exhibit reviews the three elements of a personnel loss exposure.

If the key person is viewed in terms of his or her family, the loss exposure associated with the loss of that key person is often called a **personal loss exposure** or human loss exposure. Although the terminology is slightly different, the definition is almost the same. For example, a family would face a personal loss exposure with the possibility of the primary wage earner dying.

Elements of Personnel Loss Exposures

1. **Asset Exposed to Loss**

   The asset exposed to loss for a personnel loss exposure is the value that the key person adds to the organization.

2. **Cause of Loss**

   Circumstances that can lead to a personnel loss exposure include the following:

   - Death
   - Disability
   - Retirement
   - Voluntary separation, such as resignation
   - Involuntary separation, such as layoff or firing

3. **Financial Consequences of Loss**

   The financial consequences of a personnel loss vary based on the cause of loss and can be partial or total as well as temporary or permanent. For example, the death of a key employee is a total, permanent loss. If the personnel loss is caused by a disability, the loss of value to the organization may only be a partial loss if the employee is able to continue to add some value to the organization. It may also only be temporary, if a full recovery from the disability is expected.

[DA02387]

Net Income Loss Exposures

A **net income loss exposure** is a condition that presents the possibility of loss caused by a reduction in net income. Net income equals revenues minus expenses and income taxes in a given time period. If you consider income taxes to be part of an organization's expenses, a net income loss is a reduction in revenue, an increase in expenses, or a combination of the two. Both individuals and organizations have net income loss exposures. See the exhibit "Elements of Net Income Loss Exposures."

For example, a fire at an organization's production facilities could not only destroy the facilities (a property loss exposure) but also force the organization to stop operations for a few weeks, resulting in a loss of sales revenue (a net income loss exposure). Similarly, if a tornado damages the retail store of a self-employed business owner, the inability to earn income while the store is being repaired represents a net income loss exposure. The exhibit reviews the three elements of a net income loss exposure.

Net income losses are often the result of a property, liability, or personnel loss (all of which are direct losses). Therefore, net income losses are considered to be indirect losses. A direct loss is a loss that occurs immediately as the result

Net income loss exposure
A condition that presents the possibility of loss caused by a reduction in net income.

Elements of Net Income Loss Exposures

1. **Asset Exposed to Loss**

    The asset exposed to loss for a net income loss exposure is the future stream of net income cash flows of the individual or organization.

2. **Cause of Loss**

    Circumstances that can lead to a net income loss exposure include the following:

    *   Property loss
    *   Liability loss
    *   Personnel loss
    *   Losses stemming from business risks; for example, losses resulting from poor strategic planning

3. **Financial Consequences of Loss**

    The financial consequences of a net income loss vary based on the cause of loss. A reduction in revenues, an increase in expenses, or a combination of the two can have financial consequences. The worst case scenario for a net income loss is a decrease in revenues to zero and a significant increase in expenses for a prolonged period.

[DA02388]

of a particular cause of loss, such as the reduction in the value of a building that has been damaged by fire.

An indirect loss is a loss that results from, but is not directly caused by, a particular cause of loss. For example, the reduction in revenue an organization suffers as a result of fire damage to one of its buildings is an indirect loss. Estimating indirect losses is often challenging because of the difficulty in projecting the effects that a direct loss will have on revenues or expenses. For example, a risk management professional working at a restaurant chain may be able to project the amount needed to settle a lawsuit brought by a customer accusing the restaurant of food poisoning (direct liability loss) with some certainty. However, projecting the effect that any negative publicity relating to the lawsuit would have on future restaurant sales (indirect loss) would be more difficult.

In the insurance industry, the term "net income losses" is usually associated with property losses, and some insurance policies provide coverage for net income losses related to property losses. However, there are many other causes of net income losses.

Some net income losses are associated with the liability or personnel loss exposures that have traditionally been the focus of risk management. Other net income losses are associated with organizational activities that have not traditionally been the focus of risk management, such as strategic marketing or branding decisions. Besides these, other potential net income losses that may affect individuals or organizations include these:

- Loss of goodwill—Organizations are concerned with maintaining goodwill among customers and other stakeholders. Goodwill can be lost in many ways, including providing poor service, offering obsolete products, or mismanaging operations. For a not-for-profit organization, goodwill is equivalent to reputation. Goodwill has broader implications than just reputation in for-profit organizations, because goodwill may have a monetary value. To maintain goodwill, many organizations choose to pay for certain accidents for which they are not legally responsible. For example, if a guest sustains an injury on an organization's premises, and the organization did not cause or contribute to the injury, that organization might still choose to pay any medical bills in order to maintain goodwill and avoid adverse publicity.

- Failure to perform—Net income losses may occur as a result of some type of failure to perform, including a product's failure to perform as promised, a contractor's failure to complete a construction project as scheduled, or a debtor's failure to make scheduled payments.

- Missed opportunities—An organization may suffer a net income loss as a result of a missed opportunity for profit. For example, an organization that delays a decision to modify its product in response to changes in market demand might lose market share and profit that it could have made on that updated product.

RISK MANAGEMENT BENEFITS

Risk management involves the efforts of individuals or organizations to efficiently and effectively assess, control, and finance risk in order to minimize the adverse effects of losses or missed opportunities. Properly managing risk reduces its negative financial consequences and thereby benefits individuals, organizations, and society.

An organization with an effective risk management program should experience smaller expected losses (less frequent or less severe) and experience less residual uncertainty than a comparable organization that does not practice good risk management. For example, an organization that installs a state-of-the-art security system would expect to have fewer thefts (and therefore lower expected losses) and a better sense of security (less residual uncertainty).

For individuals and families, risk management is usually an informal series of efforts, not a formalized process. Individual or personal risk management may be viewed as part of the financial planning process that encompasses broader matters such as capital accumulation, retirement planning, and estate planning.

In small organizations, risk management is not usually a dedicated function, but one of many tasks carried out by the owner or senior manager. In many larger organizations, the risk management function is conducted as part of a formalized risk management program. A risk management program is a system for planning, organizing, leading, and controlling the resources and activities that an organization needs to protect itself from the adverse effects of accidental losses. See the exhibit "Risk Management Benefits."

Risk Management Benefits

	Component	
	Lower Expected Losses	Less Residual Uncertainty
Individuals	Preserves financial resources	Reduces anxiety
Organizations	Preserves financial resources Makes an organization more attractive as an investment opportunity	Reduces deterrence effect
Society	Preserves financial resources	Improves allocation of productive resources

[DA02293]

The exhibit summarizes the benefits of risk management for individuals, organizations, and society in terms of its reduction of expected losses and residual uncertainty. An efficient risk management program helps to minimize the total of all three components of risk's costs.

Reducing the Financial Consequences of Risk

The overall financial consequence of risk for a given asset or activity is the sum of three costs: (1) the cost of the value lost because of actual events that cause a loss, (2) the cost of the resources devoted to risk management for that asset or activity, and (3) the cost of residual uncertainty. However, because it is difficult to assign a specific value to the cost of residual uncertainty, it is also difficult to establish a benchmark against which the performance of the risk management program can be assessed. As a result, organizations typically evaluate a subset of costs that form part of the financial consequences of risk and refer to this subset of costs as the cost of risk.

For a particular asset or activity, the cost of risk can be broken down in this way:

- Cost of losses not reimbursed by insurance or other external sources
- Cost of insurance premiums
- Cost of external sources of funds—for example, the interest payments to lenders or the transaction costs associated with noninsurance indemnity

- Cost of measures to prevent or reduce the size of potential losses
- Cost of implementing and administering risk management

Each year, the Risk and Insurance Management Society (RIMS), a global organization of risk management professionals, conducts a survey to determine the cost of risk for industry categories in the United States and Canada. The survey reveals trends in different industries and is used as a benchmarking tool to compare cost of risks between organizations in the same industry. The survey also provides benchmarking measures in areas such as risk management staffing, insurance coverages, and insurance broker compensation.

By reducing the long-term, overall cost of risk and devoting a minimum of resources to the actual process of managing risk without interfering with normal activities, risk management helps an individual or an organization to be more productive, promotes safety, and enhances profitability.

Benefits to Individuals

Risk management can preserve an individual's financial resources by reducing his or her expected losses. Most individuals have limited financial resources and are therefore not able—or willing—to bear the financial consequences of substantial risks.

For example, most people cannot afford to pay thousands (or millions) of dollars in damages if they seriously injure or kill someone in an auto accident. For some, avoiding loss is a viable alternative, and they choose not to drive. However, for most individuals, driving is a necessity.

Purchasing auto liability insurance enables them to transfer this liability loss exposure to the insurer. Although auto liability insurance is required in most states, many individuals purchase liability coverage well above the minimum required limits.

The second benefit of risk management for individuals is that it reduces the residual uncertainty associated with risk. Most individuals are at least some-what risk averse. Risk aversion means that, all else being equal, individuals prefer certainty to uncertainty, or less risk to more risk.

For example, if given a choice between the 100 percent certainty of paying $100 or a 20 percent chance of paying $500 (and, therefore, an 80 percent chance of paying nothing), a risk-averse individual would choose the 100 percent certainty of paying $100. Risk management allows an individual to invest time and money into managing risks in order to reduce uncertainty and its associated anxiety.

Benefits to Organizations

Organizations tend to have more resources than individuals and therefore are better equipped to bear risk. Consequently, organizations do not exhibit the same degree of risk aversion as individuals. Nonetheless, organizations usually choose to manage their risks, because they, too, benefit from preserving their financial resources.

Preservation of financial resources adds value to the organization and makes it a safer and more attractive investment, because shareholders or other investors want to know that their equity is safe and will generate future income and creditors seek assurance that the money they have loaned the organization will be repaid on time with interest. Risk management can protect the financial resources necessary to satisfy these parties and other stakeholders.

The protection that risk management affords an organization's financial resources can, in turn, provide confidence that capital is protected against future costs such as property loss, interruption of future income, liability judgments, or loss of key personnel. This sense of confidence is attractive both to suppliers and customers. As a result, suppliers may be more willing to allow the organization to buy on credit, and customers may purchase more products or services the organization offers.

Risk management also can reduce the deterrence effect of risk; that is, it can improve an organization's capacity to engage in business activities by minimizing the adverse effects of risk. Consequently, the organization can plan for its future with less uncertainty about potential outcomes. The fear of possible future losses tends to make senior management reluctant to undertake activities or investments it considers too risky, thereby depriving the organization of their associated benefits.

By making losses less frequent, less severe, or more predictable, risk management can alleviate management's fears about potential losses. This increases the feasibility of activities such as research and development, joint ventures, or investment in other organizations, which previously appeared too risky.

Benefits to Society

Society also faces a cost of risk, as well as uncertainty about future losses. Its cost of risk is slightly different from that of an individual or organization. Nonetheless, risk management benefits society in the same ways that it does individuals and organizations, by lowering expected losses and reducing residual uncertainty.

A nation's economy has limited resources with which to produce goods and services. When, for example, a fire or an earthquake demolishes a factory or destroys a highway, that economy's overall productive resources are reduced. Beyond the resources directly consumed in a loss, a significant portion of a nation's productive resources is devoted to preventing, repairing, or compensating for the results of losses.

When losses are possible, some portion of the economy's resources must be devoted to risk management for the benefit of society as a whole. Minimizing the resources consumed in running an economy's risk management program is analogous to an organization minimizing the administrative costs of its risk management department.

By reducing residual uncertainty, risk management also improves the allocation of productive resources. Risk management makes those who own or run an organization more willing to undertake risky activities, because they are better protected against losses that those activities might have produced. This makes executives, workers, and suppliers of financial capital more able to pursue activities that maximize profits; returns on investments; and, ultimately, wages. Such shifts increase productivity within an economy and improve the overall standard of living.

RISK MANAGEMENT PROGRAM GOALS

Senior management support is essential to an effective and efficient risk management program. To gain that support, a risk management program should promote the organization's overall goals. With a clear understanding of the organization's overall goals, a risk management program's goals can be tailored to support the organization's goals.

Risk management program goals are typically divided into two categories: pre-loss goals and post-loss goals. Possible **pre-loss goals** include economy of operations, tolerable uncertainty, legality, and social responsibility. **Post-loss goals** broadly describe the degree of recovery that an organization will strive to reach following a loss. Possible post-loss goals include survival, continuity of operations, profitability, earnings stability, social responsibility, and growth.

Pre-loss goals

Goals to be accomplished before a loss, involving social responsibility, externally imposed goals, reduction of anxiety, and economy.

Post-loss goals

Risk management program goals that should be in place in the event of a significant loss.

Pre-Loss Goals

Regardless of loss experience, every organization has operational goals that are vital to its success that the risk management program should support. Four such operational goals include these:

- Economy of operations
- Tolerable uncertainty
- Legality
- Social responsibility

Although these are not the only possible operational goals, they are typical of the types of operational goals that pre-loss risk management activities are designed to support.

Economy of Operations

A risk management program should operate economically and efficiently; that is, the organization generally should not incur substantial costs in exchange for slight benefits. One way to measure the economy of a risk management program is through benchmarking, in which an organization's risk management costs are compared with those of similar organizations. One such study, conducted annually, is the *Risk and Insurance Management Society (RIMS) Benchmark Survey.*

Tolerable Uncertainty

Tolerable uncertainty involves keeping managers' uncertainty about losses at tolerable levels. Managers should be able to make and implement decisions effectively without being unduly affected by uncertainty. Therefore, risk management professionals typically seek to implement a risk management program that assures managers that whatever might happen will be within the bounds of what was anticipated and will be effectively treated by the risk management program.

Although a risk management program should make all personnel aware of potential loss exposures, the program should also provide assurances through both risk control and risk financing that loss exposures are being managed well.

Legality

The risk management program should help to ensure that the organization's legal obligations are satisfied. These legal obligations will typically be based on:

- Standard of care that is owed to others
- Contracts entered into by the organization
- Federal, state, and local laws and regulations

A risk management professional has an essential role in helping the organization avoid liability by meeting the standard of care that it owes to others. The risk management professional and the organization's legal counsel manage lawsuits brought by others that arise from the organization's wrongful or negligent acts or omissions.

Some public and charitable entities are immune from negligence claims because of long-standing constitutional and other judicial doctrines that exempt them. However, such immunities have eroded over time, and many entities that might be eligible for such immunity choose to purchase liability insurance rather than invoke it.

The risk management professional should be aware of the organization's contractual obligations as well as the contractual obligations that others owe to it. If the organization does not fulfill its obligations under a contract, the other party may bring a lawsuit against the organization for breach of contract. If the other party does not fulfill its obligation and the organization does not pursue the matter, the other party may be relieved of its obligations under the contract.

Risk management professionals also need to be aware of the federal, state, and local laws and regulations that apply to their organizations and should work with other employees to ensure compliance. Examples of laws and regulations of particular concern to the risk management function are occupational health and safety regulations, labeling requirements for consumer products, regulations about hazardous waste disposal, and statutes establishing mandatory insurance requirements.

Social Responsibility

Social responsibility, which is both a pre-loss and a post-loss goal for many organizations, includes acting ethically and fulfilling obligations to the community and society as a whole. Beyond the altruistic interests of the organization's owners, many organizations justify pursuing this goal because of its potential to enhance the organization's reputation.

For public entities and not-for-profit organizations, social responsibility might be the overriding pre-loss goal, even surpassing the need for economy of operations. Public entities exist to fulfill the needs of their constituents, so their purpose is to promote social goals. Similarly, not-for-profit organizations are chartered to meet the needs of members, subscribers, or students, and this often requires a social responsibility focus.

Post-Loss Goals

Post-loss goals are based on the operating and financial conditions that the organization's senior management would consider acceptable after a significant foreseeable loss. These are six possible post-loss goals:

- Survival
- Continuity of operations
- Profitability
- Earnings stability
- Social responsibility
- Growth

After a severe loss, the most basic goal is survival, while the most ambitious goal is uninterrupted growth. The more ambitious a particular post-loss goal, the more difficult and costly it is to achieve.

Survival

Survival is a fundamental post-loss goal. For individuals, survival means staying alive. For organizations, survival means resuming operations to some extent after an adverse event. Survival does not necessarily mean returning to the condition that existed before loss. Within that context, an organization survives a loss whenever that loss does not permanently halt its production and the incomes of those who work for or own it.

Examples of losses that could prevent an organization's survival include these:

• Its only office or plant is destroyed.

• A legal liability judgment or an out-of-court settlement drains its cash and credit resources.

• The death or disability of a key employee (such as an executive or a technician) deprives it of essential leadership or of some vital expertise.

Continuity of Operations

Continuity of operations is an important post-loss goal for many private organizations and an essential goal for all public entities. Although the survival goal requires that no loss (no matter how severe) permanently shut down an organization, the goal of continuity of operations is more demanding. With continuity as a goal, no loss can be allowed to interrupt the organization's operations for any appreciable time.

Within the context of continuity, "appreciable" is a relative term and depends on the goods or services produced. One organization may be unable to tolerate even a few days' shutdown, whereas another organization's output might be continuous even when some of its activities halt for a month or more.

When an organization's senior management sets continuity of operations as a goal, its risk management professional must have a clear, detailed understanding of the specific operations whose continuity is essential and the maximum tolerable interruption interval for each operation.

Any organization for which continuous operation is essential must take steps, and probably incur additional expenses, to forestall an intolerable shutdown. Such steps include these:

• Identify activities whose interruptions cannot be tolerated

• Identify the types of events that could interrupt such activities

• Determine the standby resources that must be immediately available to counter the effects of those losses

• Ensure the availability of the standby resources at even the most unlikely and difficult times

The last step, ensuring the availability of standby resources, is likely to add to an organization's expenses, and, accordingly, achieving the continuity of operations goal tends to be more costly than the more basic goal of survival. However, for organizations that give high priority to continuity of operations, this added cost is preferable to the alternative of business interruption.

For public entities—particularly cities, counties, and other governing bodies, as well as schools and public utilities—maintaining public services without interruption is perhaps the most important risk management goal. Any sustained interruption in police or fire protection, supplies of clean water, removal of trash or sewage, or public education can be catastrophic. The essential purpose of most public entities is to provide some service, and therefore they are willing to commit significant resources to comprehensive contingency plans.

Profitability

As well as considering the physical effects a loss might have on an organization's operations, senior management may also be concerned with how such a loss would affect the organization's profitability. In a for-profit organization, the goal is to generate net income (profit). In a not-for-profit organization, the goal is to operate within the budget. An organization's senior management might have established a minimum amount of profit (or surplus in not-for-profit organizations) that no loss can be allowed to reduce.

To achieve the specified minimum amount of profit, the risk management program is likely to emphasize insurance and other means of transferring the financial consequences of loss so that actual financial results fall within an acceptable range. An organization that requires a minimum profit tends to spend more on risk management, particularly risk financing, than does an organization that is prepared to tolerate an occasional unprofitable financial result.

Earnings Stability

Rather than strive for the highest possible level of profit (or surplus) in a given period, some organizations emphasize earnings stability over time. Striving for earnings stability requires precision in forecasting risk management costs, as well as lower retention levels and a willingness on the part of the organization to spend more on risk transfer mechanisms. A risk management professional focusing on earnings stability would seek ways of creating consistent results over time rather than choose actions that might produce fluctuating results.

Social Responsibility

Losses affect an organization's ability to fulfill its real or perceived obligations to the community and to society as a whole. Organizational disruptions have implications for relationships with customers, suppliers, employees, taxpayers, and other members of the public. These relationships, even though they may not involve legal obligations, are often the focus of the organization's overall mission.

Many not-for-profit organizations and public entities are unable to distinguish between the post-loss goals of survival and social responsibility because of their focus on community service. However, the post-loss goal of social responsibility does not apply only to not-for profit and public entities.

For example, consider an organization with strong ties to the local community that relies heavily on the support of the customers and suppliers in its neighborhood. If such an organization makes a social commitment, such as sponsoring a local charity event, then the failure to honor that commitment could seriously damage its reputation and correspondingly affect its future business operations. Such an organization would want to ensure that its risk management program provided sufficient protection against losses so that the organization's ability to meet its social responsibilities would not be seriously diminished in the event of a loss.

Growth

Emphasizing the post-loss goal of growth—for example, increasing market share, the size and scope of activities or products, or assets—might have two distinctly opposing effects on an organization's risk management program. Those effects depend on the managers' and owners' tolerance for uncertainty.

If striving to expand makes managers and owners more willing to accept greater uncertainty in exchange for minimizing risk management costs, the organization's explicit costs for risk management could be fairly low. Such an organization's risk management professional might find it difficult to obtain a budget adequate to protect against expanding loss exposures. Moreover, if such an organization suffers a severe loss for which it was not adequately prepared, its real cost of risk management—more accurately, its real cost of not effectively managing loss exposures—might be significant and involve sacrificing much of the growth it has attained.

In contrast, the goal of risk management in a growing organization might be to protect its expanding resources so that its path of expansion is not blocked or reversed by a substantial loss. Risk management costs in this scenario are likely to be high because such an organization might seek increased earnings (growth) rather than survival or earnings stability. Consequently, the organization lowers its tolerance for unanticipated loss and requires greater emphasis on risk control and risk financing.

Conflict Between Goals

Pre-loss and post-loss goals are interrelated and sometimes conflict with each other. Although conflicts may arise between post-loss goals, it is more common for post-loss goals to conflict with pre-loss goals, or for pre-loss goals to compete with each other. Therefore, an organization might discover that fully achieving all risk management program goals simultaneously is impossible.

Achieving any post-loss goal involves expending risk management resources, which may conflict with the pre-loss goal of economy of operations. The more ambitious and costly the post-loss goal, the greater the conflict with the economy of operations goal. The economy of operations goal may also conflict with the tolerable uncertainty goal.

To provide management with the desired level of assurance, the risk management professional must be confident that certain organizational post-loss goals will be achieved. Gaining that confidence requires allocating some of the organization's limited resources, including money, to risk management efforts such as purchasing insurance, installing guards on machinery to prevent industrial accidents, or maintaining duplicate copies of records in case originals are destroyed.

The legality and social responsibility goals may also conflict with the economy of operations goal. Some externally imposed obligations, such as safety standards dictated by building codes, may be nonnegotiable. Therefore, the costs imposed by legal obligations must be accepted as unavoidable, regardless of the economy of operations goal.

Obligations imposed by social responsibility, such as employee benefits subject to collective bargaining agreements, may be negotiable. However, although meeting social responsibility might raise costs in the short term, it can have worthwhile long-term benefits that make the costs acceptable.

THE RISK MANAGEMENT PROCESS

To fulfill the goals of a risk management program, insurance and risk management professionals use the risk management process, a series of six steps that can be applied to any set of loss exposures.

Application of this process can be initiated by events such as an insurance renewal, a serious claim, a merger or an acquisition, or a new law or regulation that affects the organization. However, the risk management process need not be initiated by events such as these, because it is continuous. The last step in the process, monitoring results and revising the existing risk management program, may lead to the identification of new or additional loss exposures. See the exhibit "The Risk Management Process."

Step 1: Identifying Loss Exposures

A wide variety of methods, such as those listed in the "Identifying Loss Exposures" exhibit, can be used to identify the specific loss exposures that could interfere with the achievement of the organization's goals. These methods offer a systematic approach to identifying loss exposures. They also can enable risk management professionals to identify missed opportunities.

Although loss exposure identification methods are applied individually, they can overlap in their use and function. Despite this overlap, using different methods helps the risk management professional avoid overlooking important loss exposures. For example, loss history documents may not reveal the possibility of loss exposures related to flood, but studying a flood insurance rate map or a cause of loss checklist would. See the exhibit "Identifying Loss Exposures."

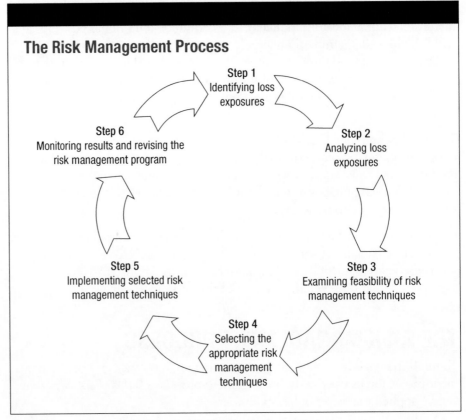

The Risk Management Process

Step 1
Identifying loss
exposures

Step 2
Analyzing loss
exposures

Step 3
Examining feasibility of risk
management techniques

Step 4
Selecting the
appropriate risk
management
techniques

Step 5
Implementing selected risk
management techniques

Step 6
Monitoring results and revising the
risk management program

[DA02595]

Step 2: Analyzing Loss Exposures

Analyzing loss exposures is completed by estimating the likely significance of possible losses identified in step one. Together, these two steps constitute the process of assessing loss exposures and are therefore probably the most important steps in the risk management process, because only a properly assessed loss exposure can be appropriately managed. Once a loss exposure has been assessed, the best ways to manage it often become immediately apparent. The remaining steps of the risk management process flow from this assessment.

Loss exposures are analyzed along these four dimensions:

- Loss frequency—the number of losses (such as fires, auto accidents, or liability claims) within a specific time period
- Loss severity—the amount, in dollars, of a loss for a specific occurrence
- Total dollar losses—the total dollar amount of losses for all occurrences during a specific time period
- Timing—when losses occur and when loss payments are made

Reviewing these dimensions enables a risk management professional to develop loss projections and prioritize loss exposures so that resources can be properly allocated. Analyzing loss exposures is, in itself, expensive. The

---

Identifying Loss Exposures

No single method exists for identifying loss exposures. Risk management professionals may use some or all of the following:

- Document analysis (including any or all of the following):
    - Risk assessment questionnaires and checklists
    - Financial statements and underlying accounting records
    - Contracts
    - Insurance policies
    - Organizational policies and procedures
    - Flowcharts and organizational charts
    - Loss histories
- Compliance reviews
- Inspections
- Expertise within and beyond the organization

[DA02597]

cost of risk includes the cost of acquiring risk-related information used in loss forecasts, estimates of future cash flows, and other planning activities. In some cases, this information can actually reduce losses.

For example, recent advances in satellite technology and meteorology provide advance warning that enables people in a hurricane's path to board up windows, evacuate, and implement other loss reduction measures. Such detailed information improves forecast accuracy and can lead to better risk management decisions.

Step 3: Examining the Feasibility of Risk Management Techniques

Loss exposures arise from activities and circumstances that are essential to individuals and to organizations. These loss exposures can be addressed through the risk control techniques and risk financing techniques shown in the "Risk Management Techniques" exhibit. Broadly speaking, risk control techniques are those risk management techniques that minimize the frequency or severity of losses or make losses more predictable. Risk financing techniques are those risk management techniques that generate funds to finance losses that risk control techniques cannot entirely prevent or reduce. See the exhibit "Risk Management Techniques."

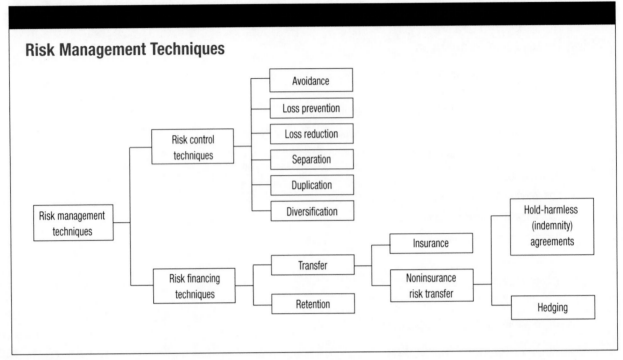

Risk Management Techniques

[DA02598]

Risk management techniques are not usually used in isolation. Unless the loss exposure is avoided, organizations typically apply at least one risk control technique and one risk financing technique to each of their significant loss exposures. The risk control technique alters the estimated frequency and severity of loss, and the financing technique pays for losses that occur despite the controls. Most risk control and risk financing techniques can be used with any other control or financing technique.

Step 4: Selecting the Appropriate Risk Management Techniques

Once loss exposures have been identified and analyzed and possible risk management techniques considered, risk management professionals can select those techniques that best prevent or reduce losses and that will adequately finance losses that occur despite prevention and reduction efforts. Selecting the most appropriate mix of risk management techniques is usually based on quantitative financial considerations as well as qualitative, nonfinancial considerations. See the exhibit "Summary of Risk Control and Risk Financing Techniques."

Financial Considerations

Most private, for-profit organizations choose risk management techniques by using financial criteria, that is, they choose those techniques with the greatest

---

Summary of Risk Control and Risk Financing Techniques

Risk Control Techniques

Avoidance eliminates any possibility of loss. The probability of loss from an avoided loss exposure is zero because an entity decides not to assume a loss exposure in the first place (proactive avoidance) or to eliminate one that already exists (abandonment).

Loss prevention involves reducing the frequency of a particular loss.

Loss reduction involves reducing the severity of a particular loss.

Separation involves dispersing a particular activity or asset over several locations. Separation involves the routine, daily reliance on each of the separated assets or activities, all of which regularly form a portion of the organization's working resources.

Duplication involves relying on backups, that is, spares or duplicates, used only if primary assets or activities suffer loss.

Diversification involves providing a range of products and services used by a variety of customers.

Risk Financing Techniques

Retention involves generating funds from within the organization to pay for losses.

Transfer involves generating funds from outside the organization to pay for losses and includes insurance and noninsurance transfer.

[DA02599]

positive (or least negative) effect on the organization's value. The risk management techniques selected should be effective and economical. A technique is effective if it enables an organization to achieve its desired goals, such as to maximize organizational value. A technique is economical if it is the least expensive of the possible effective options.

For all organizations, the potential costs if loss exposures are left completely untreated must be compared with the costs of possible risk management techniques when considering whether a technique is economical. A financial analysis of a risk management technique may be based on three different forecasts.

Based on those considerations, an organization can perform a cost/benefit analysis that identifies the risk management technique, or combination of techniques, that will maximize the organization's value while allowing it to stay within budgetary constraints.

The three forecasts a financial analysis of a risk management technique may be based on are these:

- A forecast of the dimensions of expected losses (frequency, severity, timing of payment, and total dollar losses).

- A forecast, for each feasible combination of risk management techniques, of the effect on the frequency, severity, and timing of these expected losses.

- A forecast of the after-tax costs involved in applying the various risk management techniques. These costs include, for example, the cost of insurance premiums or the expenses associated with installing and maintaining various risk control devices.

Nonfinancial Considerations

Although an organization's goal should be to determine a level of risk management that will maximize its financial value, an organization's value may also stem from ethical and other nonfinancial considerations. Data based on objective risk factors usually are not the only criteria considered in determining appropriate risk management techniques. An organization might also place a great deal of value on maintaining operations or on peace of mind.

An organization's nonfinancial goals can constrain its financial goals, leading to the selection of risk management techniques that, although best for that organization, might be inconsistent with its value maximization goal. For example, a private, family-owned organization might emphasize stability of earnings over time, rather than maximum earnings in any one period. Consequently, the organization might over-invest in loss prevention devices or safety practices rather than absorb the minor losses that these devices or practices are designed to prevent. For similar reasons, a private, family-owned organization would be likely to insure against losses that, from a value maximization standpoint, might be better to retain.

Step 5: Implementing the Selected Risk Management Techniques

After an organization decides which risk management technique(s) to use, the next step is to implement them, which requires cooperation among its departments. Implementing risk management techniques may involve any of these measures:

- Purchasing loss reduction devices
- Contracting for loss prevention services
- Funding retention programs
- Implementing and continually reinforcing loss control programs

- Selecting agents or brokers, insurers, third-party administrators, and other providers for insurance programs
- Requesting insurance policies and paying premiums

Implementing risk management techniques does not necessarily end with the initial implementation of the selected technique. For example, if an organization purchases a building, it almost certainly will also decide to purchase property insurance. However, additional details, such as the exact placement of fire extinguishers, the terms and cost of insurance and noninsurance contract revisions, which insurer to use, the timing of insurance premium payments, or the actual deposit of funds for a retention program or to cover deductibles, must be addressed as the program is implemented.

Step 6: Monitoring Results and Revising the Risk Management Program

Once implemented, a risk management program must be monitored and periodically revised as necessary in order to ensure that it is achieving expected results and to adjust it to accommodate changes in loss exposures and the availability or cost-effectiveness of alternative risk management techniques. Monitoring and revising the risk management program requires four steps: (1) establishing standards of acceptable performance, (2) comparing actual results with these standards, (3) correcting substandard performance or revising standards that prove to be unrealistic, and (4) evaluating standards that have been substantially exceeded.

Establishing Standards of Acceptable Performance

Because of year-to-year variations and the random nature of fortuitous events, the best way to monitor a risk management program may be to combine standards that consider both results and activities. A results standard focuses on actual achievement of goals, regardless of the effort required to achieve them.

For example, a risk management professional might judge a risk management program's performance in terms of a decline in the frequency or severity of employee injuries. However, those results depend largely on fortuitous events, which, by definition, are unpredictable. In contrast, an activity standard focuses on efforts made to achieve a goal regardless of actual results. These independent standards focus mainly on the quality and quantity of the risk management department's activities, such as the installation of new safety equipment designed to protect employees from injury, rather than the actual outcomes.

Risk management professionals often contend that their contribution is as great in years in which there are many losses as in years in which there are few losses, because the losses themselves are beyond their control. In fact, risk management professionals may be even more valuable to their organizations when losses are severe because of the assistance that they can give to the organization in dealing with those losses. Therefore, risk management professionals have sought performance standards that are not solely dependent on the organization's somewhat uncontrollable loss record. Although results standards are important, activities standards are necessary to obtain a complete picture of the success or failure of a risk management program.

Comparing Actual Results With Standards

A proper standard for evaluating risk management performance includes specifications for how results or performance will be measured. A good standard includes target activity levels or results, or at least desired directions of change.

For example, if an organization had a risk management goal of preventing accidents involving its employees, a results standard could be formulated as a maximum number of accidents per employee hour worked, or at least as a decrease in the number of accidents from one year to the next. A comparison of the actual number of accidents that occur with the number established in the results standard will indicate whether risk management activities are achieving the desired results.

Alternatively, an activity standard relating to the same employee accidents could specify, and provide a schedule for, when an organization's employees should receive safety training updates. The comparison of results against this activity standard would not consider the number of employee accidents, but instead determine whether all employees received the level of training established by the standard.

Correcting Substandard Performance

The risk management professional should also develop a plan for addressing substandard performance. For example, if the number of safety inspections is below that required by the standard, the risk management professional should include a plan to increase their frequency. If retained losses are growing faster than expected, then the risk management professional should determine how retention levels and, perhaps, risk control techniques should be reevaluated.

Substandard performance does not necessarily indicate that the performance itself is the problem. The standard may, in fact, be inappropriate. A risk management program should change when loss exposures change.

Similarly, the standards by which that program is evaluated must be reexamined and possibly altered if the environment within which the risk management program operates also changes. For example, increases in inflation, changes in the volume or nature of an organization's activities, and cyclical or long-term movements in insurance markets or money markets may require adjustments in standards by which acceptable risk management performance is evaluated.

Although changes in risk management standards should not be arbitrary, the continuing need for change should be recognized. Therefore, when monitoring a risk management program, the standards for evaluating that program should also be evaluated, and, when appropriate, revised to accommodate new situations.

Evaluating Standards That Have Been Substantially Exceeded

Performance should ideally meet or exceed a standard. However, if performance substantially exceeds a standard, then the risk management professional should determine why. One reason may be the superior skills of the employee or employees involved in implementing the standard. Another alternative is that the standard is not sufficiently demanding. The risk management professional should, if appropriate, revise the standard so that it more accurately reflects the performance potential of the employees and the organization.

Although monitoring results and revising the risk management program is listed as the final step of the risk management process, it is often the first step for a risk management professional who is taking control of an organization's risk management program. Unless the organization is a start-up, it probably has some (either formal or informal) risk management program in place. Once the risk management program has been properly evaluated, the risk management professional begins the risk management process again. The steps of the risk management process are applied under the revised risk management program, which may now have different program goals or face a new set of organizational risks.

SUMMARY

The word risk can have many different meanings. In this section, risk is defined as the uncertainty about outcomes, some of which can be negative. The two elements within this definition of risk are uncertainty of outcome (uncertainty about what will actually occur, when the outcome will occur, or a combination of the two) and the possibility of a negative outcome.

Possibility means that an outcome or event may or may not occur. This is not the same as probability, which is the likelihood that an outcome or event will occur. Unlike possibility, probability is measurable and has a value between zero and one.

Classifying the various types of risk can help organizations manage risk. Some of the most commonly used classifications are pure and speculative risk, subjective and objective risk, and diversifiable and nondiversifiable risk. An organization's risks can also be categorized into quadrants as hazard risk, operational risk, financial risk, and strategic risk.

When managing risk, it is useful to consider the financial consequences of risk. The financial consequences of risk faced by individuals or organizations can be broken into three components: (1) expected cost of losses or gains, (2) expenditures on risk management, and (3) the cost of residual uncertainty.

Risk management can differ markedly for individuals, small organizations, and large organizations. At whatever level it is practiced, risk management is aimed at dealing economically with risk, whether through an individual's informal efforts or through an organizations's formalized risk management program. Traditionally, risk management has been concerned almost exclusively with pure risk. A new approach, called enterprise-wide risk management, is concerned with all risks, pure and speculative, that an organization faces.

Individuals and organizations incur losses when assets they own decrease in value. Situations or conditions that expose assets to loss are called loss exposures. The elements of any loss exposure are an asset exposed to loss, the cause of loss (or peril), and the financial consequences of the loss. Property loss exposures, liability loss exposures, personnel loss exposures, and net income loss exposures each contain the three elements.

For an individual, the specific benefits of risk management are preservation of financial resources and reduction of anxiety. For an organization, the benefits are preservation of financial resources, increased attractiveness to investors, and reduction of the deterrence effect of risk. For society as a whole, the benefits are preservation of financial resources and an improved allocation of productive resources.

Risk management program goals are typically divided into two categories: pre-loss goals and post-loss goals. Pre-loss goals include economy of operations, tolerable uncertainty, legality, and social responsibility. Post-loss goals include survival, continuity of operations, profitability, earnings stability, social responsibility, and growth.

The risk management process consists of six steps that can be applied to any set of loss exposures:

1. Identifying loss exposures
2. Analyzing loss exposures
3. Examining the feasibility of risk management techniques
4. Selecting the appropriate risk management techniques
5. Implementing the selected risk management techniques
6. Monitoring results and revising the risk management program

ASSIGNMENT NOTE

1. Herbert W. Heinrich, *Industrial Accident Prevention*, 4th ed. (New York: McGraw-Hill Book Co., 1959), pp. 51–52. In 1980, a fifth edition of *Industrial Accident Prevention* was published, containing revisions by Dan Peterson and Nester Roos.

Direct Your Learning ▶▶

2

Risk Assessment

Educational Objectives

After learning the content of this assignment, you should be able to:

▷ Describe the following methods of loss exposure identification:

- Document analysis

- Compliance review

- Personal inspections

- Expertise within and beyond the organization

▷ Explain why data used in risk management decisions need to be relevant, complete, consistent, and organized.

▷ Describe the nature of probability with respect to theoretical and empirical probability and the law of large numbers.

▷ Explain how the information provided in a simple probability distribution can be used in making basic risk management decisions.

▷ Describe the various measures of central tendency and how they can be used in analyzing the probabilities associated with risk.

▷ Describe the measures of dispersion and how they can be used in analyzing the probabilities associated with risk.

▷ Describe the characteristics of normal distributions and how they can be used to analyze loss exposures and project future losses more accurately.

▷ Explain how to analyze loss exposures considering the four dimensions of loss and data credibility.

Risk Assessment

IDENTIFYING LOSS EXPOSURES

For individuals, common property and liability exposures can be identified by a property-casualty insurance producer as part of an assessment of insurance needs. Similarly, individuals' net income loss exposures can be identified by life insurance producers as part of a needs assessment for life and health insurance products. For organizations, loss exposure identification is typically more complex, using a variety of methods and sources of information.

The methods of information that enable an organization to take a systematic approach to identifying loss exposures include these:

- Document analysis
- Compliance review
- Inspections
- Expertise within and beyond the organization

Document Analysis

The variety of documents used and produced by an organization can be a key source of information regarding loss exposures. Some of these documents are standardized and originate from outside the organization, such as questionnaires, checklists, and surveys. These standardized documents broadly categorize the loss exposures that most organizations typically face and are completed with information that is exclusive to the organization.

Other documents are organization-specific, such as financial statements and accounting records, contracts, insurance policies, policy and procedure manuals, flowcharts and organizational charts, and loss histories. Although the use and function of the various documents may overlap, causing possible duplication in loss exposure identification, reviewing multiple documents is necessary to avoid failing to identify important loss exposures.

In addition to the documents discussed in this section, virtually any document connected to an organization's operations also reveals something about its loss exposures. For example, Web sites, news releases, or reports from external organizations such as A.M. Best or D&B may indicate something about an organization's loss exposures. Although it is not feasible to review every document that refers to an organization, some of these additional sources may be useful.

Risk Assessment Questionnaires and Checklists

Standardized documents published outside an organization, such as insurance coverage checklists and risk assessment questionnaires, broadly categorize the loss exposures that most organizations typically face. A variety of checklists and questionnaires have been published by insurers, the American Management Association (AMA), the International Risk Management Institute (IRMI), the Risk and Insurance Management Society (RIMS), and others.

Although some organizations or trade associations have developed specialized checklists or questionnaires for their members, most are created by insurers and concentrate on identifying insurable hazard risks. Some focus on listing the organization's assets, whereas others focus on identifying potential causes of loss that could affect the organization.

Checklists typically capture less information than questionnaires. Although checklists can help an organization identify its loss exposures, they do not show how those loss exposures support or affect specific organizational goals. Linking loss exposures with the goals they support can be useful in analyzing the potential financial consequences of loss. Therefore, checklists are of limited benefit in the analysis step of the risk management process.

A questionnaire captures more descriptive information than a checklist. For example, as well as identifying a loss exposure, a questionnaire may capture information about the amounts or values exposed to loss. The questionnaire can be designed to include questions that address key property, liability, net income, and at least some personnel loss exposures.

Questionnaire responses can enable an insurance or a risk management professional to identify and analyze an organization's loss exposures regarding real property, equipment, products, key customers, neighboring properties, operations, and so on. Additionally, the logical sequencing of questions helps in developing a more detailed examination of the loss exposures an organization faces.

Both checklists and questionnaires may be produced by insurers (such questionnaires are known as insurance surveys). Most of the questions on these surveys relate to loss exposures for which commercial insurance is generally available.

Risk management or risk assessment questionnaires have a broader focus and address both insurable and uninsurable loss exposures. However, a disadvantage of risk assessment questionnaires is that they typically can be completed only with considerable expense, time, and effort and still may not identify all possible loss exposures.

Standardizing a survey or questionnaire has both advantages and disadvantages. Standardized questions are relevant for most organizations and can be answered by persons who have little risk management expertise.

However, no standardized questionnaire can be expected to uncover all the loss exposures particularly characteristic of a given industry, let alone those unique to a given organization. Additionally, the questionnaire's structure might not stimulate the respondent to do anything more than answer the questions asked; that is, it will elicit only the information that is specifically requested. Consequently, it may not reveal key information. Therefore, questionnaires should ideally be used in conjunction with other identification and analysis methods.

Because even a thoroughly completed checklist or questionnaire does not ensure that all loss exposures have been recognized, experienced insurance and risk management professionals often follow up with additional questions that are not on the standardized document. See the exhibit "Follow-Up to Questionnaire: Shipton's Auto Body Shop."

Follow-Up to Questionnaire: Shipton's Auto Body Shop

Insurance producer Amy Chung used a questionnaire when interviewing Damon Shipton for his property insurance application. The questionnaire was specially developed by the insurer for use with organizations in the auto business and asked whether the body shop had a spray-painting booth. The answer was "no," which was unusual for a modern body shop. Amy asked a few more questions and learned that this shop was using a newly developed air filtration system that was better than the standard spray-painting booth.

When Amy submitted the insurance application, not only was this account not rejected because of the "no spray-painting booth" response on the questionnaire, but the answer prompted the property underwriter, James Day, to also visit the shop. James then granted a preferential insurance rate based on additional information his visit uncovered as well as Amy's information about the new air filtration system.

[DA04880]

Financial Statements and Underlying Accounting Records

Risk management professionals with accounting or finance expertise sometimes begin the loss exposure identification process by reviewing an organization's financial statements, including the balance sheet, income statement, statement of cash flows, and supporting statements. As well as identifying current loss exposures, financial statements and accounting records can be used to identify any future plans that could lead to new loss exposures.

An organization's **balance sheet** is the financial statement that reports the assets, liabilities, and owners' equity of the organization as of a specific date. Owners' equity, or net worth, is the amount by which assets exceed liabilities. Asset entries indicate property values that could be reduced by loss. Liability entries show what the organization owes and enable the risk management professional to explore two types of loss exposures: (1) liabilities that could be increased or created by a loss and (2) obligations (such as mortgage payments)

Balance sheet

The financial statement that reports the assets, liabilities, and owners' equity of an organization as of a specific date.

that the organization must fulfill, even if it were to close temporarily as a result of a business interruption.

The **income statement** is particularly useful in identifying net income loss exposures; that is, those loss exposures that reduce revenue or increase expenses.

The **statement of cash flows** (also called the statement of sources and uses of funds) is the financial statement that summarizes the cash effects of an organization's operating, investing, and financing activities during a specific period.

Funds-flow analysis on the statement of cash flows can identify the amounts of cash either subject to loss or available to meet continuing obligations. For example, the statement of cash flows would indicate the amount of cash that is typically on hand to pay for any losses resulting from loss exposures that have been retained by the organization.

Financial statements can reveal that an organization is subject to significant financial risks, such as fluctuations in the value of investments, interest rate volatility, foreign exchange rate changes, or commodity price swings. However, the primary advantage of financial statements from a risk management professional's perspective is that they help to identify major categories of loss exposures.

For example, property loss exposures can be seen in the asset section of the balance sheet. Some liability loss exposures, especially contractual obligations such as loans or mortgages, can be seen in the liabilities section of the balance sheet. The potential effects of net income loss exposures can be seen by comparing revenues with expenses on the income statement.

The major disadvantage of using financial statements for identifying loss exposures is that although they identify most of the major categories of loss exposures (property, liability and net income are identified but personnel loss exposures are not), they do not identify or quantify the individual loss exposures. For example, the balance sheet may show that there is $5 million in property exposed to loss, but it does not specify how many properties make up that $5 million, where those properties are located, or how much each individual property is worth. Moreover, the real and personal property values recorded in financial statements are based on accounting conventions and are not accurate for purposes of insurance or risk management.

Another disadvantage is that financial statements depict past activities—for example, revenue that has already been earned, expenses that have already been incurred, prior valuations of assets and liabilities, and business operations that have already taken place. They are of limited help in identifying projected values or future events. Therefore, even after using financial statements for loss exposure identification, insurance and risk management professionals still need to project what events might occur in the future, determine how these future events could change loss exposures, and analyze and quantify potential losses accordingly.

Contracts

A contract is an agreement entered into by two or more parties that specifies the parties' responsibilities to one another. Analyzing an organization's contracts may help identify its property and liability loss exposures and help determine who has assumed responsibility for which loss exposures. It is often necessary to consult with legal experts when interpreting contracts.

Contract analysis can both identify the loss exposures generated or reduced by an organization's contracts and ensure that the organization is not assuming liability that is disproportionate to its stake in the contract. Ongoing contract analysis is part of monitoring and maintaining a risk management program.

Entering into contracts can either increase or reduce an organization's property and liability loss exposures. For example, a contract to purchase property or equipment will increase the organization's property loss exposures, whereas a contract to sell property or equipment will reduce property loss exposures.

A contract can generate liability loss exposures in two ways. First, the organization can accept the loss exposures of another party through a contract, such as a **hold-harmless agreement** (sometimes referred to as an indemnity agreement). For example, an organization may enter into a hold-harmless agreement with its distributor under which the organization agrees to indemnify the distributor (pay the losses for which the distributor is liable) if the distributor is found liable for a products liability claim. **Indemnification** is the process of restoring an individual or organization to a pre-loss financial condition.

The second way a contract may generate a liability loss exposure is if the organization fails to fulfill a valid contract. For example, if an organization agrees to deliver manufactured goods to a distributor and then fails to deliver those goods, the distributor is entitled to bring a legal claim against the organization. The distributor's claim presents a liability loss exposure for the organization.

Alternatively, an organization can reduce or eliminate liability loss exposures by entering into a contract that transfers its liability to another organization. For example, an organization can enter into a hold-harmless agreement under which the second party agrees to indemnify the organization in the event of a liability claim.

Insurance Policies

Although insurance is a means of risk financing, reviewing insurance policies can also be helpful in risk assessment.

Analyzing insurance policies reveals many of the insurable loss exposures that an organization faces. However, this analysis may either indicate the organization is insured for more loss exposures than it really has, or, alternatively, may not show all the loss exposures the organization faces.

Hold-harmless agreement (or indemnity agreement)
A contractual provision that obligates one of the parties to assume the legal liability of another party.

Indemnification
The process of restoring an individual or organization to a pre-loss financial condition.

As insurance policies typically are standardized forms, an organization does not necessarily face every loss exposure covered by its policies. Furthermore, the organization may face many other loss exposures that either cannot be covered by insurance policies or are covered by policies the organization has chosen not to purchase.

To identify insurance coverage that an organization has not purchased, and therefore potentially identify insurable loss exposures that have not been insured, a risk management professional can compare his or her organization's coverage against an industry checklist of insurance policies currently in effect.

Organizational Policies and Records

Loss exposures can also be identified using organizational policies and records, such as corporate by-laws, board minutes, employee manuals, procedure manuals, mission statements, and risk management policies. For example, policy and procedure manuals may identify some of the organization's property loss exposures by referencing equipment, or pinpoint liability loss exposures by referencing hazardous materials with which employees come into contact. See the exhibit "Internal Documents as Loss Exposures."

Internal Documents as Loss Exposures

Internal documents, in addition to identifying loss exposures, need to be analyzed to determine their appropriateness and consistency with external publications. An organization's internal documents are not typically written in anticipation that they will be viewed outside the organization. However, many internal documents are used during legal proceedings and therefore may present a potential liability loss exposure to the organization. This illustrates the need for internal documents to be consistent with external information the organization releases.

[DA02555]

As well as identifying existing loss exposures, some documents may indicate impending changes in loss exposures. For example, board minutes may indicate management's plans to sell or purchase property, thereby either reducing or increasing its property loss exposures.

One drawback to using policies and records to identify loss exposures is the sheer volume of documents that some organizations generate internally. It may be virtually impossible to have one employee or a group of employees examine every internal document. In these instances, insurance and risk management professionals would need to examine a representative sample of documents. This makes the task manageable, but increases the likelihood that not all loss exposures will be identified.

Flowcharts and Organizational Charts

A flowchart is a diagram that depicts the sequence of activities performed by a particular organization or process. An organization can use flowcharts to show the nature and use of the resources involved in its operations as well as the sequence of and relationships between those operations.

A manufacturer's flowchart might start with raw material acquisition and end with the finished product's delivery to the ultimate consumer. Individual entries on the flowchart, including the processes involved and the means by which products move from one process to the next, can help identify loss exposures—particularly critical loss exposures.

For example, the flowchart might illustrate that every item produced must be spray-painted during the production process. This activity presents a critical property loss exposure, because an explosion at the spray-painting location might disable the entire production line. The simplified flowchart in the exhibit reveals that difficulties with getting the furniture through customs at the Los Angeles Port could disrupt the entire furniture supply chain. See the exhibit "Furniture Manufacturer Flowchart."

Information can also be obtained from organizational charts. An organizational chart depicts the hierarchy of an organization's personnel and can help to identify key personnel for whom the organization may have a personnel loss exposure. This chart can also help track the flow of information through an organization and identify any bottlenecks that may exist. Although organizational charts can be fundamental in properly identifying personnel loss exposures, an individual's place on an organizational chart does not guarantee that he or she is a key employee. The organizational chart does not necessarily reflect the importance of the individual to the continued operation or profitability of the organization.

Loss Histories

Loss history analysis, that is, reviewing an organization's own losses or those suffered by comparable organizations, can help a risk management or an insurance professional to both identify and analyze loss exposures. Loss histories of comparable organizations are particularly helpful if the organization is too small or too new to have a sizeable record of its own past losses, or if the organization's own historical loss records are incomplete.

Any past loss can recur unless the organization has had a fundamental change in operations or property owned. Accordingly, loss histories are often an important indicator of an organization's current or future loss exposures. However, loss histories will not identify any loss exposures that have not resulted in past losses. Therefore, use of loss histories alone is inadequate.

Furniture Manufacturer Flowchart

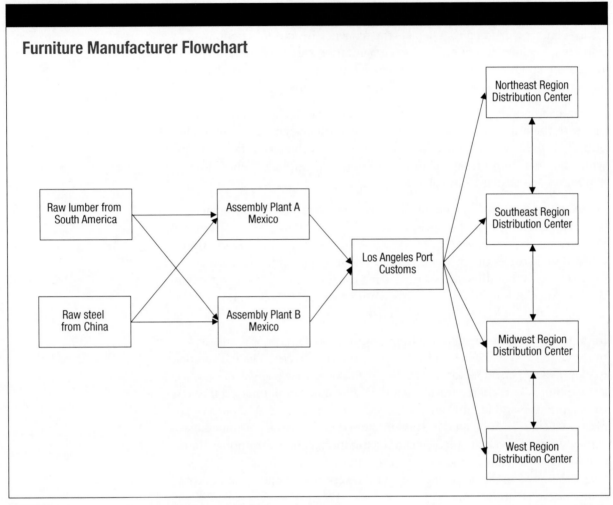

[DA02556]

Compliance Review

In addition to document analysis, insurance and risk management professionals may also conduct compliance reviews to identify loss exposures. A compliance review determines an organization's compliance with local, state, and federal statutes and regulations. The organization can conduct most of the compliance review itself if it has adequate in-house legal and accounting resources. Otherwise, it may have to use outside expertise.

The benefit of compliance reviews is that they can help an organization minimize or avoid liability loss exposures. However, a drawback of compliance reviews is that they are expensive and time consuming. Furthermore, because regulations are often changing, remaining in compliance requires ongoing monitoring. As a result, conducting a compliance review simply to identify loss exposures is often impractical. However, because noncompliance is a liability loss exposure, loss exposure identification can be part of the justification of the cost of a compliance review and is an ancillary benefit once a review has been completed.

Personal Inspections

Some loss exposures are best identified by personal inspections, that is, information-gathering visits to critical sites both within and outside an organization. Such visits often reveal loss exposures that would not appear in written descriptions of the organization's operations and therefore should lead to a more complete list of loss exposures.

Personal inspections should ideally be conducted by individuals whose background and skills equip them to identify unexpected, but possible, loss exposures. Additionally, the person conducting the inspection should take the opportunity to discuss the particular operations with front-line personnel, who are often best placed to identify nonobvious loss exposures. Therefore, a personal inspection can overlap with consulting expertise within and beyond the organization.

Expertise Within and Beyond the Organization

Thorough loss exposure identification should include soliciting expertise both inside and outside the organization. Doing so renders a more complete and objective picture of the organization's loss exposures.

Interviews with employees can be conducted to gather information about their jobs and departments. Whereas an inspection can only reveal what is happening during the inspection, interviews can elicit information about what occurred before the inspection, what might be planned for the future, or what could go or has gone wrong that has not been properly addressed.

Interviews should include a range of employees from every level of the organization. Questionnaires can be designed for use in conjunction with these interviews to ensure that they are comprehensive and are eliciting as much information as possible.

To obtain an external perspective, practitioners in fields such as law, finance, statistics, accounting, auditing, and the technology of the organization's industry can be consulted. The special knowledge of experts in identifying particular loss exposures is an invaluable resource.

One area of specialization that often requires such expert services is **hazard analysis**. For example, a business consultant might identify conditions that cause the organization to overlook opportunities for growth. Alternatively, concerns about environmental hazards might require a specialist to take air or water samples and a specialized laboratory to analyze them. Although hazard analysis is focused on loss exposures that have already been identified, the results of the analysis often identify previously overlooked loss exposures.

Hazard analysis
A method of analysis that identifies conditions that increase the frequency or severity of loss.

DATA REQUIREMENTS FOR EXPOSURE ANALYSIS

Loss exposure analysis is often based on probability and the statistical analysis of data. The statistical analysis of loss exposures starts with gathering sufficient data in a suitable form. Once these data have been collected, they can be subjected to a variety of probability and statistical techniques that are frequently used by insurance and risk management professionals.

The most common basis of an analysis of current or future loss exposures is information about past losses arising from similar loss exposures. To accurately analyze loss exposures using data on past losses, the data should meet four criteria. They should be relevant, complete, consistent, and organized.

Relevant Data

To analyze current loss exposures based on historical data, the past loss data for the loss exposures in question must be relevant to the current or future loss exposures the insurance or risk management professional is trying to assess. For example, if an organization was trying to assess its auto physical damage loss exposures for the next twelve months, it may examine its auto physical damage losses for the last four or five years and then take into account any changes in the makeup of its auto fleet and the rate of increase for repairs to determine potential losses for the next twelve months.

Although the organization may have auto physical damage records for the last twenty or thirty years, much of that data may no longer be relevant because of advances in auto engineering. Modern cars use different designs and materials that provide more for passenger safety at the expense of increased physical damage to the auto in the event of an accident. Therefore, data from ten years ago may not be relevant to today's auto physical damage loss exposures.

Similarly, relevant data for property losses include the property's repair or replacement cost at the time it is to be restored, not the property's historical or book value. For liability losses, the data should relate to past claims that are substantially the same as the potential future claims being assessed.

Even relatively minor differences in the factual and legal bases of claims can produce substantially different outcomes and costs. Data to analyze personnel loss exposures must relate to personnel with similar experience and expertise as those being considered as future loss exposures. The appropriate data for considering net income loss exposures would depend on the type of loss exposure being analyzed. Those data should involve similar reductions in revenue and similar additional expenses as would those loss exposures under consideration.

Complete Data

Obtaining complete data about past losses for particular loss exposures often requires relying on others, both inside and outside the organization. What constitutes complete data depends largely on the nature of the loss exposure being considered.

Having complete information helps to isolate the causes of each loss. Furthermore, having complete data enables the risk management professional to make reasonably reliable estimates of the dollar amounts of the future losses.

For example, considering loss exposures related to employee injuries would require historical loss data to include information regarding loss amounts, the employee's experience and training, the time of day of the loss, the task being performed, and the supervisor on duty at the time. Similarly, complete data on a property loss to a piece of machinery would include the cost of repairing or replacing any damaged or inoperative machinery, the resulting loss of revenue, any extra expenses, or any overtime wages paid to maintain production.

Consistent Data

To reflect past patterns, loss data must also be consistent in at least two respects. If data are inconsistent in either respect, the future loss exposures could be significantly underestimated or overestimated.

First, the loss data must be collected on a consistent basis for all recorded losses. Loss data are often collected from a variety of sources, each of which may use different accounting methods. Consequently, these data are likely to be inconsistent in their presentation.

For example, one common source of inconsistency results when some of the loss amounts being analyzed are reported as estimates and others are reported as actual paid amounts. Similarly, data will be inconsistent if some amounts are reported at their original cost and others are reported at their current replacement cost.

Second, data must be expressed in constant dollars, to adjust for differences in price levels. Differences in price levels will also lead to inconsistency. Two physically identical losses occurring in different years will probably have different values. Inflation distorts the later loss, making it appear more severe because it is measured in less valuable dollars.

To prevent this distortion, historical losses should be adjusted (indexed) so that loss data is expressed in constant dollars. To express data in constant dollars means that the amounts reported are comparable in terms of the value of goods and services that could be purchased in a particular benchmark year. Price indices are used to adjust data so that they are in constant dollars. See the exhibit "When a Dollar Is Not Worth a Dollar."

> ### When a Dollar Is Not Worth a Dollar
>
> When referring to historical values, a variety of terms are used, such as nominal dollars, current dollars, and real or constant dollars.
>
> Nominal dollars—dollar values at the time of the loss. For example, if a fire destroyed a building in 1995 and it cost $100,000 to repair the building in 1995, then the loss in nominal dollars is $100,000.
>
> Current dollars—dollar values today. This value involves inflating all historical dollar values to today's value by using some measure of inflation (such as the Consumer Price Index). For example, the $100,000 loss in 1995 is actually a $125,000 loss in today's (current) dollars.
>
> Real or constant dollars—dollar values in some base year. This value enables comparison of losses that have occurred in different time periods. The choice of base year does not matter. For convenience, the most recent year is often chosen. For example, suppose losses were reported over the four-year window 2002-2005. To determine real or constant dollars, multiply 2002 values by 1.08 (to account for the 8 percent increase in prices from 2002 to 2005) to convert the 2002 values into 2005 values for comparison. Similarly, 2003 losses would have to be multiplied by 1.06 and 2004 losses by 1.03.

[DA02571]

Organized Data

Even if data are relevant, complete, and consistent, if they are not appropriately organized they will be difficult for the insurance or risk management professional to use to identify patterns and trends that will help to reveal and quantify potential future loss exposures. Data can be organized in a variety of different ways, depending on which is most useful for the analysis being performed.

For example, listing losses for particular loss exposures by calendar dates may be useful for detecting seasonal patterns but may not disclose patterns that could be revealed by listing such losses by size. An array of losses—amounts of losses listed in increasing or decreasing value—could reveal clusters of losses by severity and could also focus attention on large losses, which are often most important for insurance and risk management decisions. Organizing losses by size is also the foundation for developing loss severity distributions or loss trends over time.

NATURE OF PROBABILITY

The probability of an event is the relative frequency with which the event can be expected to occur in the long run in a stable environment. Determining the probability that a certain event will occur can be an important part of exposure analysis in the risk management process.

Concepts affecting the basic nature of probability include theoretical probability, empirical probability, and the law of large numbers.

Theoretical Probability and Empirical Probability

Any probability can be expressed as a fraction, percentage, or decimal. For example, the probability of a head on a coin toss can be expressed as 1/2, 50 percent, or .50. The probability of an event that is totally impossible is 0 and the probability of an absolutely certain event is 1.0. Therefore, the probabilities of all events that are neither totally impossible nor absolutely certain are greater than 0 but less than 1.0.

Probabilities can be developed either from theoretical considerations or from historical data. **Theoretical probability** is probability that is based on theoretical principles rather than on actual experience. Probabilities associated with events such as coin tosses or dice throws can be developed from theoretical considerations and are unchanging. For example, from a description of a fair coin or die, a person who has never seen either a coin or a die can calculate the probability of flipping a head or rolling a four.

Empirical probability is probability that is based on actual experience. For example, the probability that a sixty-two-year-old male will die in a particular year cannot be theoretically determined, but must be estimated by studying the loss experience of a sample of men aged sixty-two. The empirical probabilities deduced solely from historical data may change as new data are discovered or as the environment that produces those events changes.

Empirical probabilities are only estimates whose accuracy depends on the size and representative nature of the samples being studied. In contrast, theoretical probabilities are constant as long as the physical conditions that generate them remain unchanged.

Although it may be preferable to use theoretical probabilities because of their unchanging nature, they are not applicable or available in most of the situations that insurance and risk management professionals are likely to analyze, such as automobile accidents or workers' compensation claims. As a result, empirical probabilities must be used.

Law of Large Numbers

Probability analysis is particularly effective for projecting losses in organizations that have (1) a substantial volume of data on past losses and (2) fairly stable operations so that (except for price level changes) patterns of past losses presumably will continue in the future. In organizations with this type of unchanging environment, past losses can be viewed as a sample of all possible losses that the organization might suffer.

The larger the number of past losses an organization has experienced, the larger the sample of losses that can be used in the analysis. Consequently, the forecasts of future losses are more reliable (consistent over time) because the forecast is based on a larger sample of the environment that produced the losses. This is an application of the **law of large numbers**.

Theoretical probability
Probability that is based on theoretical principles rather than on actual experience.

Empirical probability (a posteriori probability)
A probability measure that is based on actual experience through historical data or from the observation of facts.

Probability analysis
A technique for forecasting events, such as accidental and business losses, on the assumption that they are governed by an unchanging probability distribution.

Law of large numbers
A mathematical principle stating that as the number of similar but independent exposure units increases, the relative accuracy of predictions about future outcomes (losses) also increases.

As an example, suppose an urn holds four marbles. One of the marbles is red and three are black. Assume that the number of red or black marbles is not known. The task is to estimate the theoretical probability of choosing a red marble on one draw (sample) from the urn by repeatedly sampling the marbles and replacing each in the urn after the sampling.

After twenty samples a red marble has been chosen eight times, which yields an empirical frequency of 40 percent (8/20). However, this estimate is inaccurate because the theoretical probability is 25 percent (1/4), given that only one of the four marbles is red.

According to the law of large numbers, the relative inaccuracy between the empirical frequency (40 percent in this case) and the theoretical probability (25 percent) will decline, on average, as the sample size increases. That is, as the number of samples increases from 20 to 200 or 2,000, the empirical frequency of choosing a red marble gets closer and closer to 25 percent.

The law of large numbers has some limitations. It can be used to more accurately forecast future events only when the events being forecast meet all three of these criteria:

- The events have occurred in the past under substantially identical conditions and have resulted from unchanging, basic causal forces.

- The events can be expected to occur in the future under the same, unchanging conditions.

- The events have been, and will continue to be, both independent of one another and sufficiently numerous.

USING PROBABILITY DISTRIBUTIONS

Once empirical probabilities are determined, probability distributions can be constructed. The information provided by probability distributions can be instrumental in analyzing loss exposures and making risk management decisions.

Probability distribution

A presentation (table, chart, or graph) of probability estimates of a particular set of circumstances and of the probability of each possible outcome.

A properly constructed **probability distribution** always contains outcomes that are both mutually exclusive and collectively exhaustive. There are two forms of probability distributions: discrete and continuous. Discrete probability distributions have a finite number of possible outcomes and are typically used as frequency distributions. Continuous probability distributions have an infinite number of possible outcomes and are typically used as severity distributions.

Outcomes of a Properly Constructed Probability Distribution

Both theoretical probabilities (such as those involving tossing coins or rolling dice) and empirical probabilities (such as those involving the number or size of losses) have outcomes that are mutually exclusive and collectively exhaustive. For example, on a particular flip of a coin, only one outcome is possible: heads or tails. Therefore, these outcomes are mutually exclusive.

Similarly, these two outcomes are the only possible outcomes and, therefore, are collectively exhaustive. A properly constructed probability distribution always contains outcomes that are both mutually exclusive and collectively exhaustive. For example, the exhibit shows the hypothetical probability distribution of the number of hurricanes making landfall in Florida during any given hurricane season. Each outcome (hurricane) is mutually exclusive and the sum of the outcomes is 1.0, so they are collectively exhaustive. The second exhibit shows the distribution as a pie chart. See the exhibit "Number of Hurricanes Making Landfall in Florida During One Hurricane Season."

Number of Hurricanes Making Landfall in Florida During One Hurricane Season

Number of Hurricanes Making Landfall	Probability
0	.300
1	.350
2	.200
3	.147
4	.002
5+	.001
Total Probability	1.000

[DA02572]

Theoretical Probability Distributions

Consider the probability distribution of the total number of points on one throw of two dice, one red and one green. There are thirty-six equally likely outcomes (green 1, red 1; green 1, red 2; ... green 6, red 6). The exhibit shows three alternate presentations of this probability distribution—a table, a chart and a graph.

- All possible outcomes are accounted for (they are collectively exhaustive), and the occurrence of any possible outcome (such as green 1, red 1) excludes any other outcome.

- Eleven point values are possible (ranging from a total of two points to a total of twelve points), and the probability of each of these eleven possible point values is proportional to the number of times each point value appears in the table of outcomes.

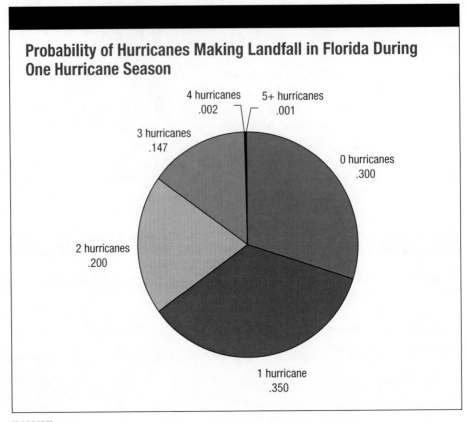

Probability of Hurricanes Making Landfall in Florida During One Hurricane Season

- 4 hurricanes .002
- 5+ hurricanes .001
- 3 hurricanes .147
- 0 hurricanes .300
- 2 hurricanes .200
- 1 hurricane .350

[DA02573]

- As the chart in the exhibit indicates, the probability of a total of two points is 1/36 because only one of the thirty-six possible outcomes (green 1, red 1) produces a total of two points.

- Similarly, 1/36 is the probability of a total of twelve points. The most likely total point value, seven points, has a probability of 6/36, represented in the table of outcomes by the diagonal southwest-northeast row of sevens. When the outcomes are presented as a graph, the height of the vertical line above each outcome indicates the probability of that outcome.

Although insurance and risk management professionals work with theoretical distributions on occasion, relatively few of the loss exposures they analyze involve theoretical probabilities. Therefore, most of the work they do involves empirical probability distributions. See the exhibit "Probability Distribution of Total Points on One Roll of Two Dice."

Empirical Probability Distributions

Empirical probability distributions (estimated from historical data) are constructed in the same way as theoretical probability distributions. The exhibit shows a hypothetical empirical probability distribution for auto physical damage losses. See the exhibit "Estimated Probability Distribution of Auto Physical Damage Losses."

Probability Distribution of Total Points on One Roll of Two Dice

A.   Table of Outcomes

		Red Die				
	1	2	3	4	5	6
Green Die 1	2	3	4	5	6	7
2	3	4	5	6	7	8
3	4	5	6	7	8	9
4	5	6	7	8	9	10
5	6	7	8	9	10	11
6	7	8	9	10	11	12

B.   Chart Format

Total Points Both Dice	Probability				
2	1/36	or	.028	or	2.8%
3	2/36	or	.056	or	5.6
4	3/36	or	.083	or	8.3
5	4/36	or	.111	or	11.1
6	5/36	or	.139	or	13.9
7	6/36	or	.167	or	16.7
8	5/36	or	.139	or	13.9
9	4/36	or	.111	or	11.1
10	3/36	or	.083	or	8.3
11	2/36	or	.056	or	5.6
12	1/36	or	.028	or	2.8
Total	36/36	or	1.000	or	100.0%

Note: Total may not sum to 1 or 100% because of rounding.

C.   Graph Format

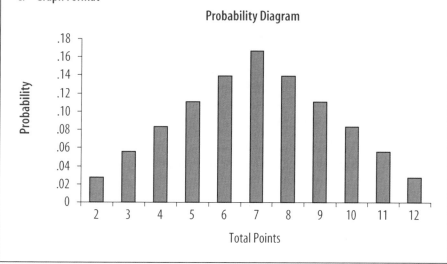

Probability Diagram

Estimated Probability Distribution of Auto Physical Damage Losses

(1)	(2)	(3)	(4)	(5)
Size Category of Losses (bins)	Number of Losses	Percentage of Number of Losses	Dollar Amount of Losses	Percentage of Dollar Amount
$0–$5,000	7	36.84%	$18,007	10.64%
$5,001–$10,000	7	36.84	51,448	30.39
$10,001–$15,000	2	10.53	27,298	16.13
$15,001–$20,000	1	5.26	15,589	9.21
$20,001–$25,000	1	5.26	21,425	12.66
$25,001+	1	5.26	35,508	20.98
Total	19	100.00%	$169,275	100.00%

Mean dollar amount = $8,909

[DA02575]

Because the first requirement of a probability distribution is that it provide a mutually exclusive, collectively exhaustive list of outcomes, loss categories (bins) must be designed so that all losses can be included. One method is to divide the bins into equal sizes, similar to the exhibit, with each bin size being a standard size (in this case, $5,000).

The second requirement of a probability distribution is that it define the set of probabilities associated with each of the possible outcomes. The exhibit shows empirical probabilities for each size category in Column 3.

To determine the empirical probabilities in Column 3, the number of losses for each category (Column 2) is divided by the total number of losses. The sum of the resulting empirical probabilities is 100 percent (that is, the outcomes are collectively exhaustive) and any given loss falls into only one category (the outcomes are mutually exclusive). Therefore, the empirical probability distribution for losses is described by Columns 1 and 3 and satisfies all the requirements of a probability distribution.

The empirical probability distribution for auto physical damage losses presented in the exhibit differs in two ways from the theoretical probability distributions of the dice rolls shown in the "Probability Distribution of Total Points on One Roll of Two Dice" exhibit:

- First, the outcomes shown in Column 1 of the auto physical damage exhibit (size categories of losses) are arbitrarily defined boundaries, whereas the outcomes of a roll of dice are specific and observable.

- Second, whereas the maximum possible dice total is twelve, the largest size of auto physical damage losses ($25,000+) has no evident upper limit.

Discrete and Continuous Probability Distributions

Probability distributions come in two forms: discrete probability distributions and continuous probability distributions. Discrete probability distributions have a finite number of possible outcomes, whereas continuous probability distributions have an infinite number of possible outcomes.

Discrete probability distributions are usually displayed in a table that lists all possible outcomes and the probability of each outcome. These distributions are typically used to analyze how often something will occur; that is, they are shown as frequency distributions. The number of hurricanes making landfall in Florida (shown in the "Number of Hurricanes Making Landfall in Florida During One Hurricane Season" exhibit) is an example of a frequency distribution.

Discrete probability distributions have a countable number of outcomes. For example, it is impossible to have 2.5 outcomes. In contrast, continuous probability distributions have an infinite number of possible outcome values and are generally represented in one of two ways: either as a graph or by dividing the distribution into a countable number of bins (shown in the "Estimated Probability Distribution of Auto Physical Damage Losses" exhibit).

The "Continuous Probability Distributions" exhibit illustrates two representations of continuous probability distributions. The possible outcomes are presented on the horizontal axes, and the likelihood of those outcomes is shown in the vertical axes. The height of the line or curve above the outcomes indicates the likelihood of that outcome. The outcomes in a continuous probability distribution are called probability density functions. Continuous probability distributions are typically used for severity distributions—they depict the value of the loss rather than the number of outcomes.

Figure (a) in the "Continuous Probability Distributions" exhibit, which has a flat line above the interval $0 to $1,000, illustrates that all of the outcomes between $0 and $1,000 are equally likely. Figure (b), which has a curve that starts at $0 and increases until it reaches a peak at $500 and then declines to $0 again at $1,000, illustrates that the very low (close to $0) and very high (close to $1,000) outcomes are unlikely and that the outcomes around $500 are much more likely. See the exhibit "Continuous Probability Distributions."

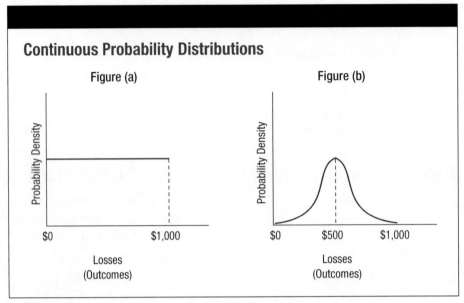

Continuous Probability Distributions

[DA02576]

The other way of presenting a continuous probability distribution is to divide the distribution into a countable number of bins. The "Estimated Probability Distribution of Auto Physical Damage Losses" exhibit displays auto physical damage losses in a continuous probability distribution that has been divided into six bins described by various ranges of losses. Although the auto physical damage distribution is a continuous probability distribution, the dividing of the losses into bins makes the continuous distribution resemble a discrete probability distribution with several outcomes.

In continuous probability distributions used as severity distributions, the value lost can take any value between $0 and some upper limit (such as $1,000,000). By definition, continuous probability distributions have an infinite number of possible outcomes (otherwise they are discrete distributions). Therefore, the probability of any given outcome is zero, as there are an uncountable number of other outcomes.

As a result, an insurance or risk management professional has to divide the continuous distribution into a finite number of bins. When divided into bins, a probability of an outcome falling within a certain range can be calculated.

For example, in a discrete frequency distribution, the probability of a high-rise office building not having a fire (zero fires) may be .50, of having one fire—.35, and of having two fires—.15. If a fire occurs, the damage may be anywhere between $0 and $1,000,000,000, which is a continuous severity distribution.

It is almost impossible for an insurance or risk management professional to assign a probability to the likelihood of having a loss amount of $35,456.32. However, if the severity distribution is divided into a finite number of bins,

$0–$1,000,000, $1,000,001–$2,000,000, and so on, it is possible to assign a probability to each bin.

For example, the probability of the damage being between $0 and $1,000,000 is .25, and the probability of the damage being between $1,000,001 and $2,000,000 is .30. By dividing a continuous distribution into bins, the insurance or risk management professional simplifies the analysis necessary to develop a forecast of future losses using frequency and severity distributions.

USING CENTRAL TENDENCY

In analyzing a probability distribution, the measures of central tendency represent the best guess as to what the outcome will be. For example, if a manager asked an underwriter what the expected losses from fire would be on a store that the underwriter had insured, the underwriter's best guess would be one of the measures of central tendency of the frequency distribution multiplied by one of the measures of central tendency of the severity distribution. So, if the expected number of fires was two, and each fire had an expected severity of $5,000, the underwriter would expect $10,000 in losses.

After determining empirical probabilities and constructing probability distributions, the insurance or risk management professional can use **central tendency** to compare the characteristics of those probability distributions. Many probability distributions cluster around a particular value, which may or may not be in the exact center of the distribution's range of values. The three most widely accepted measures of central tendency are the expected value or mean, the median, and the mode.

Central tendency
The single outcome that is the most representative of all possible outcomes included within a probability distribution.

Expected Value

The **expected value** is the weighted average of all of the possible outcomes of a theoretical probability distribution. The weights are the probabilities of the outcomes. The outcomes of a probability distribution are symbolized as *x1, x2, x3, ... xn* (*xn* represents the last outcome in the series), having respective probabilities of *p1, p2, p3, ... pn*. The distribution's expected value is the sum of *(p1 × x1) + (p2 × x2) + (p3 × x3) + ... (pn × xn)*. See the exhibit "Calculating the Expected Value of a Probability Distribution—The Two Dice Example."

Expected value
The weighted average of all of the possible outcomes of a probability distribution.

In the example of a probability distribution of total points on one roll of a pair of dice, the distribution's expected value of 7.0 is shown in the exhibit as the sum of the values in Column 3.

The procedure for calculating the expected value applies to all theoretical discrete probability distributions, regardless of their shape or dispersion. For continuous distributions, the expected value is also a weighted average of the possible outcomes. However, calculating the expected value for a continuous distribution is much more complex and therefore is not discussed here.

Calculating the Expected Value of a Probability Distribution—The Two Dice Example

(1) Total Points— Both Dice (x)	(2) Probability (p)	(3) p × x	(4) Cumulative Probability (sum of p's)
2	1/36	2/36	1/36
3	2/36	6/36	3/36
4	3/36	12/36	6/36
5	4/36	20/36	10/36
6	5/36	30/36	15/36
7	6/36	42/36	21/36
8	5/36	40/36	26/36
9	4/36	36/36	30/36
10	3/36	30/36	33/36
11	2/36	22/36	35/36
12	1/36	12/36	36/36 or 100%
Total	36/36 = 1	252/36 = 7.0	

Expected Value = 252/36 = 7.0
Median = 7 (There is an equal number of outcomes (15) above and below 7.)
Mode = 7 (The most frequent outcome.)

[DA02577]

Mean

Probabilities are needed to calculate a theoretical distribution's expected value. However, when considering an empirical distribution constructed from historical data, the measure of central tendency is not called the expected value, it is called the **mean**. In other words, the mean is the numeric average. Just as the expected value is calculated by weighting each possible outcome by its probability, the mean is calculated by weighting each observed outcome by the relative frequency with which it occurs.

Mean
The sum of the values in a data set divided by the number of values.

For example, if the observed outcome values are 2, 3, 4, 4, 5, 5, 5, 6, 6, and 8, then the mean equals 4.8, which is the sum of the values, 48, divided by the number of values, 10. The mean is only a good estimate of the expected outcome if the underlying conditions determining those outcomes remain constant over time.

Unlike the expected value, which is derived from theory, the mean is derived from experience. If the conditions that generated that experience have changed, the mean that was calculated may no longer be an accurate estimate of central tendency. Nonetheless, an insurance or a risk management professional will often use the mean as the single best guess as to forecasting future events.

For example, the best guess as to the number of workers compensation claims that an organization will suffer in the next year is often the mean of the frequency distribution of workers compensation claims from previous years.

Median and Cumulative Probabilities

Another measure of central tendency is the **median**. In order to determine a data set's median, its values must be arranged by size, from highest to lowest or lowest to highest. In the array of nineteen auto physical damage losses in the exhibit, the median loss has an adjusted value of $6,782. This tenth loss is the median because nine losses are greater than $6,782 and nine losses are less than $6,782. See the exhibit "Array of Historical and Adjusted Auto Physical Damage Losses."

A probability distribution's median has a cumulative probability of 50 percent. For example, seven is the median of the probability distribution of points in rolling two dice because seven is the only number of points for which the probability of higher outcomes (15/36) is equal to the probability of lower outcomes (15/36). That is, there are fifteen equally probable ways of obtaining an outcome higher than seven and fifteen equally probable ways of obtaining an outcome lower than seven.

The median can also be determined by summing the probabilities of outcomes equal to or less than a given number of points in rolling two dice, as in the "Calculating the Expected Value of a Probability Distribution—The Two Dice Example" exhibit. The cumulative 50 percent probability (18/36) is reached in the seven-points category (actually, in the middle of the seven-point class of results). Therefore, seven is the median of this distribution.

The cumulative probabilities in Column 4 of the exhibit indicate the probability of a die roll yielding a certain number of points or less. For example, the cumulative probability of rolling a three or less is 3/36 (or the sum of 1/36 for rolling a two and 2/36 for rolling a three). Similarly, the cumulative probability of rolling a ten or less is 33/36, calculated by summing the individual Column 2 probabilities of outcomes of ten points or less.

With probability distributions of losses, calculating probabilities of losses equal to or less than a given number of losses or dollar amounts of losses, individually and cumulatively, can be helpful in selecting retention levels. Similarly, calculating individual and cumulative probabilities of losses equal to or greater than a given number of losses or dollar amounts can help in selecting upper limits of insurance coverage.

The "Cumulative Probabilities" exhibit shows how to derive a cumulative probability distribution of loss sizes from the individual probabilities of loss

Median

The value at the midpoint of a sequential data set with an odd number of values, or the mean of the two middle values of a sequential data set with an even number of values.

Array of Historical and Adjusted Auto Physical Damage Losses

(1) Date	(2) Historical Loss Amount	(3) Adjusted Loss Amount*	(4) Rank
09/29/X3	$ 155	$ 200	19
04/21/X3	1,008	1,300	18
03/18/X4	1,271	1,500	17
12/04/X3	1,783	2,300	16
07/27/X5	3,774	4,000	15
06/14/X6	4,224	4,224	14
04/22/X6	4,483	4,483	13
02/08/X5**	5,189	5,500	12
05/03/X3	4,651	5,999	11
01/02/X6**	6,782	6,782	10
07/12/X4	6,271	7,402	9
05/17/X5**	7,834	8,303	8
08/15/X4	7,119	8,403	7
06/10/X6	9,059	9,059	6
12/19/X5	12,830	13,599	5
08/04/X5	12,925	13,699	4
11/01/X4	13,208	15,589	3
01/09/X6	21,425	21,425	2
10/23/X6	35,508	35,508	1

*   Adjusted amount column is the historical loss amount adjusted to current year dollars using a price index.

** Loss for which adjustment of historical amount to current year dollars changes ranking in array.

[DA02578]

size in the exhibit. See the exhibit "Cumulative Probabilities That Auto Physical Damage Losses Will Not Exceed Specified Amounts."

Column 3 of the "Cumulative Probabilities" exhibit indicates that, on the basis of the available data, 36.84 percent of all losses are less than or equal to $5,000 and that another 36.84 percent are greater than $5,000 but less than or equal to $10,000. Therefore, the probability of a loss being $10,000 or less is calculated as the sum of these two probabilities, or 73.68 percent, as shown in Column 4 of the "Cumulative Probabilities" exhibit. Similarly, as shown in Column 7 of the same exhibit, individual losses of $10,000 or less can be expected to account for 41.03 percent of the total dollar amount of all losses.

Cumulative Probabilities That Auto Physical Damage Losses Will Not Exceed Specified Amounts

(1) Loss Size Category	(2) Number of Losses	(3) Percentage of Number of Losses	(4) Cumulative Percentage of Number of Losses Not Exceeding Category	(5) Dollar Amount of Losses	(6) Percentage of Dollar Amount	(7) Cumulative Percentage of Dollar Amount of Losses Not Exceeding Category
$0–$5,000	7	36.84%	36.84%	$18,007	10.64%	10.64%
$5,001–$10,000	7	36.84	73.68	51,448	30.39	41.03
$10,001–$15,000	2	10.53	84.21	27,298	16.13	57.16
$15,001–$20,000	1	5.26	89.47	15,589	9.21	66.37
$20,001–$25,000	1	5.26	94.74	21,425	12.66	79.02
$25,001+	1	5.26	100.00	35,508	20.98	100.00
Total		100.00%			100.00%	

Understanding the cumulative probability distribution will enable an insurance or risk management professional to evaluate the effect of various deductibles and policy limits on insured loss exposures. For example, if an insurance policy has a $5,000 deductible, the insurance or risk management professional would know that 36.84 percent of losses covered by that policy would be below the deductible level and therefore would not be paid by the insurer.

The summed probabilities in Column 4 of the "Cumulative Probabilities" exhibit indicate that the median individual loss is between $5,001 and $10,000, the category in which the 50 percent cumulative probability is reached. This result is consistent with the $6,782 median loss found by examining the "Array of Historical and Adjusted Auto Physical Damage Losses" exhibit.

Mode

Mode

The most frequently occurring value in a distribution.

In addition to mean and median, a further measure of central tendency is the **mode**. For a continuous distribution, the mode is the value of the outcome directly beneath the peak of the probability density function. In the distribution of total points of two dice throws, the mode is seven points. In the empirical distribution of auto physical damage losses shown in the "Cumulative Probabilities" exhibit, the mode is the $0–$5,000 range or the $5,001–$10,000 range, because those ranges have the highest frequency of losses (seven).

Knowing the mode of a distribution allows insurance and risk management professionals to focus on the outcomes that are the most common. For example, knowing that the most common auto physical damage losses are in the $0–$10,000 range may influence the risk financing decisions regarding deductible levels for potential insurance coverages.

The relationships among the mean (average), median, and mode for any data set are illustrated by the distribution's shape. The shape of a particular relative frequency or severity probability distribution can be seen by graphing a curve of the data as shown in the "Typical Shapes" exhibit and can be either symmetrical or asymmetrical. See the exhibit "Typical Shapes of Symmetrical and Skewed Distributions Showing Relative Locations of Mean, Median, and Mode."

In a symmetrical distribution, one side of the curve is a mirror image of the other. The distribution in Figure (a) of the exhibit is the standard (normal) distribution commonly called a bell-shaped curve, but the distributions in both Figure (a) and Figure (b) are symmetrical. In a symmetrical distribution, the mean and median have the same value. In a standard bell-shaped distribution, the mode also has the same value as that of the mean and the median.

If a distribution is asymmetrical, it is skewed. Skewed distributions are shown in both Figure (c) and Figure (d) of the exhibit. Many loss distributions are

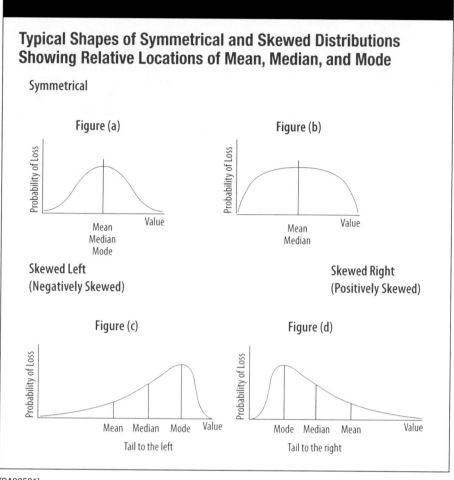

Typical Shapes of Symmetrical and Skewed Distributions Showing Relative Locations of Mean, Median, and Mode

[DA02581]

skewed because the probability of small losses is large whereas the probability of large losses is small. Asymmetrical distributions are common for severity distributions where most losses are small losses but there is a small probability of a large loss occurring. If the distribution is skewed, the mean and median values will differ and the median value of the distribution is often a better guess than the mean as to what is most likely to occur.

For example, if the distribution of workers compensation claims was skewed by two years in which an organization experienced an unusually high level of claims, the mean would be higher than the median. In that situation, the median is more likely a better estimate of next year's claims than the mean. See the exhibit "Practice Exercise."

Practice Exercise

Based on the mean of the total workers compensation losses for each year, the risk manager of an airline company expects the total amount of such losses next year to be $2 million. The chief financial officer has assured the risk manager that the company can afford to retain half of that amount ($1 million) in an effort to reduce the insurance premium. Using the values provided in the chart, what is the highest aggregate annual deductible the risk manager should consider?

Loss Size Category	Dollar Amount of Losses	Percentage of Total Dollar Amount of Losses
$0 – $10,000	$500,000	25%
$10,001 – $20,000	$300,000	15%
$20,001 – $50,000	$300,000	15%
$50,001 – $100,000	$400,000	20%
$100,001 +	$500,000	25%
Total	$2,000,000	100%

Answer

By adding the percentages of total dollar amounts to obtain cumulative percentages (shown in the new column, far right), the risk manager can see that 50 percent, or $1 million, will likely be retained by the company if it chooses a deductible of slightly less than $50,000. The risk manager may want to resize the loss size categories to derive a more accurate number.

Loss Size Category	Dollar Amount of Losses	Percentage of Total Dollar Amount of Losses	Cumulative Percentage of Dollar Amount of Losses Not Exceeding Category
$0 – $10,000	$500,000	25%	25%
$10,001 – $20,000	$300,000	15%	40%
$20,001 – $50,000	$300,000	15%	55%
$50,001 – $100,000	$400,000	20%	75%
$100,001 +	$500,000	25%	100%
Total	$2,000,000	100%	

[DA05840]

USING DISPERSION

When analyzing probability distributions, insurance and risk management professionals use measures of dispersion to assess the credibility of the measures of central tendency used in analyzing loss exposures.

Measures of central tendency for a distribution of outcomes include the expected value (or mean), which can provide useful information for comparing characteristics of distributions. However, another important characteristic of a distribution is its **dispersion**. Dispersion describes the extent to which the distribution is spread out rather than concentrated around the expected value. The less dispersion around the distribution's expected value, the greater the likelihood that actual results will fall within a given range of that expected value.

Therefore, less dispersion means less uncertainty about the expected outcomes. Insurance professionals may be able to use measures of dispersion around estimated losses to determine whether to offer insurance coverage to a possible insured. Dispersion also affects the shape of a distribution. The more dispersed a distribution (larger standard deviation), the flatter the distribution. A less dispersed distribution forms a more peaked distribution. Two symmetrical distributions with the same mean but with different standard deviations are shown in the "Dispersion" exhibit. See the exhibit "Dispersion."

Dispersion

The variation among values in a distribution.

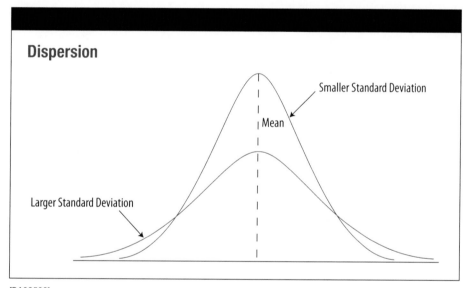

Dispersion

Smaller Standard Deviation

Mean

Larger Standard Deviation

[DA02582]

For example, if an underwriter is choosing between two accounts, both with the same expected loss, but one account has more variation in possible losses then the other, the underwriter will likely choose to insure the account with less variation (lower dispersion). In general, the less dispersion around the central tendency, the less risk is involved in the loss exposure.

There are two widely used statistical measures of dispersion:

- Standard deviation
- Coefficient of variation

Standard Deviation

Standard deviation

A measure of dispersion between the values in a distribution and the expected value (or mean) of that distribution, calculated by taking the square root of the variance.

The **standard deviation** is the average of the differences (deviations) between the values in a distribution and the expected value (or mean) of that distribution. The standard deviation therefore indicates how widely dispersed the values in a distribution are.

To calculate the standard deviation of a probability distribution, one must perform these steps:

1. Calculate the distribution's expected value or mean
2. Subtract this expected value from each distribution value to find the differences
3. Square each of the resulting differences
4. Multiply each square by the probability associated with the value
5. Sum the resulting products
6. Find the square root of the sum

The "Calculation of Standard Deviation of the Probability Distribution of Two Dice" exhibit illustrates how to calculate a standard deviation for the distribution of values in rolling two dice. The distribution's expected value or mean is seven. See the exhibit "Calculation of Standard Deviation of the Probability Distribution of Two Dice."

The standard deviation of auto physical damage losses can be estimated using the individual loss amounts shown in Column (1) of the "Calculation of Standard Deviation of Individual Outcomes" exhibit. Calculating a standard deviation using a sample of actual outcomes is done in much the same way as for a probability distribution. To calculate the standard deviation using the actual sample of outcomes, it is not necessary to know the probability of each outcome, just how often each outcome occurred. See the exhibit "Calculation of Standard Deviation of Individual Outcomes."

The steps for calculating the standard deviation of a set of individual outcomes not involving probabilities are these:

1. Calculate the mean of the outcomes (the sum of the outcomes divided by the number of outcomes)
2. Subtract the mean from each of the outcomes
3. Square each of the resulting differences
4. Sum these squares
5. Divide this sum by the number of outcomes minus one (this value is called the variance)
6. Calculate the square root of the variance

The "Calculation of Standard Deviation of Individual Outcomes" exhibit illustrates how to calculate a standard deviation using actual loss data rather than a theoretical probability distribution. Insurance and risk management

Calculation of Standard Deviation of the Probability Distribution of Two Dice

(1) Points (x_i)	(2) Probability (p)	(3) Step 1 EV	(4) Step 2 $x_i - EV$	(5) Step 3 $(x_i - EV)^2$	(6) Step 4 $(x_i - EV)^2 \times p$
2	1/36	7	−5	25	25/36
3	2/36	7	−4	16	32/36
4	3/36	7	−3	9	27/36
5	4/36	7	−2	4	16/36
6	5/36	7	−1	1	5/36
7	6/36	7	0	0	0
8	5/36	7	1	1	5/36
9	4/36	7	2	4	16/36
10	3/36	7	3	9	27/36
11	2/36	7	4	16	32/36
12	1/36	7	5	25	25/36
			Step 5	Total	210/36
			Step 6	$\sqrt{(210/36)} =$	2.42*

*Rounded

[DA02583]

professionals use measurements of dispersion of the distributions of potential outcomes to gain a better understanding of the loss exposures being analyzed.

For example, knowing the expected number of workers compensation claims in a given year is important, but it is only one element of the information that can be gleaned from a distribution. The standard deviation can be calculated to provide a measure of how sure an insurance or risk management professional can be in his or her estimate of number of workers compensation claims.

Coefficient of Variation

The **coefficient of variation** is a further measure of the dispersion of a distribution. For example, the coefficient of variation for the distribution of total points in rolling two dice equals 2.4 points (the standard deviation of the distribution) divided by 7.0 points (the mean or expected value), which is 0.34. Similarly the coefficient of variation of the sample of outcomes in the "Calculation of Standard Deviation of Individual Outcomes" exhibit is $8,430 divided by $8,909, or approximately 0.95.

Coefficient of variation

A measure of dispersion calculated by dividing a distribution's standard deviation by its mean.

Calculation of Standard Deviation of Individual Outcomes

(1) Adjusted Loss Amount (ALA)	(2) Step 1 Mean Loss (ML)	(3) Step 2 ALA-ML	(4) Step 3 (ALA-ML)^2
$ 200	$8,909	$-8,709	$ 75,846,681
1,300	8,909	−7,609	57,896,881
1,500	8,909	−7,409	54,893,281
2,300	8,909	−6,609	43,678,881
4,000	8,909	−4,909	24,098,281
4,224	8,909	−4,685	21,949,225
4,483	8,909	−4,426	19,589,476
5,500	8,909	−3,409	11,621,281
5,999	8,909	−2,910	8,468,100
6,782	8,909	−2,127	4,524,129
7,402	8,909	−1,507	2,271,049
8,303	8,909	−606	367,236
8,403	8,909	−506	256,036
9,059	8,909	150	22,500
13,599	8,909	4,690	21,996,100
13,699	8,909	4,790	22,944,100
15,589	8,909	6,680	44,622,400
21,425	8,909	12,516	156,650,256
35,508	8,909	26,599	707,506,801
Step 4 Sum			$1,279,202,694
Step 5 Variance [sum ÷ (n − 1)]			71,066,816
Step 6 Standard deviation (sqrt variance)			$8,430

[DA02584]

In comparing two distributions, if both distributions have the same mean (or expected value), then the distribution with the larger standard deviation has the greater variability. If the two distributions have different means (or expected values), the coefficient of variation is often used to compare the two distributions to determine which has the greater variability relative to its mean (or expected value).

For insurance and risk management professionals, comparing two distinct distributions with different means and standard deviations is difficult. In the example of an underwriter trying to determine to which account to offer coverage, if the means are the same, all else being equal, the underwriter should choose the account with the lower standard deviation. If the accounts have different means and standard deviations, the underwriter could compare the two accounts using the coefficient of variation and choose the account with the lower coefficient of variation.

Insurance and risk management professionals can use the coefficient of variation to determine whether a particular loss control measure has made losses more or less predictable (that is, whether the distribution is more or less variable).

For example, an insurance or a risk management professional may calculate that an organization's theft losses have a severity distribution with a mean of $3,590 and a standard deviation of $3,432 for a coefficient of variation of 0.96. If the organization installs a new security system, the theft losses may have a severity distribution with a mean of $2,150 and a standard deviation of $2,950 for a coefficient of variation of 1.37.

Although the security system has reduced the mean severity, it has actually made the losses less predictable because the new severity distribution is relatively more variable than the old distribution without the security system.

The coefficient of variation is useful in comparing the variability of distributions that have different shapes, means, or standard deviations. The distribution with the largest coefficient of variation has the greatest relative variability. The higher the variability within a distribution, the more difficult it is to accurately forecast an individual outcome.

USING NORMAL DISTRIBUTIONS

Insurance and risk management professionals use normal probability distributions to predict future losses, which enables them to marshal the resources to control losses that can be prevented or mitigated and to finance those that cannot.

The **normal distribution** is a probability distribution that, when graphed, generates a bell-shaped curve. This particular probability distribution can help to accurately forecast the variability around some central, average, or expected value and has therefore proven useful in accurately forecasting the variability of many physical phenomena.

Normal distribution

A probability distribution that, when graphed, generates a bell-shaped curve.

Characteristics of Normal Distributions

The exhibit illustrates the typical bell-shaped curve of a normal distribution. Note that the normal curve never touches the horizontal line at the base of the diagram. In theory, the normal distribution assigns some probability greater than zero for every outcome, regardless of its distance from the mean. The exhibit also shows the percentage of outcomes that fall within a given number of standard deviations above or below the mean of a distribution. See the exhibit "The Normal Distribution—Percentages of Outcomes Within Specified Standard Deviations of the Mean."

The Normal Distribution—Percentages of Outcomes Within Specified Standard Deviations of the Mean

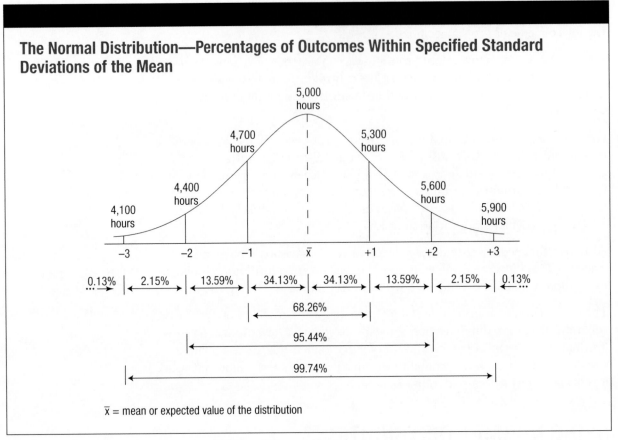

$\bar{x}$ = mean or expected value of the distribution

[DA02585]

For example, for all normal distributions, 34.13 percent of all outcomes are within one standard deviation above the mean and, because every normal distribution is symmetrical, another 34.13 percent of all outcomes fall within one standard deviation below the mean. By addition, 68.26 percent of all outcomes are within one standard deviation above or below the mean. The portion of a normal distribution that is between one and two standard deviations above the mean contains 13.59 percent of all outcomes, as does the portion between one and two standard deviations below the mean. Hence, the area between the mean and two standard deviations above the mean contains 47.72 percent (34.13 percent + 13.59 percent) of the outcomes, and another 47.72 percent are two standard deviations or less below the mean.

Consequently, 95.44 percent of all outcomes are within two standard deviations above or below the mean, and fewer than 5 percent of outcomes are outside two standard deviations above or below the mean. Taking this a step further, 2.15 percent of all outcomes are between two and three standard deviations above the mean, and another 2.15 percent are between two and three standard deviations below the mean. Therefore, 49.87 percent (34.13 percent + 13.59 percent + 2.15 percent) of all outcomes are three standard deviations or less above the mean, and an equal percentage are three standard deviations or less below the mean.

Consequently, the portion of the distribution between three standard deviations above the mean and three standard deviations below it contains 99.74 percent (49.87 percent × 2) of all outcomes. Therefore, only 0.26 percent (100 percent – 99.74 percent) of all outcomes lie beyond three standard deviations from the mean. Half of these outcomes (0.13 percent) are more than three standard deviations below the mean, and the other half (0.13 percent) are more than three standard deviations above the mean.

Practical Application

The relationship between the expected value and the standard deviation of a normal distribution can have useful practical application. For example, suppose that a plant uses 600 electrical elements to heat rubber. The useful life of each element is limited, and an element that is used for too long poses a substantial danger of exploding and starting an electrical fire. An insurance professional underwriting the plant's fire insurance would look for evidence that proper maintenance is performed and the elements are replaced to ensure proper fire safety.

The issue is determining when to replace the elements. Replacing them too soon can be costly, whereas replacing them too late increases the chance of fire. The characteristics of the normal probability distribution provide a way of scheduling maintenance so that the likelihood of an element becoming very dangerous before it is replaced can be kept below a particular margin of safety that is specified by the organization based on its willingness to assume risk.

Assume that the expected safe life of each element conforms to a normal distribution having a mean of 5,000 hours and a standard deviation of 300 hours. Even if the maintenance schedule requires replacing each element after it has been in service only 5,000 hours (the mean, or expected, safe life), a 50 percent chance exists that it will become unsafe before being changed, because 50 percent of the normal distribution is below this 5,000-hour mean.

If each element is changed after having been used only 4,700 hours [one standard deviation below the mean (5,000 – 300)], a 15.87 percent (50 percent – 34.13 percent) chance still exists that an element will become unsafe before being changed. If this probability of high hazard is still too high, changing each element after 4,400 hours [two standard deviations below the mean (5,000 – (2 × 300))] reduces the probability of high hazard to only 2.28 percent, the portion of a normal distribution that is more than two standard deviations below the mean.

A still more cautious practice would be to change elements routinely after only 4,100 hours [three standard deviations below the mean (5,000 – (3

× 300))], so that the probability of an element becoming highly hazardous before replacement would be only 0.13 percent, slightly more than one
chance in 1,000.

Using this analysis, management can select an acceptable probability that an
element will become unsafe before being replaced and can schedule maintenance accordingly. See the exhibit "Practice Exercise."

Practice Exercise

An insurer is beginning to write policies in a new state. The insurer's claim manager
wants to know how many new claim representatives to hire. The insurer's marketing
department has provided an estimate of additional premium volume from the new
state. Based on that estimate and industry data, the manager has determined the mean
number of new claims to be 8,000, with a standard deviation of 2,000 in a normal
distribution. If a claim representative can adjust 600 claims per year and the manager
wants to be approximately 98 percent certain that she has enough representatives,
how many will she need to hire?

Answer

As shown in the exhibit titled "The Normal Distribution—Percentages of Outcomes
Within Specified Standard Deviations of the Mean," 2.28 percent of all outcomes (2.15
percent + 0.13 percent) are more than two standard deviations above the mean, and
97.72 percent (100 percent – 2.28 percent) of all outcomes fall under the normal
distribution below two standard deviations above the mean. Therefore, by rounding up
the 97.72 percent, the claim manager can be approximately 98 percent certain that the
actual number of claims will fall at or below two standard deviations above the mean.
In the claim manager's distribution, two standard deviations above the mean is 12,000
claims (calculated as 8,000 + 2,000 + 2,000). Because each claim representative
can adjust 600 claims per year, the manager will need to hire 12,000/600 or 20 new
representatives.

[DA05841]

ANALYZING LOSS EXPOSURES

Analyzing loss frequency, loss severity, total dollar losses, and timing helps
insurance and risk management professionals develop loss projections, and,
therefore, also helps them prioritize loss exposures so that risk management
resources can be concentrated where they are needed most.

The analysis step of the risk management process involves considering the
four dimensions of a loss exposure:

- Loss frequency—the number of losses (such as fires, auto accidents, or
  liability claims) that occur during a specific period.

- Loss severity—the dollar amount of loss for a specific occurrence.

- Total dollar losses—the total dollar amount of losses for all occurrences during a specific period.

- Timing—the points at which losses occur and loss payments are made. (The period between loss occurrence and loss payment can be lengthy.)

If any of these dimensions of loss exposure analysis involve empirical distributions developed from past losses, the credibility of the data being used needs to be determined. Data credibility is the level of confidence that available data are accurate indicators of future losses.

Loss Frequency

Loss frequency is the number of losses—such as fires, thefts, or floods—that occur during a specific period. Relative loss frequency is the number of losses that occur within a given period relative to the number of exposure units (such as the number of buildings or cars exposed to loss).

For example, if an organization experiences, on average, five theft losses per year, five is the mean of an empirical frequency distribution. If the organization has only one building, then both the loss frequency and the relative frequency of losses from theft is five per year. However, if the organization has five buildings, then the organization still has a loss frequency of five theft losses per year, but the relative frequency is one loss per year per building. Two of the most common applications of relative frequency measures in risk management are injuries per person per hour in workers compensation and auto accidents per mile driven.

Frequency distributions are usually discrete probability distributions based on past data regarding how often similar events have happened. For example, the "Skewness of Number of Hurricanes Making Landfall in Florida During Hurricane Season" exhibit contains the frequency distribution of the number of hurricanes that make landfall in Florida during a single hurricane season. One way of describing the frequency of hurricanes is to report a mean frequency of occurrence, such as approximately 1.2 hurricanes making landfall per year. See the exhibit "Skewness of Number of Hurricanes Making Landfall in Florida During One Hurricane Season."

However, this figure does not incorporate some of the other information available from the entire frequency distribution. For example, the most likely outcome may be one hurricane per year (35.0 percent of the time). However, having zero hurricanes per year is also reasonably likely (30.0 percent of the time), but having five or more hurricanes make landfall in Florida is reasonably unlikely (0.1 percent of the time). Therefore, an insurance or risk management professional should supplement the mean of 1.2 with other information from the frequency distribution, such as the standard deviation (which is approximately 1.04) and skewness measures.

Loss frequency can be projected with a fairly high degree of confidence for some loss exposures in large organizations. For example, a company that

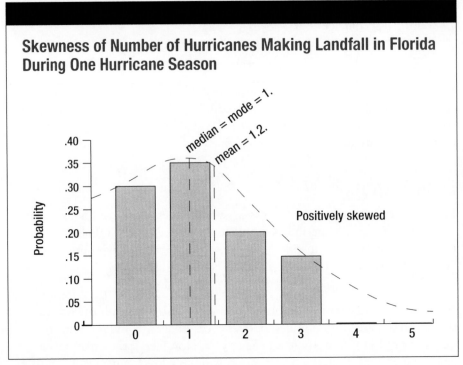

Skewness of Number of Hurricanes Making Landfall in Florida During One Hurricane Season

[DA02586]

ships thousands of parcels each day probably can more accurately project the number of transit losses it will sustain in a year, based on past experience and adjusted for any expected changes in future conditions, than can a company that ships only hundreds of parcels each month.

Most organizations do not have enough exposure units to accurately project low-frequency, high-severity events (such as employee deaths). However, an estimate with a margin for error is better than no estimate at all, as long as its limitations are recognized.

Loss Severity

The purpose of analyzing loss severity is to determine how serious a loss might be. For example, how much of a building could be damaged in a single fire? Alternatively, how long might it take for an organization to resume operations after a fire?

Maximum Possible Loss

Effectively managing risk requires identifying the worst possible outcome of a loss. The maximum possible loss (MPL) is the total value exposed to loss at any one location or from any one event. For example, in the case of fire damage to a building and its contents, the maximum possible loss is typically the value of the building plus the total value of the building's contents.

To determine MPL for multiple exposure units, such as a fleet of cars, an insurance or risk management professional may consider factors such as whether multiple vehicles travel together (a circumstance that could cause one event, such as a collision, to affect several vehicles at once) or whether several vehicles are stored in the same location (a circumstance that could cause one event, such as a fire, flood, or theft, to affect several vehicles). This helps determine the maximum number of vehicles that could be involved in any one loss and therefore the event's MPL.

Although maximum possible property losses can be estimated based on the values exposed to loss, this estimation is not necessarily appropriate or possible for assessing maximum possible liability losses. In theory, liability losses are limited only by the defendant's total wealth. Therefore, some practical assumptions must be made about the MPL in liability cases to properly assess that loss exposure. Instead of focusing on the defendant's total wealth, a common assumption is that the maximum amount that would be exposed to liability loss 95 percent (or 98 percent) of the time in similar cases is the MPL.

Frequency and Severity Considered Jointly

In order to fully analyze the significance of a particular loss exposure, it is important to consider both severity and frequency distributions and how they interact. One method of jointly considering both loss frequency and loss severity is the Prouty Approach, which identifies four broad categories of loss frequency and three broad categories of loss severity. Another method is more statistically based and involves combining frequency and severity distributions to create a single total claims distribution. See the exhibit "The Prouty Approach."

As shown in the exhibit, the Prouty Approach entails four categories of loss frequency:

- Almost nil—extremely unlikely to happen; virtually no possibility
- Slight—could happen but has not happened
- Moderate—happens occasionally
- Definite—happens regularly

There are three categories of loss severity:

- Slight—Organization can readily retain each loss exposure.
- Significant—Organization cannot retain the loss exposure, some part of which must be financed.
- Severe—Organization must finance virtually all of the loss exposure or endanger its survival.

These broad categories of loss frequency and loss severity are subjective. One organization may view losses that occur once a month as moderate, while another would consider such frequency as definite. Similarly, one organization

The Prouty Approach

		Loss Frequency			
		Almost Nil	**Slight**	**Moderate**	**Definite**
Loss Severity	**Severe**	Reduce or prevent / Transfer	Reduce or prevent / Transfer	Reduce or prevent / Retain	Avoid
	Significant	Reduce or prevent / Transfer	Reduce / Transfer	Reduce or prevent / Retain	Avoid
	Slight	Reduce or prevent / Retain	Reduce / Retain	Reduce or prevent / Retain	Prevent / Retain

[DA02588]

may view a $1 million loss as slight, while another might view it as severe. However, these categories can help insurance and risk management professionals prioritize loss exposures.

A loss exposure's frequency and severity tend to be inversely related. That is, the more severe a loss tends to be, the less frequently it tends to occur. Conversely, the more frequently a loss occurs to a given exposure, the less severe the loss tends to be.

Loss exposures that generate minor but definite losses are typically retained and incorporated in an organization's budget. At the other extreme, loss exposures that generate intolerably large losses are typically avoided. Therefore, most risk management decisions, such as whether to adopt the risk control and risk financing techniques shown in the "Prouty Approach" exhibit, concern loss exposures for which individual losses, although tolerable, tend to be either significant or severe and have a moderate, slight, or almost nil chance of occurring.

A given loss exposure might generate financially significant losses because of either high individual loss severity or high-frequency, low-severity losses that aggregate to a substantial total. Organizations may be tempted to focus on high-profile "shock events," such as a major fire, a violent explosion, or a huge liability claim. However, smaller losses, which happen so frequently that they become routine, can eventually produce much larger total losses than a single dramatic event. For example, many retail firms suffer greater total losses from shoplifting, which happens regularly, than they do from large fires that might happen once every twenty years. Minor, cumulatively significant losses usually deserve as much risk management attention as large individual losses.

Another way of jointly considering frequency and severity is to combine both frequency and severity distributions into a total claims distribution, which can provide additional information about potential losses that may occur in a given period. Combining distributions can be difficult because as the number of possible outcomes increases, the possible combinations of frequency and severity grow exponentially. See the exhibit "Total Claims Distribution for Hardware Store Shoplifting Losses."

Total Claims Distribution for Hardware Store Shoplifting Losses

Frequency

	Number of Losses	Probability
F0	0	.33
F1	1	.33
F2	2	.34

Severity

	Dollar Loss	Probability
S1	$100	.33
S2	$250	.33
S3	$500	.34

Total Claims Distribution

Dollar Loss	Probability*	Probability Calculation	
$ 0	.33	p(F0)	← There is only one possible way to have $0 losses: the frequency = 0. That happens 33% of the time.
100	.11	p(F1) × p(S1)	
200	.04	p(F2) × p(S1) × p(S1)	
250	.11	p(F1) × p(S2)	
350	.07	p(F2) × p(S1) × p(S2)	
500	.15	[p(F2) × p(S2) × p(S2)] + [p(F1) × p(S3)]	← There are two possible ways to have $500 in losses in a given year: two $250 losses or one $500 loss.
600	.08	p(F2) × p(S1) × p(S3)	
750	.08	p(F2) × p(S2) × p(S3)	
1,000	.04	p(F2) × p(S3) × p(S3)	← There is only one possible way to have $1,000 in losses: two $500 losses.

*Rounded

[DA02589]

The "Total Claims Distribution for Hardware Store Shoplifting Losses" exhibit presents a simple example of three possible frequencies (0, 1, and 2) and three possible severities ($100, $250, and $500) that represent shoplifting losses from a hardware store. The frequency and severity distributions for a given year are shown in the exhibit, along with the total claims distribution created by considering all the possible combinations of the frequency and severity distributions.

For example, a 33 percent chance exists of a loss not occurring during the year (frequency = 0). Therefore, in the total claims distribution, a 33 percent chance exists of the total losses being $0. There is only one possible way for a $100 loss to occur: a frequency of 1 and a severity of $100. Therefore, that probability is .11 [.33 (frequency 1) × .33 (severity $100) = .11]. There are two ways that the total claims for the year could equal $500. Either the organization could have one loss of $500, or it could have two losses of $250. Therefore, the probability of a $500 loss is the probability of one $500 loss plus the probability of two $250 losses.

A total claims distribution can be used to calculate the measures of central tendency and dispersion and evaluate the effect that various risk control and risk financing techniques would have on this loss exposure.

Total Dollar Losses

The third dimension to consider in analyzing loss exposures is total dollar losses, calculated by multiplying loss frequency by loss severity. Total dollar losses represent a simplified version of combining frequency and severity distributions and can be used when analyzing frequency and severity distributions that have multiple possible outcomes. See the exhibit "Total Dollar Losses."

Expected total dollar losses can be projected by multiplying expected loss frequency by expected loss severity, while worst-case scenarios can be calculated by assuming both high frequency and the worst possible severity. For example, the "Total Dollar Losses" exhibit includes the frequency and severity distributions that were shown in the "Total Claims Distribution for Hardware Store Shoplifting Losses" exhibit if they were expanded to include more possible outcomes.

Combining the frequency and severity distributions in the exhibit would be difficult given the total number of possible combinations. An insurance or risk management professional could make some simpler calculations to determine what the potential total dollar losses may be. In this example, expected total dollar losses would be $1,878.33, and the worst-case scenario could be calculated as $7,950.00, using F9 in the exhibit. (F10 was not used, given its low probability.) These estimates could then be used in managing these loss exposures, such as evaluating whether to insure the loss exposures for the premium an insurer is quoting.

Total Dollar Losses

Frequency

	Number of Losses	Probability
F0	0	.03
F1	1	.05
F2	2	.08
F3	3	.10
F4	4	.15
F5	5	.20
F6	6	.15
F7	7	.10
F8	8	.08
F9	9	.05
F10	10	.01

Expected value = 4.9.

Severity

	Dollar Loss	Probability
S1	$100	.30
S2	$250	.25
S3	$500	.20
S4	$683	.15
S5	$883	.10

Expected value = $383.33.

Expected total dollar losses = 4.9 × $383.33 = $1,878.33.

Worst case total dollar losses = 9 × $883.00 = $7,950.00.

[DA02590]

Timing

The fourth dimension to consider in analyzing loss exposures is timing of losses. Risk assessment requires considering not only when losses are likely to occur, but also when payment for those losses will likely be made. The timing dimension is significant because money held in reserve to pay for a loss can earn interest until the actual payment is made. Whether a loss is counted when it is incurred or when it is paid is also significant for various accounting and tax reasons that are beyond the scope of this discussion.

Funds to pay for property losses are generally disbursed relatively soon after the event occurs. In contrast, liability losses often involve long delays between the occurrence of the adverse event, when an occurrence is recognized, the period of possible litigation, and the time when payment is actually made. Damages for disability claims, for example, might be paid over a long period. In some cases, especially those involving environmental loss exposures or health risks, the delay can span several decades. Although this delay increases the uncertainty associated with the loss amount, it allows reserves to earn interest or investment income over a longer period of time.

Data Credibility

After analyzing the four dimensions of a loss exposure, an insurance or risk management professional then evaluates the credibility of the projections of loss frequency, loss severity, total dollar losses, and timing. The term data credibility refers to the level of confidence that available data can accurately indicate future losses. Two related data credibility issues may prevent data from being good indicators of future losses—the age of the data and whether the data represent actual losses or estimates of losses. See the exhibit "How Credible Are Your Data?."

How Credible Are Your Data?

There are several factors, both internal and external, that may influence data credibility for an organization. Internally, changes in the way that an organization operates, such as alterations to manufacturing processes or changes in data collection methods, may significantly reduce the credibility of previously collected data. Externally, events such as natural catastrophes, large liability awards, or terrorist attacks not only alter the data that are collected in that time frame, but also may cause shifts in the operating environment that render previously collected data less credible.

[DA02591]

Ideally, data used to forecast losses are generated in the same environment that will apply to the projected period. However, the environment for most loss exposures changes, even if those changes happen slowly. The changing environment renders more recent data a more credible predictor of future losses than older data. However, because of delays in reporting and paying of claims, more recent data are not always actual losses, but estimates of what the ultimate losses will be.

This leaves insurance and risk management professionals with a dilemma: Is it better to use older data, which are accurate but may have been generated in an environment that is substantially different from that of the period for which they are trying to predict, or to use more recent data and sacrifice some accuracy to maintain the integrity of the environment?

Once the projections are made along the four dimensions of loss exposures, the analysis of the loss exposures will often dictate which type of risk control or risk financing measures should be implemented. See the exhibit "Transportation Losses for a Large Shipper."

For example, the pattern shown in the "Transportation Losses for a Large Shipper" exhibit illustrates the expected transportation losses for a large shipper that has been in business for ten years and that has a steadily increasing volume of transportation services.

The average losses during the coming years might be projected to fall along the line labeled "projected," and the probable maximum loss might be pro-

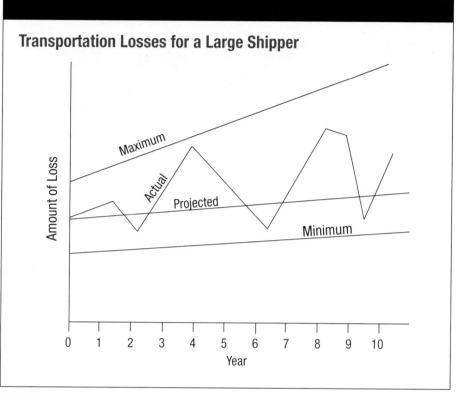

Transportation Losses for a Large Shipper

Amount of Loss

Maximum

Actual

Projected

Minimum

Year

0   1   2   3   4   5   6   7   8   9   10

[DA02592]

jected to fall along the line labeled "maximum." Probable minimum loss levels might also be projected, as shown by the "minimum" line.

If such projections can be made with a high degree of confidence in the data used for the projections, actual losses would be expected to follow a pattern like the "actual" line on the graph, deviating from the average from one year to the next but in no case exceeding the maximum or falling below the minimum. Because the shipper can reasonably anticipate the degree of uncertainty, it may choose to retain these losses instead of insuring them. See the exhibit "Product Liability Losses for a Large Manufacturer."

Similarly, the "Product Liability Losses for a Large Manufacturer" exhibit represents products liability losses experienced by a large manufacturer. A few losses usually occur each year. However, in Year 4, almost no losses occurred, whereas, in Year 8, at least one major loss occurred. (The losses in Year 8 are so high that total losses exceeded even maximum projections.) It may have been possible to project these losses to a certain extent at lower levels, but possibilities existed for substantial losses above the expected and maximum levels. It might be disastrous to attempt to finance such losses solely out of the organization's operating budget.

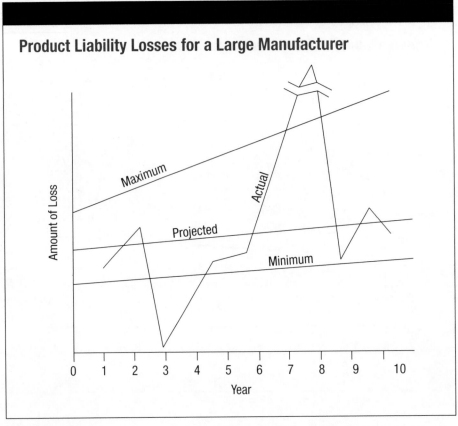

Product Liability Losses for a Large Manufacturer

[DA02593]

SUMMARY

Because identifying loss exposures is the beginning of the risk management process, it should be done thoroughly and systematically. Various methods can be used to identify loss exposures, including document analysis, compliance review, inspections, and expertise within and beyond the organization.

To accurately analyze loss exposures using data on past losses, the data should be relevant, complete, consistent, and organized.

Concepts affecting the use of probability in risk analysis include theoretical probability, empirical probability, and the law of large numbers. Although it may be preferable to use theoretical probabilities because of their unchanging nature, theoretical probabilities are not applicable or available in most situations that insurance and risk management professionals are likely to analyze. Applying the law of large numbers to probability reveals that a forecast of future losses will be more reliable if the forecast is based on a larger sample of the losses used in the analysis.

A properly constructed probability distribution always contains outcomes that are both mutually exclusive and collectively exhaustive. All probability distributions can be classified as either discrete or continuous.

The central tendency is the single outcome that is the most representative of all possible outcomes included within a probability distribution. The three most widely accepted measures of central tendency are expected value or mean, median, and mode.

Dispersion, which is the variation between values in a distribution, can be used as well as central tendency to compare the characteristics of probability distributions. The less dispersion around a distribution's expected value, the greater the likelihood that actual results will fall within a given range of that expected value. Two widely used statistical measures of dispersion are standard deviation and the coefficient of variation.

The normal distribution is a probability frequency distribution that, when graphed, generates a bell-shaped curve. This particular probability distribution can help to accurately forecast the variability around some central, average, or expected value and has therefore proven useful in accurately forecasting the variability of many physical phenomena.

The analysis step of the risk management process involves considering the four dimensions of a loss exposure: loss frequency, loss severity, total dollar losses, and timing.

Direct Your Learning ▶▶

Risk Control

Educational Objectives

After learning the content of this assignment, you should be able to:

▷ Describe the six categories of risk control techniques in terms of the following:

- Whether each reduces loss frequency, reduces loss severity, or makes losses more predictable

- How each can be used to address a particular loss exposure

- How they differ from one another

▷ Explain how an organization can use risk control techniques and measures to achieve the following risk control goals:

- Implement effective and efficient risk control measures

- Comply with legal requirements

- Promote life safety

- Ensure business continuity

▷ Explain how risk control techniques can be applied to property, liability, personnel, and net income loss exposures.

▷ Describe business continuity management in terms of its scope, the process used to implement it, and the contents of a typical business continuity plan.

Risk Control

RISK CONTROL TECHNIQUES

To select the most appropriate risk management techniques, insurance and risk management professionals consider the various techniques available so that they can then determine which of those techniques most effectively address an organization's or individual's loss exposures.

All risk management techniques fall into one of two categories: risk control or risk financing. The focus of this section is on **risk control**. Risk control techniques can be classified using these six broad categories:

- Avoidance
- Loss prevention
- Loss reduction
- Separation
- Duplication
- Diversification

Each of the techniques in these six categories aims to reduce either loss frequency or severity, or make losses more predictable. See the exhibit "Target of Risk Control Techniques."

Risk control
A conscious act or decision not to act that reduces the frequency and/or severity of losses or makes losses more predictable.

Avoidance

The most effective way of managing any loss exposure is to avoid the exposure completely. If a loss exposure has successfully been avoided, then the probability of loss from that loss exposure is zero.

The aim of **avoidance** is not just to reduce loss frequency, but also to eliminate any possibility of loss. Avoidance should be considered when the expected value of the losses from an activity outweighs the expected benefits of that activity. For example, a toy manufacturer might decide not to produce a particular toy because the potential cost of products liability claims would outweigh the expected revenue from sales, no matter how cautious the manufacturer might be in producing and marketing the toy.

Avoidance can either be proactive or reactive.

Proactive avoidance seeks to avoid a loss exposure before it exists, such as when a medical student chooses not to become an obstetrician because he or

Avoidance
A risk control technique that involves ceasing or never undertaking an activity so that the possibility of a future loss occurring from that activity is eliminated.

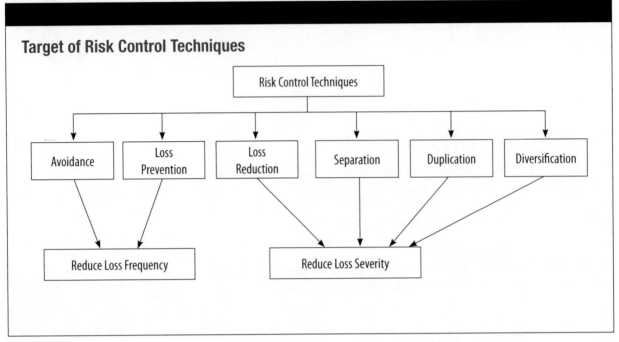

Target of Risk Control Techniques

[DA02648]

she wants to avoid the large professional liability (malpractice) claims associated with that specialty.

Reactive avoidance seeks to eliminate a loss exposure that already exists, such as when manufacturers of hand-held hair dryers stopped using asbestos insulation in their dryers once the cancer-causing properties of asbestos became known.

Reactive avoidance, that is, discontinuing an existing activity, avoids loss exposures from future activities but does not eliminate loss exposures from past activities. For example, the hair dryer manufacturer may avoid claims from consumers who purchase the hair dryers produced after asbestos is no longer used, but would remain legally liable for associated harm suffered by prior consumers.

Because loss exposures do not exist in a vacuum, avoiding one loss exposure can create or enhance another. For example if an individual is concerned about dying in an airplane crash, he or she can choose not to travel by air. However, by avoiding air travel, the individual increases the loss exposure to injury or death from the other means of transport chosen in its place.

Complete avoidance is not the most common risk control technique and is typically neither feasible nor desirable. Loss exposures arise from activities that are essential to individuals and to organizations. Therefore, it is not possible to avoid these core activities. For instance, if a manufacturer's principal product is motorcycle safety helmets, it could not stop selling them in order to avoid liability loss exposures. Similarly, an organization cannot decline to occupy office space in order to avoid property loss exposures. Nonfinancial concerns also can render avoidance impossible. For example, a municipality cannot arbitrarily stop providing police protection or water to its inhabitants in order to avoid the associated liability loss exposures.

Loss Prevention

Loss prevention is a risk control technique that reduces the frequency of a particular loss. For instance, pressure relief valves on a boiler are intended to prevent explosions by keeping the pressure in the boiler from reaching an unsafe level. The valve is a type of loss prevention, not avoidance, because a boiler explosion is still possible, just not as likely.

Loss prevention
A risk control technique that reduces the frequency of a particular loss.

To illustrate a loss prevention measure, consider a hypothetical manufacturing company, Etchley Manufacturing (Etchley). Etchley has 500 employees working at a single plant. The workers' compensation loss history for this plant shows a significant number of back injuries. Etchley is considering hiring a back injury consultant to host a series of educational seminars for its employees. The consultant estimates that, based on the results of his past seminar series, Etchley will see a 20 percent reduction in the frequency of back injuries. See the exhibit "Example of a Loss Prevention Measure: Etchley Manufacturing."

The chart in the exhibit shows the frequency distributions of back injuries both with and without the educational seminar in order to demonstrate the estimated effect of this loss prevention measure. The frequency distribution without the educational seminar has a mean of 30, a standard deviation of 5.48 and a coefficient of variation of 0.1827.

The frequency distribution with the educational seminar has a lower mean of 24, a lower standard deviation of 4.20, and a lower coefficient of variation of 0.1750. Based on these figures, not only would the consultant's educational seminar reduce the expected frequency of back injuries, it would also reduce their variability from year to year, which would allow Etchley to budget more effectively for those injuries that do occur.

Loss prevention measures that reduce frequency may also affect the loss severity of the specified loss exposures. For example, as a result of the educational seminar, both the number of back injuries that occur and their severity may be reduced.

Generally, a loss prevention measure is implemented before a loss occurs in order to break the sequence of events that leads to the loss. Because of the close link between causes of loss and loss prevention, determining effective loss prevention measures usually requires carefully studying how particular losses are caused.

For example, according to Heinrich's domino theory, as described in the exhibit, most work-related injuries result from a chain of events that includes an unsafe act or an unsafe condition. Workplace safety efforts have therefore

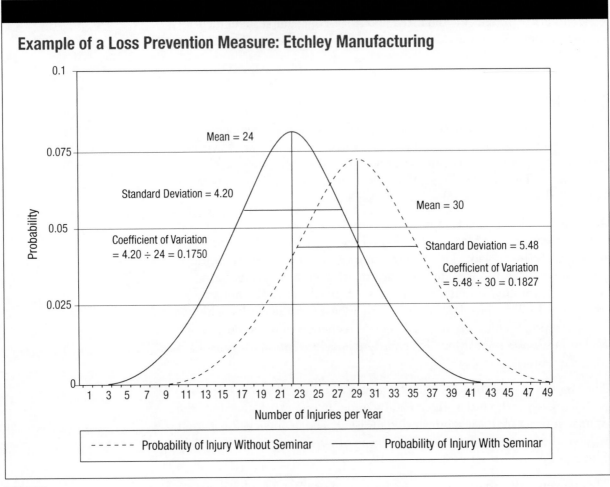

Example of a Loss Prevention Measure: Etchley Manufacturing

Mean = 24

Standard Deviation = 4.20

Coefficient of Variation
= 4.20 ÷ 24 = 0.1750

Mean = 30

Standard Deviation = 5.48

Coefficient of Variation
= 5.48 ÷ 30 = 0.1827

Probability

Number of Injuries per Year

- - - - - Probability of Injury Without Seminar　————— Probability of Injury With Seminar

[DA02649]

focused on trying to eliminate specific unsafe acts or unsafe conditions to break this chain of events and prevent injuries.

As is the case with avoidance, a loss prevention measure may reduce the frequency of losses from one loss exposure but increase the frequency or severity of losses from other loss exposures. For example, a jewelry store that installs security bars on its windows would likely reduce the frequency of theft. These same bars, however, might make it impossible for firefighters to enter the building through the windows or might trap employees inside the store if a fire occurs. See the exhibit "Heinrich's Domino Theory."

Loss Reduction

Loss reduction

A risk control technique that reduces the severity of a particular loss.

Loss reduction is a risk control technique that reduces the severity of a particular loss. Automatic sprinkler systems are a classic example of a loss reduction measure; sprinklers do not prevent fires from starting, but can limit or extinguish fires that have already started. Some loss reduction measures can prevent losses as well as reduce them.

Heinrich's Domino Theory

In 1931, H. W. Heinrich published the first thorough analysis of work injuries caused by accidents. He determined that work injuries were actually a result of a series of unsafe acts and/or mechanical or physical hazards (dominoes) that occurred in a specific order. Furthermore, he concluded that if any one of these dominoes could be removed from the chain, the work injury could be prevented. Heinrich's theory included the following five dominoes: (1) social environment and ancestry, (2) the fault of persons, (3) personal or mechanical hazards, (4) the accident, and (5) the injury. For example, if risk control measures could minimize mechanical hazards, the domino chain would be broken and fewer injuries would occur. Many of the principles that Heinrich outlined in his publication became the basis of modern risk control measures.

H.W. Heinrich, Industrial Accident Prevention, 4th edition (New York: McGraw-Hill, 1959). [DA02650]

For example, using burglar alarms is generally considered a loss reduction measure because the alarm is activated only when a burglary occurs. However, because burglar alarms also act as a deterrent, they can prevent loss as well as reduce it.

As an example of a loss reduction measure, assume the consultant Etchley hired to conduct the educational seminars suggested that Etchley provide back braces for all of its employees because back braces help prevent back injuries and reduce the severity of back injuries that do occur.

The exhibit contains the original severity distribution for Etchley and the new severity distribution with all employees using back braces. As with most severity distributions, the severity distribution for back injuries is not symmetrical, but skewed. Most back injuries are grouped in the left-hand portion of the distribution (lower severity values), with some very serious injuries grouped as outliers to the right. This positively skewed distribution pulls the tail of the distribution to the right and increases the mean.

Note the difference between the means and modes with and without back braces. The use of back braces lowers the average severity (mean) by $15,792 ($29,800 − $14,008 = $15,792) as well as the severity of the injuries that would occur most often (mode) by $5,000 ($8,000 − $3,000 = $5,000).

The two broad categories of loss reduction measures are pre-loss measures, applied before the loss occurs, and post-loss measures, applied after the loss occurs. The aim of pre-loss measures is to reduce the amount or extent of property damaged and the number of people injured or the extent of injury incurred from a single event.

For example, Etchley's use of back braces is a pre-loss measure erecting fire-walls to limit the amount of damage and danger that can be caused by a single fire is also a pre-loss measure. See the exhibit "Example of a Loss Reduction Measure: Etchley Manufacturing."

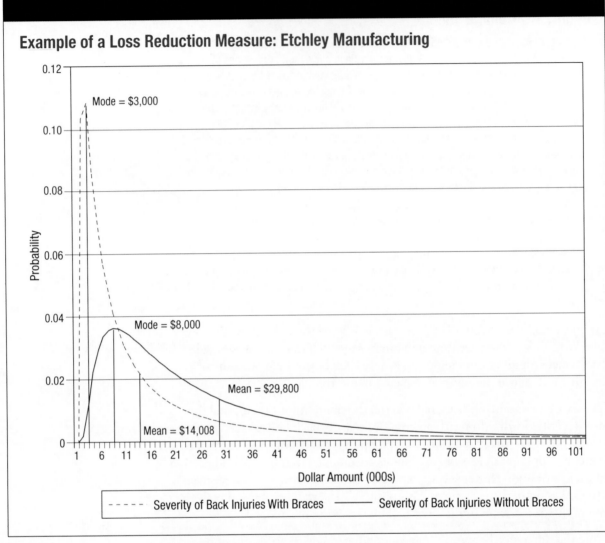

Example of a Loss Reduction Measure: Etchley Manufacturing

[DA02651]

Post-loss measures typically focus on emergency procedures, salvage operations, rehabilitation activities, public relations, or legal defenses to halt the spread or to counter the effects of loss. An example of a post-loss loss reduction measure is to temporarily move an organization's operations to a new location following a fire so that operations can continue while the main premises is repaired, thus reducing loss severity.

Disaster recovery planning is a specialized aspect of loss reduction. A **disaster recovery plan**, also called catastrophe recovery plan or contingency plan, is a plan for backup procedures, emergency response, and post-disaster recovery to ensure that critical resources are available to facilitate the continuity of operations in an emergency situation. For many organizations, disaster recovery planning is especially important in addressing the risks associated with those systems without which the organization could not function. Disaster recovery

Disaster recovery plan

A plan for backup procedures, emergency response, and post-disaster recovery to ensure that critical resources are available to facilitate the continuity of operations in an emergency situation.

plans typically focus on property loss exposures and natural hazards, not on the broader array of risks and associated loss exposures that may also threaten an organization's survival.

Separation

Separation is appropriate if an organization can operate with only a portion of these separate units left intact. If one unit suffers a total loss, the portion of the activity or assets at the other unit must be sufficient for operations to continue. Otherwise, separation has not achieved its risk control goal.

Separation is rarely undertaken for its own sake, but is usually a byproduct of another management decision. For example, few organizations build a second warehouse simply to reduce the potential loss severity at the first warehouse. However, if an organization is considering constructing a second warehouse to expand production, the risk control benefits of a second warehouse could support the argument in favor of the expansion.

The intent of separation is to reduce the severity of an individual loss at a single location. However, if an organization is considering constructing a second warehouse to expand production, the risk control benefits of a second warehouse could support the argument in favor of the expansion. The intent of separation is to reduce the severity of an individual loss at a single location. However, by creating multiple locations, separation most likely increases loss frequency. For example, using two distantly separated warehouses instead of one reduces the maximum possible loss at each individual location, but increases loss frequency, because two units are exposed to loss. The insurance or risk management professional should be confident that the benefits of reduced loss severity from separation more than offset the increased loss frequency.

As an example of separation, consider a hypothetical organization, Ryedale Shipping Company (Ryedale), which has to decide between these options for shipping its clients' products:

• Option A—use one central warehouse.

• Option B—use two warehouses.

Under Option A, the central warehouse would contain $500,000 worth of merchandise and have a 5 percent chance of experiencing a fire in any given year. For simplicity, assume that only one fire per year can occur and that if a fire occurs, all of the warehouse's merchandise is completely destroyed. Under Option B, the two warehouses would each have the same probability of a fire (5 percent), but would each house $250,000 worth of merchandise. For simplicity, assume that the two locations are independent of one another. See the exhibit "Example of Separation: Ryedale Shipping Company."

The exhibit shows the severity distributions for these options and how the expected loss is calculated.

Separation

A risk control technique that isolates loss exposures from one another to minimize the adverse effect of a single loss.

Example of Separation: Ryedale Shipping Company

Option A

	Central Warehouse
Value of merchandise	$500,000
Probability of a fire	.05

Severity distribution (maximum loss in a fire)	$500,000
Probability of a fire in the central warehouse	.05
Expected loss (.05 × $500,000)	$25,000

Option B

	Warehouse 1 (W1)	Warehouse 2 (W2)
Value of merchandise	$250,000	$250,000
Probability of a fire	.05	.05

Severity distribution (maximum loss in a fire)	$250,000
Probability of fire at W1 and fire at W2 (.05 × .05)	.0025
Probability of fire in W1 but not W2 [.05 × (1 − .05)]	.0475
Probability of fire in W2 but not in W1 [(1 − .05) × .05]	.0475
Probability of one fire in either W1 or W2 (.0475 + .0475)	.095
Probability of zero fires (1 − .05) × (1 − .05)	.9025
Expected loss [(.0025 × $500,000) + (.095 × $250,000)]	$25,000

[DA02652]

Under Option A, the severity distribution is just the single outcome of a loss of $500,000. There are two possible outcomes in any one year: a fire at the central warehouse or no fire at the central warehouse. Given a probability of fire of .05 (5 percent), Ryedale would expect a $500,000 loss 5 percent of the time and a $0 loss 95 percent of the time. Therefore, the expected loss in any given year is $25,000 (.05 × $500,000 = $25,000).

Under Option B, only $250,000 worth of merchandise is at risk in any one fire. Therefore, having two warehouses reduces Ryedale's severity distribution from $500,000 to $250,000.

Increasing the number of warehouses increases the number of possible outcomes. One of these situations will occur:

- No fire at either location.
- There will be a fire at the first warehouse (W1) but not at the second warehouse (W2).

- There will be a fire at W2 but not at W1.
- There will be a fire at both W1 and W2.

The probability of each of these possible outcomes is shown in the exhibit. Given a probability of fire of .05, Ryedale would expect these outcomes:

- $500,000 loss (fires at both W1 and W2) 0.25 percent of the time
- $250,000 loss at W1 4.75 percent of the time
- $250,000 loss at W2 4.75 percent of the time
- $0 loss 90.25 percent of the time

The expected loss remains $25,000, but the likelihood of suffering a $500,000 loss has fallen from 5 percent to 0.25 percent, whereas the likelihood of suffering a $250,000 loss has increased from 0 percent to 9.5 percent.

This results in a total claims distribution for Option B that has a lower standard deviation than the total claims distribution for Option A. The standard deviation of losses under Option A would be $108,973, and the standard deviation for Option B falls to $77,055.18, which makes losses under Option B more predictable than Option A.

Duplication

Duplication is a risk control technique that uses backups, spares, or copies of critical property, information, or capabilities and keeps them in reserve. Examples of duplication include maintaining a second set of records, spare parts for machinery, and copies of keys.

Duplication differs from separation in that duplicates are not a part of an organization's daily working resources. Duplication is only appropriate if an entire asset or activity is so important that the consequence of its loss justifies the expense and time of maintaining the duplicate.

For example, an organization may make arrangements with more than one supplier of a key raw material. That alternative supplier would be used only if a primary supplier could not provide needed materials because of, for example, a major fire at the primary supplier's plant.

Like separation, duplication can reduce an organization's dependence on a single asset, activity, or person, making individual losses smaller by reducing the severity of a loss that may occur. Duplication is not as likely as separation to increase loss frequency because the duplicated unit is kept in reserve and is not as exposed to loss as is the primary unit. For example, a duplicate vehicle that is ordinarily kept garaged is not as vulnerable to highway accidents as the primary vehicle.

Duplication is likely to reduce the average expected annual loss from a given loss exposure because it reduces loss severity without increasing loss frequency. Similar to separation, duplication can also make losses more predictable by reducing the dispersion of potential losses.

Duplication

A risk control technique that uses backups, spares, or copies of critical property, information, or capabilities and keeps them in reserve.

There are several measures an organization can implement that are similar to duplication and that incorporate nonowned assets.

One option is for an organization to contractually arrange for the acquisition of equipment or facilities in the event that a loss occurs. For example, a plant that manufactures aircraft can pay an annual fee for a contract in which a supplier agrees to deliver within thirty days the hydraulic tools and scaffolding required to continue operations in a rented hangar if the manufacturer's assembly plant incurs a loss. In this way, the aircraft manufacturer can continue operations with minimal business interruptions and avoid the expense associated with the ownership or storage of the duplicate equipment.

Diversification

Although **diversification** closely resembles the risk control techniques of duplication and separation, it is more commonly applied to managing business risks, rather than hazard risks.

Diversification

A risk control technique that spreads loss exposures over numerous projects, products, markets, or regions.

Organizations engage in diversification of loss exposures when they provide a variety of products and services that are used by a range of customers.

For example, an insurer might diversify its exposures by type of business and geographically by selling both personal and commercial insurance and both property-casualty and life insurance in multiple regions. Investors employ diversification when they allocate their assets among a mix of stocks and bonds from companies in different industry sectors. An investor might diversify investments by purchasing stock in a bank and stock in a pharmaceutical manufacturer. Because these are unrelated industries, the investor hopes that any losses from one stock might be more than offset by profits from another.

As with separation and duplication, diversification has the potential to increase loss frequency, because the organization has increased the number of loss exposures. However, by spreading risk, diversification reduces loss severity and can make losses more predictable.

Organizations implement risk control techniques and the measures that support them to address one or more specific loss exposures. Each measure should be tailored to the specific loss exposure under consideration. Furthermore, the application of risk control techniques should serve to support an organization's overall goals, pre-loss and post-loss risk management goals, and risk control goals.

RISK CONTROL GOALS

Individuals and organizations have a variety of goals when implementing a risk management program. Just as the risk management program goals support the overall organizational goals, risk control goals support the risk management program goals. See the exhibit "Risk Management Goals."

Risk Management Goals

How Risk Control Goals Support:

Organizational Goals

Risk Management Program Goals

Risk Control Goals
- Implement effective and efficient risk control measures
- Comply with legal requirements
- Promote life safety
- Ensure business continuity

Risk Financing Goals

[DA02646]

Insurance and risk management professionals therefore seek to apply risk control techniques through specific risk control measures that most effectively and efficiently support the risk management program and thereby help the organization achieve its goals.

To this end, risk control techniques are used to support these risk control goals: implement effective and efficient risk control measures, comply with legal requirements, promote life safety, and ensure business continuity.

Implement Effective and Efficient Risk Control Measures

An individual or organization generally undertakes risk control measures that have a positive financial effect. Most risk control measures are implemented at a cost to the individual or organization. These costs are typically cash outlays, like the costs of the losses they aim to control, and are considered part of the cost of risk. However, so that risk control does not unduly increase the cost of risk, one of the goals of risk control is to employ measures that are effective and efficient.

A measure is effective if it enables an organization to achieve desired risk management goals, such as the pre-loss goals of economy of operations, tolerable uncertainty, legality, and social responsibility or the post-loss goals of survival, continuity of operations, profitability, earnings stability, growth, and social responsibility.

Some risk control measures will be more effective than others. For example, both a sprinkler system and employees patrolling a warehouse with fire extinguishers may be effective risk control measures. However, a sophisticated sprinkler system with heat and flame sensors will likely be more effective than employee patrols.

The effectiveness of various risk control measures is often based on both quantitative and qualitative standards. For example, determining whether measures to ensure worker safety are effective may rely not only on statistics regarding workers compensation claims, but also on employee satisfaction with the measures taken.

As well as being effective, a risk control measure should be efficient. A measure is efficient if it is the least expensive of all possible effective measures. This does not necessarily mean an organization should choose the measure that entails the least initial cash outlay.

The long-term effects should also be examined to determine which measure can be implemented with the least overall cost to the organization.

For example, consider an organization that needs to improve security at night. The organization's risk management professional determines that a new security system and stationing a night security guard are both equally effective measures from a financial perspective, but needs to determine which of these methods is most efficient. See the exhibit "Using Cash Flow Analysis to Determine the More Efficient Risk Control Measure."

There are several methods available for this comparison, one of which is cash flow analysis. Given a loss exposure and the effective alternative risk control measures, the risk management professional can use cash flow analysis to determine which measure will be most efficient. The "Using Cash Flow Analysis" exhibit illustrates a cash flow analysis of these two security measures.

In this example, both the security system and the security guard are equally effective; they both reduce annual losses by $40,000. Cash flow analysis shows that although the security system requires a larger initial investment, it costs less to operate and maintain each year.

If the risk management professional examines these choices over a ten-year period, the annual cost of the security guard eventually eclipses the initial investment required for the security system, making the security system ultimately more efficient.

The major advantage of using cash flow analysis for selecting risk control measures is that it provides the same basis of comparison for all value-maximizing decisions and thereby helps the organization achieve its value-maximization

Using Cash Flow Analysis to Determine the More Efficient Risk Control Measure

Security System

Net Cash Flow (NCF) Calculations

Reduction in annual losses:		$40,000
Less: Differential cash expenses		
System annual monitoring fees	$ 4,200	
System annual maintenance expenses	$ 400	($ 4,600)
Before-tax NCF :		$35,400

Annual savings by installing a security system.

NCF Analysis

Factors:

Initial investment	$200,000
Life of system	10 years
Differential annual cash flow	$ 35,400
Minimum acceptable rate of return (annual)	10.00%

The system's initial cost must be considered in cash flow analysis.

To discount cash flows for ten years at 10 percent discount rate, the equivalent net present value factor is 6.145.

Net Present Value (NPV) Analysis

PV of differential annual cash flow ($35,400 × 6.145)	$217,533
Less: PV of initial investment	($200,000)
Net present value:	$ 17,533

Installing a security system would be effective, in that the cost of the risk control measure is less than the savings in prevented losses. In present value terms, the security system would save the organization over $17,000.

Security Guard

NCF Calculations

Reduction in annual losses:		$40,000
Less: Differential cash expenses		
Security guard salary and benefits	$ 38,000	($38,000)
Before-tax NCF :		$2,000

Annual savings by hiring security guard.

NCF Analysis

Factors:

Initial investment	$0
Life of system	10 years
Differential annual cash flow	$ 2,000
Minimum acceptable rate of return (annual)	10.00%

The security guard does not have upfront costs like the cost of the security system.

NPV Analysis

PV of differential annual cash flow ($2,000 × 6.145)	$ 12,290
Less: PV of initial investment	($0)
Net present value:	$ 12,290

Hiring a security guard would be effective, in that the cost of the risk control measure is less than the savings in prevented losses. However, it is not as efficient as the security system.

[DA02647]

goal. It is also very useful for not-for-profit organizations that want to increase their efficiency by reducing unnecessary expenditures on risk control.

The disadvantages of cash flow analysis include the weaknesses of the assumptions that often must be made to conduct the analysis and the difficulty of accurately estimating future cash flows. Moreover, cash flow analysis works on the assumption that the organization's only goal is to maximize its economic value and does not consider any of the nonfinancial goals or selection criteria. For example, legality and social responsibility goals are not directly considered in cash flow analysis.

Comply With Legal Requirements

An organization may be required to implement certain risk control measures if a state or federal statute mandates specific safety measures, such as protecting employees from disability or safeguarding the environment against pollution. These risk control measures are a means of implementing the risk control techniques of avoidance, loss prevention, and loss reduction and they also support the risk management program pre-loss goal of legality. The cost of adhering to legal requirements becomes part of the cost of risk.

Many laws and regulations require organizations to implement specific risk control measures.

For example, the fire safety code mandates certain fire safety procedures, environmental regulations govern the nonuse or use and disposal of toxic material, workers' compensation laws require employers to provide a safe working environment, and disability laws require organizations to make certain accommodations for people with disabilities. All of these examples would include risk control measures that support avoidance (ban of some toxic substances), loss prevention (safety procedures for machinery usage), and loss reduction (fire suppression systems).

Some laws and regulations are amended fairly frequently, so it is important for the risk management professional to stay apprised of these amendments. For example, the privacy issues and enforcement regulations regarding the Health Insurance Portability and Accountability Act of 1996 (HIPAA) continue to evolve. Failure to comply with legal requirements exposes the individual or organization to additional fines, sanctions, or liability.

Promote Life Safety

Life safety
The portion of fire safety that focuses on the minimum building design, construction, operation, and maintenance requirements necessary to assure occupants of a safe exit from the burning portion of the building.

Safeguarding people from fire has grown in importance from a risk control perspective because of the emphasis legislative bodies have placed on health and safety issues and because of the increasing frequency and severity of liability claims. In the context of risk control, **life safety** is the portion of fire safety that focuses on the minimum building design, construction, operation, and maintenance requirements necessary to assure occupants of a safe exit from the burning portion of the building.

Life safety must consider both the characteristics of the people who occupy buildings and the types of building occupancies (such as residences, office work, or manufacturing). Consideration of the general characteristics of both building occupants and occupancy has led to the development of specific fire safety standards for buildings. These standards are codified in the Life Safety Code® published by the National Fire Protection Association (NFPA) and cover the risk control techniques of avoidance, loss prevention, and loss control.[1]

Promoting life safety can be expanded beyond fire safety to incorporate any cause of loss that threatens the life of employees or customers. Therefore, organizations must be concerned about other causes of loss, such as product safety, building collapse, industrial accidents, environmental pollution, or exposure to hazardous activities that may create the possibility of injury or death. For example, a toy manufacturer should have an established product recall procedure in the event that a safety issue arises with one of its toys. Alternatively, a car manufacturer should install appropriate safety guards on machinery, equip employees with appropriate safety gear, and give employees sufficient training to enable them to carry out their jobs in reasonable safety.

Ensure Business Continuity

In addition to implementing effective and efficient measures, complying with legal requirements, and promoting safety, risk control should aim to ensure business continuity—that is, minimize or eliminate significant business interruptions, whatever their cause. Business continuity is designed to meet both the primary risk management program post-loss goal of survival and the post-loss goal of continuity of operations.

Loss exposures and their associated losses vary widely by industry, location, and organization. Some organizations are more susceptible to terrorism, some are more susceptible to information technology problems, and others are more susceptible to natural disasters. Because each organization is unique in its potential losses, each must also be unique in its application of risk control measures to promote business continuity.

For example, there are many causes of loss, such as fire, theft or vandalism, that can be prevented through appropriate loss prevention measures. If left untreated, these causes of loss could easily result in a business interruption. However, there are other causes of loss (including natural disasters such as hurricanes or earthquakes) that an organization may not be able to avoid or prevent. Nonetheless, the organization may be able to minimize any business interruption that could occur during and after a natural disaster through appropriate loss reduction techniques.

APPLICATION OF RISK CONTROL TECHNIQUES

After considering alternative risk control techniques, insurance and risk management professionals decide which techniques are appropriate for a particular loss exposure and which are not.

In performing this part of the risk management process, the insurance or risk management professional can benefit from knowing which risk control techniques are usually applicable to each of these loss exposures:

- Property
- Liability
- Personnel
- Net income

Property Loss Exposures

Property loss exposures are generally divided into two categories—tangible property loss exposures (covering real property, such as land and buildings, and tangible personal property) and intangible property loss exposures. The risk control techniques that are most applicable to property loss exposures vary based on the type of property as well as the cause of loss threatening the property. For example, risk control measures to prevent or reduce damage caused by fire are substantially different than those to prevent or reduce damage resulting from theft.

Because of the broad array of property loss exposures and causes of loss, all of the categories of risk control techniques can be applied in some way to property loss exposures. Insurance producers and underwriters commonly examine commercial property loss exposures based on construction, occupancy, protection, and external exposure (known by their acronym—COPE). Each factor inherent in COPE can be addressed through the application of risk control techniques, as demonstrated in the exhibit. See the exhibit "Applications of Risk Control Techniques to COPE."

Liability Loss Exposures

To implement effective risk control for liability losses, individuals and organizations need to understand the bases of legal liability. Legal actions can be brought under torts, contracts, or statutes. The liability loss exposures facing most individuals and organizations are presented in the exhibit. Three risk control techniques can be used to control liability losses: (1) avoid the activity that creates the liability loss exposure, (2) decrease the likelihood of the losses occurring (loss prevention), and (3) if a loss does occur, minimize its effect on the organization (loss reduction). The other risk control techniques of separation, duplication, and diversification are not as effective in treating liability loss exposures. See the exhibit "Typical Liability Loss Exposures."

Applications of Risk Control Techniques to COPE

COPE Factor	Description	Risk Control Technique
Construction	Construction materials and techniques range from simple frame construction (least resistive to fire) to fire-resistive construction (most fire resistive), with a wide variety of choices in between.	Loss prevention and loss reduction through construction techniques designed to minimize frequency and severity of losses.
Occupancy	There are nine different classifications of occupancy, ranging from residential to industrial, with each classification presenting its own unique risk to real property.	Loss reduction through safety training and emergency evacuation procedures.
Protection	There are two categories of protection, internal or external. Internal protection refers to what the organization does to protect its own real property. External protection refers to what fire departments and other public facilities do to safeguard the general public, including the organization, from fire and other causes of loss.	Two loss reduction measures used for internal fire protection are fire detection and suppression. External protection could involve security systems and security guard services.
External Exposure	A building is exposed to many hazards from outside sources, such as neighboring buildings. COPE factors are used to evaluate neighboring buildings' fire risk and the risk of transfer to the organization's real property.	The loss prevention and reduction measures may include relocation away from external hazards and fire protection to the exterior of the property to prevent or reduce the likelihood of fire from another building to the organization's property.

[DA02643]

Although avoidance is sometimes an effective risk control technique for liability losses, particularly proactive avoidance, it is often either not practicable or not possible to avoid undertaking the activity or activities that can lead to liability losses. Therefore, loss prevention and loss reduction measures are more typically used.

The most common loss prevention measure is to control hazards (conditions that increase loss frequency or severity). Limiting the number or magnitude of hazards surrounding the loss exposures can prevent losses from occurring.

Typical Liability Loss Exposures

Liability Loss Exposure	Description
Premises liability	Created by having visitors to an organization's premises.
Operations liability	Created by conducting operations either on or away from an organization's premises.
Products liability	Created by manufacturing or distributing products.
Workers compensation liability	Created by state statutes to cover employees for work-related injuries and illnesses.
Professional liability	Created by common law, which imposes a higher duty of care on professionals. A professional owes a duty of care to refrain from an action that carries an undue risk of causing harm to someone else.
Completed operations liability	Created because organization is responsible for bodily injury or property damage caused by completed work when the work is completed away from the organization's premises.
Automobile liability	Created because drivers and owners of autos owe a duty to others to use their autos in a reasonable, prudent manner and to exercise care for the safety of others.
Watercraft liability	Created because drivers and owners of watercraft owe a duty to others to use their watercraft in a reasonable, prudent manner and to exercise care for the safety of others.
Management liability	Created by the various duties that those in positions of trust owe to those they serve. Directors, officers, and managers hold such positions.

[DA02644]

For example, to limit liability claims arising from employee or customer injuries that occur in a parking lot, an organization could implement loss prevention measures such as clearing ice and snow, providing adequate signs, repairing potholes and cracks in walking surfaces, or conducting periodic inspections.

After a liability loss has occurred, individuals and organizations can implement loss reduction measures to reduce the severity of the liability loss. Such measures can include these:

- Consulting with an attorney for guidance through the legal steps necessary to resolve liability claims.
- Properly responding to the liability claim and to the claimant in order to avoid feelings of ill will that may increase the claimant's demands.
- Participating in alternative dispute resolution. Litigation is a long and costly process. Some forms of alternative dispute resolution, such as mediation or arbitration, often help to resolve liability claims more quickly and more economically than litigation.

Personnel Loss Exposures

Personnel loss exposures are unavoidable, because all organizations have key employees. These loss exposures can arise from events both inside and outside the workplace.

The risk control measures that organizations find most cost-effective are those that can be instituted in the workplace. Therefore, most risk control measures regarding personnel loss exposures involve preventing and reducing workplace injury and illness.

Loss prevention measures used to control work-related injury and illnesses typically involve education, training, and safety measures. An organization may also attempt to prevent personnel causes of loss that occur outside the workplace by controlling key employees' activities through employment contracts; for example, placing restrictions on hazardous activities such as sky diving, flying personal aircraft, riding motorcycles, and so on. Alternatively, organizations may use a form of separation, such as restricting the number of key employees who can travel on the same aircraft.

Loss reduction measures include emergency response training and rehabilitation management. Although all organizations must comply with federally mandated safety measures issued by OSHA (the Occupational Safety and Health Administration), additional training and safety precautions are often cost-effective.

Net Income Loss Exposures

Net income loss exposures can be associated with property, liability, or personnel loss exposures. Therefore, any of the risk control measures that control these three categories of loss exposures also indirectly control net income loss exposures. For example, to prevent a net income loss associated with a property loss exposure, an organization needs to prevent the property loss from occurring.

In addition to reducing the immediate effect of property, liability, or personnel losses on net income, risk control efforts must also control long-term effects, such as a loss of market share that can result from the net income loss. For example, if a manufacturer conducts a product recall, that manufacturer loses sales in the short term, causing a temporary loss of revenue. If the manufacturer's customers switch to purchasing products from other organizations, permanent market share could be lost, which is a long-term effect that translates into permanent revenue loss.

Two risk control measures that are directly aimed at reducing the severity of net income losses are separation and duplication. Separation and duplication enable an organization to reduce net income losses by maintaining operations or quickly resuming operations following a loss. Diversification is also a viable risk control technique for many because it helps to ensure that an organization's entire income is not dependent on one product or customer.

BUSINESS CONTINUITY MANAGEMENT

Business continuity management is a risk control process for identifying potential threats to an organization and ensuring the organization's continued business operations. By minimizing or avoiding significant business interruptions, business continuity management is aimed at meeting the organizational post-loss goals of survival and continuity of operations.

To help ensure the survival of the organization, business continuity management relies on the business continuity process to develop and implement a business continuity plan. The business continuity process assesses the threats to critical functions and develops a methodology for handling those threats. The business continuity plan is the planned response an organization will follow once a survival-threatening loss has occurred. By assessing threats to critical functions and pre-determining the organization's response to losses associated with those threats, business continuity management maximizes the probability of an organization's survival of a critical loss.

Scope of Business Continuity Management

Business continuity management, developed during the 1990s, typically focused on information technology (IT) concerns that could disrupt operations at organizations. Business continuity management has developed beyond its initial IT focus to encompass issues such as terrorism; corporate scandals; and economic developments that have led to more outsourcing, less duplication in production, greater reliance on just-in-time delivery, and more interdependence between organizations and key suppliers or buyers. Business continuity management plans have been expanded to help an organization handle interruptions from these:

- Property losses
- IT problems
- Human failures (such as fraud, sabotage, or terrorism)
- Loss of utility services or infrastructure
- Reputation losses
- Human asset losses (personnel losses)

These risks vary widely by industry, location, and organization. Some organizations are more susceptible to a particular loss exposure than others. Because each organization is unique in its loss exposures, it will also have to be unique in its application of business continuity management.

Business Continuity Process

The business continuity process provides a systematic approach to developing and implementing a business continuity plan. The process involves these six steps:

1. Identify the organization's critical functions
2. Identify the risks (threats) to the organization's critical functions
3. Evaluate the effect of the risks on those critical functions
4. Develop a business continuity strategy
5. Develop a business continuity plan
6. Monitor and revise the business continuity process

These steps are similar to the six steps of the risk management process and are designed to assess and control risks that are significant enough to warrant special attention because of the effect they can have on the organization's survival.

The process involves identification of both the critical functions (processes) of the organization and the risks that could have a substantial effect on those functions. The duration of interruption necessary to produce a substantial effect depends on the function. For example, even a very brief loss of electricity to a hospital can seriously impede the staff's ability to provide basic medical care. After the risks have been identified and evaluated, a business continuity strategy and plan are developed to establish how to maintain critical functions during a survival-threatening loss. Finally, similar to the risk management process, the entire process must be monitored and evaluated to ensure that it is functioning properly.

The business continuity process provides organizations with the framework to develop a systematic response to a variety of risks that could potentially threaten their future viability. Although following this process cannot ensure the survival of an organization, it can help to minimize the scope of threats that can cause its demise. See the exhibit "Business Continuity Management in Practice."

Business Continuity Management in Practice

Organizations that have implemented business continuity management face some common issues. One issue is deciding whether to outsource business continuity management to an organization that specializes in business continuity on a consulting or implementation basis. Another issue is determining the location of a backup site. Ideally, the backup site is close enough to the primary site so that employees can access the site quickly, but far enough away from the primary site so that the cause of the crisis cannot affect both locations simultaneously. The backup site would ideally have different telecommunications, power, and utilities from the primary site, in case the original cause of the crisis prevented those from functioning properly. A third issue is deciding the amount of detail that should be in a business continuity plan. The plan needs to be simple enough to follow in an emergency, but detailed enough to provide guidance in a wide variety of scenarios that may evolve. Finally, organizations need to be concerned about cost. How much time, energy, and money should be invested in business continuity is difficult to determine and is unique to each organization.

[DA02641]

Business Continuity Plan

A business continuity plan details the activities the organization will take in response to an incident that interrupts its operations. An important part of the business continuity process is to develop such a plan before a significant loss occurs that disrupts business. The plan should be designed with the understanding that it is going to be used during a crisis; that is, it should be clear and able to be quickly read and understood. All relevant parties should have a copy of the plan and should receive appropriate training, including periodic rehearsals of crisis procedures. See the exhibit "Emergency Management Considerations."

Emergency Management Considerations

- Direction and Control
  - Emergency Management Group (EMG)
  - Incident Command System (ICS)
  - Emergency Operations Center (EOC)
  - Planning Considerations
  - Security
  - Coordination of Outside Response
- Communications
  - Contingency Planning
  - Emergency Communications
  - Family Communications
  - Notification
  - Warning
- Life Safety
  - Evacuation Planning
  - Evacuation Routes and Exits
  - Assembly Areas and Accountability
  - Shelter
  - Training and Information
  - Family Preparedness
- Property Protection
  - Planning Considerations
  - Protection Systems
  - Mitigation
  - Facility Shutdown
  - Records Preservation
- Community Outreach
  - Involving the Community
  - Mutual Aid Agreements
  - Community Service
  - Public Information
  - Media Relations
- Recovery and Restoration
  - Planning Considerations
  - Continuity of Management
  - Insurance
  - Employee Support
  - Resuming Operations
- Administration and Logistics
  - Administrative Actions
  - Logistics

Adapted from "Emergency Management Guide for Business and Industry," FEMA 141, section 2, www.fema.gov/pdf/business/guide/bizindst.pdf (accessed January 15, 2010). [DA02642]

Although business continuity plans vary widely by organization, some content is fairly general. Most business continuity plans contain these:

- Strategy the organization is going to follow to manage the crisis
- Information about the roles and duties of various individuals in the organization
- Steps that can be taken to prevent any further loss or damage
- Emergency response plan to deal with life and safety issues
- Crisis management plan to deal with communication and any reputation issues (reputation management) that may arise
- Business recovery and restoration plan to deal with losses to property, processes, or products
- Access to stress management and counseling for affected parties

The exhibit contains the emergency management considerations developed by a public-private partnership with the Federal Emergency Management Association (FEMA). Ultimately, both business continuity management and risk control are aimed at enabling an individual or organization to not only deal with hazards and loss exposures, but to deal with them in the most efficient and cost-effective way in order to reduce the exposure to, and cost of, risk.

SUMMARY

Risk control is a conscious act or decision not to act that reduces the frequency and severity of losses or makes losses more predictable. Risk control techniques prevent losses, reduce the severity of losses, and speed recovery following a loss.

Risk control techniques can be categorized into one of six broad categories:

- Avoidance
- Loss prevention
- Loss reduction
- Separation
- Duplication
- Diversification

The goals of risk control are these:

- Implement effective and efficient risk control measures
- Comply with legal requirements
- Promote life safety
- Ensure business continuity

The risk control techniques most applicable to property loss exposures vary based on the type of property as well as the cause of loss. Avoidance, loss prevention, and loss reduction are the risk control techniques most applicable to liability loss exposures. Most risk control measures for personnel loss exposures involve preventing and reducing workplace injury and illness. Net income exposures can be controlled by the measures that control the property, liability, or personnel losses that causes net income losses.

Business continuity management is a process that identifies potential threats to an organization and provides a methodology for ensuring an organization's continued business operations. The business continuity process assesses the threats to critical functions and develops a methodology for handling those threats. It also provides organizations with the framework to develop a systematic response to a variety of risks that could potentially threaten the future viability of the organization.

ASSIGNMENT NOTE

1. Ron Coté, PE, and Gregory E. Harrington, PE, eds., *Life Safety Code® Handbook*, 9th ed. (Quincy, Mass.: National Fire Protection Association, 2003). Life Safety Code® is a registered trademark of the National Fire Protection Association, Quincy, Mass. 02169.

Direct Your Learning ▶▶

Risk Financing

Educational Objectives

After learning the content of this assignment, you should be able to:

▹ Explain how individuals or organizations can achieve their overall and risk management goals by fulfilling the following risk financing goals:

- Pay for losses

- Manage the cost of risk

- Manage cash flow variability

- Maintain an appropriate level of liquidity

- Comply with legal requirements

▹ Describe the following aspects of retention and transfer:

- Retention funding measures

- Limitations on risk transfer measures

- The advantages of both retention and transfer

▹ Explain how the following can affect the selection of the appropriate risk financing measure:

- Ability of a risk financing measure to meet risk financing goals

- Loss exposure characteristics

- Characteristics specific to an individual or organization

▹ Explain how an organization meets its risk financing goals by using the following risk financing measures:

- Guaranteed cost insurance

- Self-insurance

- Large deductible plans

- Captives

- Finite risk plans

4

Educational Objectives, continued

- Pools
- Retrospective rating plans
- Hold-harmless agreements
- Capital market solutions

Risk Financing

4

RISK FINANCING GOALS

Different risk control measures will help an individual or organization achieve its risk financing goals with varying degrees of effectiveness and efficiency. Therefore, when assisting others in selecting risk financing measures, insurance and risk management professionals seek to first understand the risk financing goals the individual or organization is trying to achieve.

Risk management program goals are designed to support an individual's or organization's overall goals. Because risk financing is an integral part of a risk management program, risk financing goals should support risk management program goals. See the exhibit "How Risk Financing Goals Support Risk Management Goals."

How Risk Financing Goals Support Risk Management Goals

Individual or Organizational Goals

Risk Management Program Goals

Risk Control Goals

Risk Financing Goals
- Pay for losses
- Manage the cost of risk
- Manage cash flow variability
- Maintain an appropriate level of liquidity
- Comply with legal requirements

[DA02690]

Common risk financing goals include these:

- Pay for losses
- Manage the cost of risk
- Manage cash flow variability
- Maintain an appropriate level of liquidity
- Comply with legal requirements

Pay for Losses

Individuals and organizations need to ensure that funds are available to pay for losses when they occur. The availability of funds is particularly important in situations that disrupt normal activities, such as when an individual needs to replace an automobile used to commute to work or when an organization needs to replace damaged property necessary for continued operations. However, paying for losses is also important for other reasons, such as to promote public relations.

For example, an organization does not want to damage its reputation by not paying liability losses resulting from legitimate third-party claims (claims filed against the insured by a party who is not a party to the insurance contract). Similarly, it may want to launch an advertising campaign to demonstrate its commitment to resolving a product liability issue.

For many individuals or organizations, paying for losses does not only entail paying for the actual losses or portions of losses retained, it also covers transfer costs, which are costs paid in order to transfer responsibility for losses to another party.

For financial risks, transfer costs could be the price of buying options to hedge the costs associated with currency exchange rate risk. For hazard risks, transfer costs are often insurance premiums. In return for the premium, the insurer accepts the uncertainty of the cost of the insured's covered losses and agrees to reimburse the insured for covered losses or to pay covered losses on the insured's behalf. The premium would also need to cover expenses and profit margins for the insurer.

This section considers paying for losses and paying transaction costs separately. Paying for losses is one risk financing goal, whereas paying transaction costs is part of managing the cost of risk, a separate risk financing goal.

For example, an insurance premium would cover both paying for losses and the transaction costs associated with the insurance policy. These two separate goals are parallel to being effective and efficient. Risk financing measures should be effective (pay for losses that do occur) as well as efficient (pay for losses in the most economical way).

Manage the Cost of Risk

Risk financing seeks to manage an individual's or organization's cost of risk. These expenses form part of the cost of risk, regardless of whether losses are retained or transferred:

- Administrative expenses
- Risk control expenses
- Risk financing expenses

Administrative expenses include the cost of internal administration and the cost of purchased services, such as claim administration or risk management consulting. Although many of these expenses are unavoidable if a risk financing program is to be properly managed, an individual or organization may have an opportunity to save on some expenses by modifying procedures or eliminating unnecessary tasks. For example, an organization with a loss retention program might save expenses by outsourcing the claim administration function to a third party who can adjust the claims more cost effectively.

Risk control expenses are incurred to reduce frequency, reduce the severity of losses that do occur, or increase the predictability of future losses. An individual or organization can best analyze risk control expenses by conducting a cost-benefit analysis. Therefore, to ensure that risk control expenses promote an individual's or organization's long-term financial goals, resources should be devoted to risk control only if the benefit of a risk control measure exceeds its cost.

Risk financing expenses are incurred to manage the risk financing measures used to meet risk financing goals. Many of these risk financing measures involve transaction costs, including commissions paid to brokers, fees paid to banks or other investment institutions in order to establish accounts, and fees paid for trades on capital market transactions.

Depending on the transaction's size, these costs can be substantial, sometimes millions of dollars. Transaction costs vary based not only on the risk financing measure chosen but also on varying market conditions. For example, the commissions paid to brokers are often a percentage of the total insurance premium that the broker places with an insurer. If insurance prices increase, the commission paid will be higher.

If market conditions dictate lower insurance premiums, commissions will be lower as well. Managing the administrative expenses, risk control expenses, and risk financing expenses does not necessarily mean minimizing those costs in an attempt to operate economically or increase profitability. In fact, many of those costs are necessary to manage an effective risk management program. Individuals and organizations should be aware of the value of the risk financing measures used to ensure that they are receiving adequate service for the price that is being paid for them. In other words, an individual or organization should be wary of sacrificing effectiveness for efficiency.

Manage Cash Flow Variability

The level of cash flow variability that an individual or organization is able or willing to accept depends on the individual's or organization's tolerance for risk. Determining that level of tolerance can be difficult. Individuals or organizations can achieve their goals for managing cash flow variability by determining the maximum cash flow variability they are willing to tolerate and arranging their risk management programs within those parameters.

For an individual, risk tolerance often depends on financial strength, family obligations, and the individual's aversion to risk. For example, an individual with two young children may desire more stable income than an individual without children. Therefore, the individual with children may be more inclined to choose a career in which the majority of the compensation comes from salary rather than commissions.

For an organization, the maximum cash flow variability level depends on factors such as the organization's size, its financial strength, and management's own degree of risk tolerance. For example, if management is prepared to accept risk in order to gain a possible benefit, then the cash flow variability levels will be higher than if management prefers to avoid risk.

An organization's maximum cash flow variability level also depends on the degree to which the organization's other stakeholders, such as shareholders, suppliers, or customers, are willing to accept risk. For example, suppliers may be less willing to sell supplies on credit to organizations with high variability in their cash flows because of concern about the organization's ability to make its repayments.

Maintain an Appropriate Level of Liquidity

A certain level of cash liquidity (liquid assets) is required to pay for retained losses. A liquid asset is one that can easily be converted into cash. For example, marketable securities are liquid because they can readily be sold in the stock or bond markets. Assets such as real property and machinery are typically not liquid because they are difficult to sell quickly at prices close to their market values.

As an individual or organization's retention level increases, so does the level of liquidity required. Therefore, to meet risk financing goals, individuals or organizations must determine the appropriate level of liquidity for retained losses and consider both internal and external sources of capital to meet those needs. Internally, individuals or organizations can look to the liquidity of their assets and the strength of their cash flows.

Liquidity can be increased by selling assets or by retaining cash flow instead of using it to fund capital projects or to pay dividends. Externally, an organization can increase liquidity by borrowing, issuing a debt instrument (a bond), or issuing stock (for a publicly traded organization). For an individual, borrowing is typically the only external option.

One problem with maintaining high levels of liquidity is that liquid assets do not typically offer the same return on investments as other, longer-term, less liquid investments. Individuals and organizations must consider the balance between desire for long-term returns in less liquid investments and the liquidity needs of retained losses.

Comply With Legal Requirements

Individuals and organizations need to consider the legal environment when making risk financing decisions. Ultimately, the goal of complying with legal requirements is a fundamental requirement of all risk financing goals. How individuals and organizations comply with these requirements depends on the individual requirements imposed by the applicable statutory or contractual obligations.

Sometimes laws and regulations will require specific risk financing measures. For example, most states require drivers to purchase auto liability insurance policies. Similarly, state workers compensation statutes require most employers to purchase workers compensation insurance or to qualify as self-insurers.

Alternatively, legal requirements will affect how risk financing measures are implemented. For example, an organization that intends to raise its liquidity by issuing bonds may be required by the bond purchasers to insure its property for a specific amount.

Similarly, contractual obligations, such as leases on automobiles or aircraft, may also require insurance coverage on the leased property.

RETENTION AND TRANSFER

While retention and transfer are separate risk management techniques, most risk financing measures involve both retention and transfer. Therefore, after setting risk financing goals, an individual or organization should determine the best mix of retention and transfer for meeting those goals.

Determining this mix requires understanding how both retention and transfer operate, the advantages of each, and how each enables an individual or organization to meet risk financing goals. This information can be combined with consideration of the specific loss exposure characteristics, plus any characteristics specific to the individual or organization, in order to determine the most appropriate levels of retention and transfer.

Retention and Transfer in Same Risk Financing Measure

Retention

A risk financing technique by which losses are retained by generating funds within the organization to pay for the losses.

Transfer

In the context of risk management, a risk financing technique by which the financial responsibility for losses and variability in cash flows is shifted to another party.

Because most risk financing measures involve elements of both **retention** and **transfer**, the distinction between the two is eroding. Therefore, it is more appropriate to view pure retention and pure transfer as the extreme points on a continuum of risk financing measures, with almost all risk financing measures, including insurance, falling somewhere between the two extremes. That is, most risk financing measures are risk-sharing mechanisms, part retention and part transfer.

Whether any specific risk financing measure involves more retention or more transfer depends on the measure. For example, the "Insurance Risk Sharing" exhibit shows that an individual or organization that purchases an insurance policy (the insured) retains the deductible amount and any losses above the policy limit. The insured transfers to the insurer losses that are above the deductible but below the policy limit. In the example in the exhibit, the majority of the risk financing measure involves transfer. See the exhibit "Insurance Risk Sharing."

Retention

Retention can be the most economical form of risk financing. However, it also exposes the individual or organization to the most cash flow variability. Retention can be either planned or unplanned.

Provided risks have been adequately identified and analyzed (assessed), retention is an intentional form of risk financing and is called planned retention. Planned retention allows the risk management professional to choose the most appropriate retention funding measure.

Unplanned retention occurs when either losses cannot be insured or otherwise transferred or an individual or organization fails to correctly identify or assess a loss exposure. In these two situations, retention becomes the risk financing method of last resort, which is why retention is often called the default risk financing technique. Unplanned retention can have a severe effect on risk financing goals and limits the choice of retention funding techniques.

Insurance Risk Sharing

Cara has just purchased a homeowners policy from Radley Insurance with a $1,000 deductible and a $300,000 limit. It would cost Cara $350,000 to rebuild her home today using the same construction materials. Assuming a total loss of the home from fire, Cara would retain the first $1,000 in loss because of her deductible. Radley would then pay the next $300,000 (risk transfer) in losses. Cara would be responsible for the last $49,000 in losses, as she would retain any losses above the limit. With the maximum retained amount of the losses being $50,000 and the maximum transferred amount of the losses being $300,000, this example of risk financing is closer to pure transfer than pure retention.

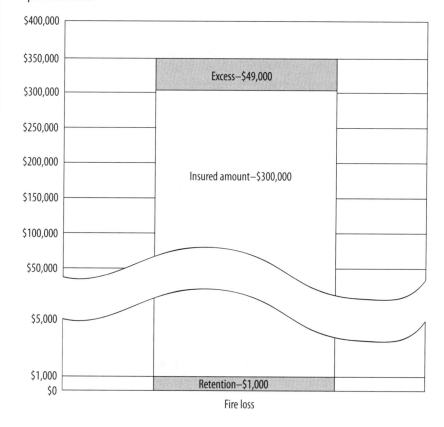

Cara can adjust the levels of retention and transfer in this example by adjusting her deductible and policy limit. Cara can decrease (increase) her retention by reducing (increasing) her deductible and raising (lowering) her policy limit.

[DA02693]

Retention Funding Measures

Retention funding measures rely on funds that originate within the organization. In order of increasing administrative complexity, these four planned retention funding measures are available to an organization:

- Current expensing of losses
- Using an unfunded reserve
- Using a funded reserve
- Borrowing funds

Current expensing of losses is the least formal funding measure (and therefore the least expensive to administer), but it also provides the least assurance that funds will be available, especially to pay for a major loss. Current expensing relies on current cash flows to cover the cost of losses.

This strategy may be feasible for losses with a low expected value but becomes less advisable as the expected value of the loss increases. Generally, the larger the potential loss an organization wants to retain relative to its cash flows, the more formal and better funded the type of retention should be.

An unfunded loss reserve appears as an accounting entry denoting potential liability to pay for a loss. Although this reserve recognizes in advance that the organization may suffer a loss, the organization does not support that potential for loss with any specific assets.

A typical example of an unfunded loss reserve is the reserve for uncollectible accounts. Organizations establish this reserve based on an estimation of the portion of accounts receivable that will not be paid.

In contrast to an unfunded loss reserve, a funded loss reserve is supported with cash, securities, or other liquid assets allocated to meet the obligations that the reserve represents. For example, a reserve for taxes payable at the end of the coming calendar quarter is usually supported by cash to pay them when they become due.

Funded loss reserves can be fairly informal, such as identifying assets that would be sold in the event of a loss, or highly complex transactions such as forming a captive insurer.

Although borrowing funds does not appear to be a retention measure, when individuals or organizations use borrowed funds to pay losses, they suffer a resulting reduction in their line of credit or ability to borrow for other purposes. This reduction ultimately depletes their resources.

Consequently, the individuals or organizations are indirectly using their own resources to pay for losses and, in time, use their own earnings to repay the loan. In the short term, the external source of capital is paying for the loss. In the long term, however, the individuals or organizations pay the entire loss.

Advantages of Retention

The advantages of using retention as a risk financing technique include these:

- Cost savings
- Control of claims process
- Timing of cash flows
- Incentives for risk control

The primary advantage that retention offers an individual or organization is cost savings. Retention is typically the most economical risk financing alternative and can generate cost savings in several ways. For example, suppose that an organization is deciding whether to retain its commercial auto liability loss exposures or transfer them through a commercial auto insurance policy. If the organization chooses to retain the risk of auto liability, then it can save money by avoiding the costs that are often included in insurance premiums:

- Administrative costs—Underwriting, claims, and investment costs incurred by the insurer as well as the additional amounts added to these costs in order to generate the profit needed by the insurer.

- Premium taxes—Taxes on insurance premiums imposed by many states.

- Moral hazard costs—Costs that are often included in underwriting and claims to verify information submitted or claims filed (often included with administrative costs).

- Social loading costs—If the state funds a residual pool through which high-risk individuals or organizations are able to purchase insurance that was unavailable from insurers, the insurers who sell insurance in that state will pass the costs of the residual pool on to all insureds who have purchased policies.

- Adverse selection costs—Cost of being pooled with high-risk policyholders. (This applies only to individuals and organizations that typically have losses below average losses.)

In addition to cost savings, retention allows an organization to maintain control of the claims process. This control allows greater flexibility in investigating and negotiating claims settlements. For example, an organization that is very concerned with its reputation may want to litigate liability claims against it, whereas an insurer may be more willing to settle the claim to reduce the payout that may be required on its part.

Another advantage of retention is the timing of cash flows. Most transfer measures require the individual or organization to make an up-front payment (such as a premium for an insurance policy). At some point after the loss occurs, the individual or organization is reimbursed by the other party.

Retention avoids the up-front payment and can shorten the delay between the time of the loss and the payment by the other party. It also allows the individual or organization to maintain any use of the funds that would have otherwise been paid. These funds can either be used in day-to-day operations or invested to generate additional income.

Retention also has the advantage of being an incentive for risk control. When individuals or organizations directly pay for their own losses, they have a strong incentive to prevent and reduce those losses. This encourages risk control in order to maximize the reduction in loss frequency and loss severity. Although not without consequences in terms of the cost of risk control measures, these efforts should ultimately reduce loss costs. See the exhibit "Industry Language—Self-Insurance and Retention."

> ### Industry Language—Self-Insurance and Retention
>
> The term "self-insurance" is sometimes used to describe a risk financing plan for which a person or an organization retains its own losses—or simply decides not to buy insurance. Used this way, the term "self-insurance" is interchangeable with the term "retention."
>
> Some argue that self-insurance is an inaccurate term because insurance involves a transfer of risk, thereby making it impossible to insure one's self. Others assert that certain forms of self-insurance are not insurance at all and that the label "self-insurance" should be applied only to a formal program in which an organization keeps records of its losses and maintains a system to pay for them. This text uses "self-insurance" in this context, that is, when an organization uses a formal program to record and pay for losses.
>
> Insurance professionals should be aware that some statutes, regulations, and contracts use "self-insurance" and "retention" interchangeably. In addition, "self-insurance" and "retention" are also used together: self-insured retention. Self-insured retentions are similar to deductibles. A self-insured retention (SIR) is defined as a risk financing measure in which the insured organization adjusts and pays its own losses up to the self-insured retention level.

[DA05016]

Transfer

The opposite of pure retention is pure transfer. A pure transfer shifts the responsibility for the entire loss from one party (transferor) to another party (transferee). However, most, if not all, transfer arrangements contain limitations that prevent them from being regarded as pure transfers.

Limitations on Risk Transfer Measures

There are two main limitations on the risk transfer measures available to individuals and organizations.

First, risk transfer measures (including insurance) are not typically pure transfers but are some combination of retention and transfer. Most, if not all, risk transfer measures involve some type of limitation on the potential loss amounts that are being transferred. These limitations can be deductibles, limits, or other restrictions so that the individual or organization (transferor) pays at least some portion of the loss.

Second, the ultimate responsibility for paying for the loss remains with the individual or organization. Risk financing does not eliminate the transferor's legal responsibility for the loss if the transferee fails to pay.

For example, if an employee gets injured at work, the employer's workers compensation insurer would pay for the medical bills of the injured employee. If the workers compensation insurer cannot or will not pay the medical bills for some reason, the employer is still responsible for paying the bills.

Therefore, the transferor is reliant on the good faith and financial strength of the transferee as well as on the judicial enforceability of the transfer agreement. The transferee might not pay because of lack of funds, a dispute about whether the loss falls within the transfer agreement's scope or financial limits, or as a result of a successful court challenge to the agreement's enforceability. See the exhibit "Risk Transfer and Counter-Party Credit Risk."

Risk Transfer and Counter-Party Credit Risk

By entering into a risk transfer agreement, one organization (Organization A) can transfer risk to another organization (Organization B). Ultimately, however, Organization A is responsible for its own losses. This creates another risk, the risk that Organization B cannot or will not pay for any losses that are incurred. In options and futures markets, this risk is often called counter-party credit risk. Counter-party credit risk is not usually an issue with exchange-traded options and futures contracts because the exchange itself typically has a clearinghouse that guarantees payment on the exchange contracts. For example, the Chicago Board of Trade (CBOT) advertises that since 1925 no contract on the CBOT has failed to pay as per the contract. When the risk transfer contracts are insurance contracts, rating organizations such as A.M. Best or Moody's assign the insurers a claims paying ability rating to help insureds identify potential counter-party credit risk. When alternative risk transfer products are used for risk transfer that is not exchange-traded, the counter-party credit risk is generally considered more substantial.

[DA05017]

Advantages of Transfer

Despite the limitations, there are significant advantages to using risk transfer measures as part of a risk financing program:

- Reducing exposure to large losses
- Reducing cash flow variability
- Providing ancillary services
- Avoiding adverse employee and public relations

The principal advantage of risk transfer measures is that they reduce an individual's or organization's exposure to large losses. Retaining large loss exposures increases the probability that the individual or organization will incur financial distress. Financial distress can have negative effects on relationships with suppliers and customers and may ultimately lead to bankruptcy.

Retaining large loss exposures also increases the probability that the individual or organization will need to either raise funds from external sources, such as a stock or bond issue, or borrow funds, which can be costly. Risk transfer measures can help lessen the variability of the cash flows of an organization or activity by reducing the effect of losses associated with retaining large loss exposures.

Many publicly traded organizations try to reduce variability of cash flows and earnings on those cash flows because this lack of variability appears to be valued by investors. Therefore, as well as achieving the risk financing goal of managing cash flow variability, risk transfers can increase an organization's attractiveness to investors and thereby potentially increase the overall value of the organization.

Risk transfer has the advantage that ancillary services can be included in the transfer arrangement; for example, insurers often offer risk assessment and control services as well as claims administration and litigation services. Being able to access these services can be a major factor in deciding to transfer some loss exposures.

The level of efficiency and expertise that some organizations, such as insurers, have developed in these areas often makes the risk transfer agreement very appealing to organizations that cannot provide these services efficiently. Although it is possible to obtain these ancillary services outside of transfer arrangements through third-party providers, this can be expensive.

Finally, risk transfer can have the advantage of avoiding adverse employee and public relations because as well as transferring responsibility for the loss itself, the organization can transfer responsibility for the claims administration process. Therefore, any issues with claims administration are less likely to harm the reputation of the organization and consequently are less likely to generate adverse employee and public relations.

Because most risk financing measures involve elements of both retention and transfer, selecting a risk financing measure involves determining how much of a particular loss exposure the individual or organization is willing to retain.

SELECTING APPROPRIATE RISK FINANCING MEASURES

To select the appropriate risk financing measures to be used in a risk management program, an individual or organization needs to evaluate the relative advantages of all the available measures and consider the ability of each to meet the risk financing goals.

The major factors influencing the ability of a risk financing measure to meet an individual's or organization's risk financing goals are these:

- The mix of retention and transfer
- Loss exposure characteristics
- Individual- or organization-specific characteristics

Mix of Retention and Transfer

An organization's risk financing program needs to balance retention and transfer in light of the specific risk financing goals that the organization is trying to accomplish. This balance can be achieved through the appropriate mix of risk financing measures.

Some loss exposures may be fully retained, others mostly transferred, and the remainder addressed with risk financing measures that balance retention and transfer. See the exhibit "Ability of Retention and Transfer to Meet Risk Financing Goals."

Because retention can be the most economical risk financing measure, it enables an organization to meet its risk financing goal of managing the cost of risk. However, depending on the magnitude of the actual losses sustained, retention programs may have difficulty paying for losses.

The ability to pay for losses depends on the structure of the retention measure implemented and the relative strength of the individual's or organization's cash flows. For example, if a loss exposure suffers a substantial loss that was retained, the ability to pay for the loss depends on whether the retention measure was pre-funded (such as funded reserve) or post-funded (such as cash flows or borrowing), how large the loss is relative to what was expected when the retention decision was made, and how large the loss is relative to cash flows or assets of the individual or organization.

Retention also generates the highest level of cash flow variability and may threaten an organization's liquidity level. Often, how an organization structures and manages its retention determines how effective it is at achieving risk financing goals compared with transfer.

Risk transfer measures typically offer the greatest certainty regarding the ability to pay losses, offer the greatest cash flow certainty, and are useful in preventing liquidity problems, but they may be costly to arrange. Furthermore, some organizations are required by statute or contractual obligation to transfer some risk.

For example, most mortgage lenders require that the property owner carry adequate limits of property insurance coverage. Similarly, many states require that motor vehicle owners, including organizations, have auto liability coverage. These requirements add to the overall cost of transfer and may therefore affect the benefit of transfer relative to retention.

Ability of Retention and Transfer to Meet Risk Financing Goals

Risk Financing Goal	Retention	Transfer
Pay for Losses	Depends on magnitude of losses and structure and management of retention measure, as well as the relative strength of cash flows	Primary benefit of transfer measures
Manage the Cost of Risk	Primary benefit of retention	Rarely the most cost-effective option
Manage Cash Flow Variability	Typically exposes the individual or organization to more variability in cash flows	Important benefit of transfer measures
Maintain an Appropriate Level of Liquidity	Depends on magnitude of losses and structure and management of retention measure, as well as the relative strength of cash flows	Generally reduces the level of liquidity needed
Comply With Legal Requirements	Depends on structure and management of retention measure	Secondary benefit of transfer measures

[DA02694]

Loss Exposure Characteristics

The frequency and severity of losses associated with each loss exposure are vital to determining whether a loss exposure should be fully retained or whether some form of transfer is appropriate. See the exhibit "The Effect of Frequency and Severity on the Retention or Transfer Decision."

Insurance products are often designed around these types of loss exposures.

The high-frequency, high-severity quadrant covers losses that occur frequently and are severe. These loss exposures should be avoided. Neither risk retention nor risk transfer is adequately designed to handle these types of loss exposures. If risk control measures can be applied to reduce the frequency or severity of the losses (or both), the loss exposure can be reclassified into the appropriate quadrant to be re-evaluated in terms of risk financing options.

The Effect of Frequency and Severity on the Retention or Transfer Decision

	Low Frequency	High Frequency
Low Severity	Retain	Retain
High Severity	Transfer	Avoid (if possible) Retain (last resort)

[DA02695]

The exhibit indicates that risk financing through retention is the appropriate technique for most loss exposures. It is only for loss exposures with low-frequency, high-severity losses that risk transfer measures are appropriate.

Individual- or Organization-Specific Characteristics

The optimal balance between retention and transfer varies for each individual or organization, depending on specific characteristics. Therefore, individuals and organizations will make different decisions in selecting the appropriate risk financing measures. Even if two organizations have the same set of loss exposures, differences between the organizations may result in vastly different selections. The individual- or organization-specific characteristics that can affect the selection of appropriate risk financing measures include these:

- Risk tolerance
- Financial condition
- Core operations
- Ability to diversify
- Ability to control losses
- Ability to administer the retention plan

Risk Tolerance

Individuals and organizations vary widely in their willingness to assume risk. A risk-averse organization may decide not to produce a certain type of product because of the high instance of associated product liability claims, whereas another organization's primary source of revenue could be that same product.

The level of risk an organization is willing to assume directly affects its optimal balance between retention and transfer. All else being equal, the higher an individual's or organization's willingness to accept risk, the higher the likelihood that more risk will be retained.

Financial Condition

The financial condition of the individual or organization has a significant effect on ability to retain risk. The more financially secure an individual or organization is, the more loss exposures can be retained without causing liquidity or cash flow variability problems.

However, even financially secure individuals or organizations need to be careful. They may experience short-term liquidity problems if a significant loss has been retained and short-term cash flow or liquid assets are not sufficient to cover the loss.

Core Operations

An organization is often better able to retain the loss exposures directly related to its core operations because it has an information advantage regarding those operations. That is, the organization knows and understands its core operations and the loss exposures associated with them better than any outside party, including insurers. Because of this information advantage, an outside party would likely need higher compensation to enter into a transfer agreement.

Ability to Diversify

If an organization can diversify its loss exposures, similar to the way many individuals and organizations diversify their investment portfolios, it can gain the advantage of offsetting losses that occur to one loss exposure with the absence of losses associated with the other loss exposures. The organization is then better able to accurately forecast future losses. This increased level of loss accuracy would reduce uncertainty about losses and therefore allow the organization to retain more loss exposures.

Ability to Control Losses

Because risk control reduces loss frequency and/or loss severity, the more risk control an organization is able to undertake, the more loss exposures it is typically able to retain. All else being equal, the reductions in frequency and/or severity make it more likely that the organization will have the ability to fund the retention of that particular loss exposure.

Ability to Administer the Retention Plan

Risk retention requires more administration than risk transfer. Such administration may include claim administration, risk management consulting, or retention fund accounting. Organizations that have a better ability to fulfill these administrative requirements are able to use retention more efficiently.

Determining the optimal balance between risk transfer and risk retention measures keeps the risk financing program aligned with the individual's or organization's overall risk management goals. For the portion of those loss exposures that an individual or organization decides to transfer, a variety of risk financing measures are available.

RISK FINANCING MEASURES

To assist an individual or organization in selecting appropriate risk financing measures, an insurance or risk management professional must understand how each measure operates and whether it will enable the person or organization to meet its risk financing goals.

Each risk financing measure is unique not only in its operation but also in its ability to meet an individual's or organization's risk financing goals. The decision to use a specific risk financing measure depends on the specific characteristics of the targeted loss exposure, as well as the characteristics of that risk financing measure.

The risk financing measures discussed here are these:

- Guaranteed cost insurance
- Self-insurance
- Large deductible plans
- Captive insurers
- Finite risk insurance plans
- Pools
- Retrospective rating plans
- Hold-harmless agreements
- Capital market solutions

Guaranteed Cost Insurance

This section uses the term "guaranteed cost insurance" to refer to insurance policies in which the premium and limits are specified in advance. The premium is guaranteed in that it does not depend on the losses incurred during the period of coverage.

Guaranteed cost insurance policies are designed to cover property, liability, personnel, and net income loss exposures from various causes of loss and have been widely offered by the insurance industry for many years. Insurance is a funded risk transfer measure. The insurance buyer (insured) transfers the potential financial consequences of certain loss exposures to an insurer.

The insured pays the insurer a relatively small, certain financial cost in the form of an insurance premium. In exchange, the insurer agrees to pay for all the organization's losses that are covered by the insurance policy, typically subject to a deductible and policy limit. The insurer also agrees to provide necessary services, such as claim handling and liability-claim defense.

Organizations that have large loss exposures often have difficulty finding a single insurer that is willing or able to supply adequate guaranteed cost insurance coverage. To solve this problem, many organizations purchase multiple guaranteed cost insurance policies as part of an overall insurance program.

An insurance program is typically divided into two or more layers—a primary layer and one or more excess layers.

Primary layer
The first level of insurance coverage above any deductible.

The **primary layer** is the first level of insurance coverage above any deductible. It is also referred to as the working layer because it is the layer used most often to pay losses.

Excess layer
A level of insurance coverage above the primary layer.

An **excess layer** is a level of insurance coverage above the primary layer. Insureds who want more insurance coverage than that offered by the primary layer usually purchase one or more excess layers. The insurance policies issued to provide coverage in excess layers are often referred to as excess coverage.

Excess coverage
Insurance that covers losses above an attachment point, below which there is usually another insurance policy or a self-insured retention.

Excess coverage is insurance that covers losses above an attachment point, below which there is usually another insurance policy or a self-insured retention. Some insurers do not provide primary layers of coverages; they specialize in supplying excess layers.

Umbrella policy
A liability policy that provides excess coverage above underlying policies and may also provide coverage not available in the underlying policies, subject to a self-insured retention.

In between primary and excess layers in an insurance program, an organization may use an **umbrella policy**. A **buffer layer** is used when the umbrella policy requires underlying coverage limits that are higher than those provided by the primary layer.

Buffer layer
A level of excess insurance coverage between a primary layer and an umbrella policy.

As an example of using layers of coverage, consider a large hotel chain that uses a layered liability insurance program to insure its large liability loss exposures:

- The primary layer of the insurance program consists of three primary (underlying) policies covering general liability, commercial auto liability, and employers liability.

- Coverage above the primary layer is provided by an umbrella policy, which provides coverage for all three areas of liability.

- For the auto liability coverage, the umbrella policy requires a buffer layer above the primary layer because the primary auto liability policy limits are below the umbrella policy's minimum requirements.

- Finally, the hotel chain has three layers of excess insurance above the umbrella policy, providing layers of coverage for loss exposures not covered by the umbrella policy.

The exhibit illustrates the hotel chain's multilayered liability insurance program. See the exhibit "Multilayered Liability Insurance Program Including a Buffer Layer."

The number of layers the insured purchases depends on both the limits the insured desires and the limits that are available from insurers. The premium per $100 of coverage (the rate) usually decreases for each layer of coverage (for example, in the preceding exhibit, excess layer 3 would probably be cheaper than excess layer 2) because there is a corresponding decrease in the probability that losses will be large enough to use higher layers. See the exhibit "Ability of Guaranteed Cost Insurance to Meet Risk Financing Goals."

Multilayered Liability Insurance Program Including a Buffer Layer

| Excess layer 3 |
| Excess layer 2 |
| Excess layer 1 |
| Umbrella policy |

| General liability (primary layer) | Buffer layer | Employers' liability (primary layer) |
| | Auto liability (primary layer) | |

[DA02696]

Before using guaranteed cost insurance for risk financing, an organization should assess the extent to which such insurance meets the organization's risk financing goals. An additional benefit offered by guaranteed cost insurance is that generally the individual or organization can deduct the insurance premium for tax purposes. See the exhibit "Alternative Risk Transfer (ART)."

Alternative Risk Transfer (ART)

The term "alternative risk transfer" or simply "ART" is widely used to refer to risk financing measures other than guaranteed cost insurance. Thus, risk financing measures that involve both insurance and retention (such as large deductible plans and retrospective rating plans) can be classified as ART.

[DA05894]

Self-Insurance

Self-insurance can be contrasted with an informal retention plan, under which an organization simply pays for its losses with its cash flow or current (liquid) assets but has no formal payment procedures or method of recording losses.

Self-insurance is particularly well-suited for financing losses that are paid out over a period of time, thereby providing a cash flow benefit (compared with guaranteed cost insurance) to the organization retaining its losses. Consequently, workers compensation, general liability, and automobile liability loss exposures are often self-insured because they have claim payouts that extend over time.

Self-insurance

A form of retention under which an organization records its losses and maintains a formal system to pay for them.

Ability of Guaranteed Cost Insurance to Meet Risk Financing Goals

Risk Financing Goal	How Guaranteed Cost Insurance Meets the Goal
Pay for Losses	Insurance can meet this goal, provided the loss exposures are covered by the guaranteed cost insurance policies.
Manage the Cost of Risk	Insurance can meet this goal, but it is not ideal because insurance premiums are designed to cover not only expected losses, but also insurer administrative costs, adverse selection and moral hazard costs, premium taxes, and any social loadings.
Manage Cash Flow Variability	Insurance can meet this goal because much of the uncertainty about future losses is transferred to the insurer.
Maintain Appropriate Level of Liquidity	Insurance can meet this goal because the organization requires less liquidity with guaranteed cost insurance compared with retention or other risk financing measures.
Comply With Legal Requirements	Insurance can meet this goal, especially regarding loss exposures that are required (by law or contractual obligation) to be transferred.

[DA02697]

Self-insurance (retention) is usually combined with a risk financing measure (transfer), such as an excess coverage insurance policy that covers any infrequent, high-severity losses that may occur. Self-insurance is usually used for high-frequency loss exposures because it is more efficient than filing many claims with an insurer.

Because of the large volume of claim transactions, self-insurance requires claim administration services similar to those provided by an insurer. Such services include these:

- Recordkeeping—A self-insured organization needs a recordkeeping system to track its self-insured claims.
- Claim adjustment—As with an insured plan, claims must be investigated, evaluated, negotiated, and paid.
- Loss reserving—A self-insured organization must determine reserve amounts needed for estimated future payments on self-insured losses that

have occurred. The reserves for self-insured loss payments can be funded or unfunded.

- Litigation management—Litigation management involves controlling the cost of legal expenses for claims that are litigated. This includes evaluating and selecting defense lawyers, supervising them during litigation, and keeping records of their costs. It also involves specific techniques such as auditing legal bills and experimenting with alternative fee-billing strategies.

- Regulatory requirements—In most states, an organization must qualify as a self-insurer in order to self-insure workers compensation or auto liability loss exposures. The qualification requirements specify items such as financial security requirements; filing fees, taxes, and assessments that must be paid; excess coverage insurance requirements; and periodic reports that the organization must submit to the regulatory body to qualify as a self-insurer.

- Excess coverage insurance—Many states require a self-insurer to purchase excess coverage insurance. Some states specify conditions for the purchase of this coverage. In other states, the state agency responsible for self-insurance reviews each applicant and decides whether to require excess coverage insurance.

Before adopting a self-insurance plan, an organization should evaluate the plan's ability to meet the organization's risk financing goals. See the exhibit "Ability of a Self-Insurance Plan to Meet Risk Financing Goals."

Large Deductible Plans

A **large deductible plan** is similar to a self-insurance plan combined with excess coverage insurance in that it exposes the organization to a relatively large amount of loss. In exchange for this exposure, the insurer provides a premium reduction relative to guaranteed cost insurance.

Large deductible plan
An insurance policy with a per occurrence or per accident deductible of $100,000 or more.

A key difference between self-insurance and large deductible plans is that with self-insurance, the insured is responsible for adjusting and paying its own losses up to the attachment point of the excess coverage insurance. Under a large deductible plan, the insurer adjusts and pays all claims, even those below the deductible level. The insurer then seeks reimbursement from the insured for those claims that fall below the deductible. In effect, the insurer is guaranteeing the payment of all claims. See the exhibit "Ability of a Large Deductible Plan to Meet Risk Financing Goals."

The insured usually must provide the insurer with a form of financial security (such as a letter of credit) to guarantee payment of covered losses up to the deductible. Both self-insurance and large deductible plans are common for workers compensation, auto liability, and general liability policies. Before adopting a large deductible plan, an organization should evaluate the plan's ability to meet the organization's risk financing goals. The exhibit describes how a large deductible plan can meet these goals.

Ability of a Self-Insurance Plan to Meet Risk Financing Goals

Risk Financing Goal	How a Self-Insurance Plan Meets the Goal
Pay for Losses	Self-insurance can help meet this goal if an organization carefully chooses the loss retention level, purchases appropriate excess coverage, and has sufficient cash flow or liquid assets.
Manage the Cost of Risk	A self-insured organization must administer its own claims (either with its own staff or a third-party administrator) but can save insurer operating expenses, profits, and risk charges. These significant savings are the primary benefit of self-insurance.
Manage Cash Flow Variability	With self-insurance, retained loss outcomes are uncertain. The higher the retention, the higher the degree of uncertainty of retained loss outcomes.
Maintain Appropriate Level of Liquidity	Self-insurance can help meet this goal if an organization carefully chooses the loss retention level, purchases appropriate excess coverage, and accurately forecasts paid amounts for retained losses.
Comply With Legal Requirements	A self-insurer must meet certain legal requirements. In most states, an organization must qualify as a self-insurer for workers compensation and auto liability.

[DA02698]

Captive Insurers

Captive insurer, or captive
A subsidiary formed to insure the loss exposures of its parent company and the parent's affiliates.

A **captive insurer**, or captive, can be owned by a single parent or by multiple parents.

A captive owned by multiple parents is called a group captive. Group captives typically operate as formalized pools in which several organizations group together to share the financial consequences associated with their collective loss exposures. Because of the sharing of loss exposures with other parents, group captives act more like transfer measures.

If a significant portion of the captives' revenues are generated by underwriting loss exposures from unrelated, third-party organizations (unaffiliated business), captives operate much more as a transfer measure than as a retention measure. Captives also have the potential to transfer the financial consequences of some of the insured loss exposures to other insurers through a variety of arrangements, including reinsurance.

Ability of a Large Deductible Plan to Meet Risk Financing Goals

Risk Financing Goal	How a Large Deductible Plan Meets the Goal
Pay for Losses	The plan meets this goal because the insurer pays for losses as they become due, including losses less than the deductible for which the insured eventually reimburses the insurer.
Manage the Cost of Risk	The plan may meet this goal because the insurer administers the claims process, even for the small claims the insured has retained. The plan will meet this goal better than guaranteed cost insurance but not as well as retention plans.
Manage Cash Flow Variability	The plan meets this goal because the organization can effectively manage cash flow uncertainty if the deductible amount is chosen carefully. The plan will meet this goal better than self-insurance but not as well as guaranteed cost insurance.
Maintain Appropriate Level of Liquidity	The plan meets this goal because liquidity is maintained if the deductible level is carefully selected. The liquidity needed is lower with a large deductible plan than with retention, but higher than the liquidity needed with guaranteed cost insurance.
Comply With Legal Requirements	The plan meets this goal because it can meet legal requirements for purchasing insurance because an insurer issues a policy guaranteeing that all covered claims will be paid.

[DA02699]

Single-parent captives, also called pure captives, typically operate as a formalized retention plan and only provide insurance coverage for their parent or sibling organizations, known as affiliated business.

Operation of a Captive

A captive requires an investment of capital by its parent(s) in order to have the ability to pay losses and to manage its accounting, auditing, legal, and underwriting expenses. Just as any other insurer does, a captive collects premiums, issues policies, invest assets and pays covered losses. Nearly 5,000 captive insurers operate worldwide, with many large organizations using one or more captives to finance their loss exposures.

Deciding how a captive will operate includes these considerations:

- What types of loss exposures the captive will insure
- Where the captive will be domiciled
- Whether the captive will accept unaffiliated business

Similar to self-insurance, captives are commonly used to cover loss exposures that substantially drain cash flow, such as workers compensation, general liability, and automobile liability. An advantage to covering these types of losses through a captive is that the captive can earn investment income on the substantial loss reserves necessary for these exposures.

Captives are also used to cover property loss exposures that are difficult to insure in the primary insurance market, as well as loss exposures that fall under specialized types of business, such as products liability and environmental liability.

The decision on the types of loss exposures covered by the captive is often made prior to the captive's formation. In that case, the captive is specifically formed to handle particular loss exposures for the parent. Once in operation, many captives expand their operations to manage a wider variety of loss exposures.

Many jurisdictions, known as domiciles, encourage captives to locate within their territories by offering favorable regulations and low (or no) taxes. These domiciles see captive insurance as an industry that boosts their economies by providing employment and income such as annual registration fees.

Examples of these domiciles include offshore locations such as Barbados, Bermuda, Dublin, Isle of Man, Guernsey, Singapore, and the Cayman Islands, as well as onshore locations such as Hawaii, Vermont, Colorado, and Tennessee.

Although a captive insurer can be domiciled anywhere in the world, most organizations choose a domicile that is favorable toward the formation and operation of captives. Corporate governance concerns about the transparency of financial transactions have increased the appeal of onshore captive domiciles and offshore domiciles that offer reputable regulatory oversight.

When selecting the domicile for a captive, the captive's parent should consider these factors:

- Initial capital requirements, taxes, and annual fees
- Reputation and regulatory environment
- Premium and investment restrictions
- Support of infrastructure in terms of accountants, bankers, lawyers, captive managers, and other third-party service providers within the domicile

Some organizations operate a captive not only to underwrite their own loss exposures, but also to insure third-party business; that is, business that is not directly related to the captive's parent and affiliates. Some organizations use their captives in this way to enable them to operate in the insurance business. Others have found a benefit to writing third-party business over which they have some control, such as warranties on the products they sell.

There are several considerations to take into account when deciding whether to insure third-party business. For example, many domiciles have different capital and regulatory requirements for captives that are involved in third-party business. Such requirements are much more restrictive than the requirements for captives writing only affiliated business.

Furthermore, writing third-party business may require additional actuarial, underwriting, and marketing expertise that the captive does not currently present. Finally, insuring third-party business adds additional risk to the captive resulting from the possibility of adverse results from that business.

Special Types of Group Captives

In addition to the single-parent and group captive structures discussed previously, there are several special types of group captives. The most common special types of group captives are these:

- Risk retention group (RRG)
- Rent-a-captive
- Protected cell company (PCC)

The Liability Risk Retention Act allows the formation of **risk retention groups** (RRG) to provide liability coverage, other than personal insurance, workers compensation, and employers' liability. Risk retention groups were formed in direct response to the lack of liability insurance coverage available in insurance markets during the mid-1980s.

A **rent-a-captive** is an arrangement under which an organization rents capital from a captive to which it pays premiums and receives reimbursement for its losses. By using a rent-a-captive, an organization can benefit from using a captive without having to supply its own capital to establish such a company.

Each insured keeps its own premium and loss account, so no risk transfer occurs among the members. However, there is no statutory separation of capital and assets in a rent-a-captive structure as there is in the protected cell company structure. Because of this, it is possible that the capital rented by the insured in a rent-a-captive structure could be diminished by losses of another insured in the structure.

A **protected cell company (PCC)** is similar in structure to a rent-a-captive. An organization pays premiums to the PCC and receives reimbursement for its losses while also receiving credit for underwriting profit and investment income.

Risk retention group

A group captive formed under the requirements of the Liability Risk Retention Act of 1986 to insure the parent organizations.

Rent-a-captive

An arrangement under which an organization rents capital from a captive to which it pays premiums and receives reimbursement for its losses.

Protected cell company (PCC)

A corporate entity separated into cells so that each participating company owns an entire cell but only a portion of the overall company.

As with a rent-a-captive, each organization keeps its own premium and loss account in a separate cell from those of other members. Because the PCC is required by statute to be separated into cells, each member is assured that other members and third parties cannot access its assets in the event that any of those other members becomes insolvent. This protection is not necessarily provided by a rent-a-captive.

Ability of a Captive to Meet Risk Financing Goals

Before forming a captive, an organization should evaluate the captive insurer plan's ability to meet the organization's risk financing goals. See the exhibit "Ability of a Captive Plan to Meet Risk Financing Goals."

Finite Risk Insurance Plans

Finite risk insurance differs from guaranteed cost insurance in that a large part of the insured's premium under a finite risk insurance agreement creates a fund (experience fund) for the insured's own losses. The remaining amount of the premium is used to transfer a limited portion of risk of loss to the insurer. The insurer under a **finite risk insurance plan** usually shares with the insured a large percentage of its profit from the plan. See the exhibit "Ethical Considerations: Accounting for Finite Risk Transactions."

Finite risk insurance plan

A risk financing plan that transfers a limited (finite) amount of risk to an insurer.

Ability of a Captive Plan to Meet Risk Financing Goals

Risk Financing Goal	How a Captive Plan Meets the Goal
Pay for Losses	The captive can meet this goal if properly capitalized and managed.
Manage the Cost of Risk	The captive can reduce an organization's costs over time if properly funded and managed, despite large start-up costs.
Manage Cash Flow Variability	The captive can meet this goal by charging level premiums to the parent and affiliates and by retaining earnings in the years with lower losses to pay for higher losses in the other years.
Maintain Appropriate Level of Liquidity	The captive can meet this goal if it is properly capitalized.
Comply With Legal Requirements	The captive can be structured to meet all legal requirements, although captives are rarely licensed to operate as a primary insurer in the United States.

[DA02701]

Ethical Considerations: Accounting for Finite Risk Transactions

Insurers have often used finite risk insurance products as a risk financing measure to manage their own risks. When insurers purchase a finite risk insurance policy from a reinsurer, it is referred to as finite risk reinsurance. Because finite risk insurance products do not involve much risk transfer, ethical questions have been raised regarding how insurers and reinsurers should account for finite risk reinsurance arrangements in their financial statements.

Premiums paid for finite risk reinsurance can be accounted for as reinsurance premiums (reinsurance accounting) if there is sufficient risk transfer; otherwise, the premiums are accounted for as a deposit (deposit accounting), similar to a deposit at a bank. Although the accounting standards (FAS #113 and SSAP #62) do not specify exactly how much risk transfer needs to occur, common interpretation of the standards is that they require at least a 10 percent chance of a loss of 10 percent or more of the coverage limits for the transaction to qualify for reinsurance accounting.

Investigations by the New York State Attorney General, the Securities and Exchange Commission, and state regulators have questioned whether the risk transfer requirements were met by certain insurers and reinsurers that accounted for some finite risk reinsurance arrangements as reinsurance transactions. These investigations are not questioning the finite risk financing measure itself. They are questioning the accounting involved in specific transactions to determine whether some of these transactions have not been properly accounted for.

[DA02703]

A finite risk insurance plan is often used for especially hazardous loss exposures (such as those leading to environmental liability and earthquake damage) for which insurance capacity is limited or unavailable.

Unlike a guaranteed cost insurance policy, the premium for a finite risk insurance plan is a very high percentage of the policy limits. For example, an insurer might provide a limit of $10 million for a $7 million premium. The insurer's risk is limited because the most it would ever have to pay is $10 million, and it has the opportunity to earn investment income on the $7 million premium until losses are paid. By charging a substantial premium for the risk and applying a relatively low policy limit, the insurer has only a small chance that its losses and expenses will exceed its premium and earned investment income.

As with most ART measures, finite risk insurance combines many of the advantages of both risk retention and risk transfer. An insured that can control its losses receives profit sharing, including investment income, on the cash flow of the experience fund. In addition, the insured is protected by a limited amount of risk transfer in the event that losses are much higher than expected.

A finite risk plan often enables an insured to obtain higher limits than it could get using guaranteed cost insurance. Underwriters are willing to provide the higher limits because premiums and limits are combined over several years under a single plan. In addition, by using a finite risk plan, an insured can certify to third parties that it has insurance that might not otherwise be available.

Before adopting a finite risk plan, an organization should evaluate the plan's ability to meet the organization's risk financing goals. See the exhibit "Ability of a Finite Risk Plan to Meet Risk Financing Goals."

Pools

Pool

A group of organizations that band together to insure each other's loss exposures.

A **pool** is a group of organizations that insure each other's loss exposures. Each insured member of the pool contributes premium based on its loss exposures and in exchange the pool pays for each insured's covered losses. In some pools, the members also contribute capital. Pools can be organized in a variety of ways, including as a stock insurer or as a not-for-profit unincorporated association governed by its members. However, the structure of most pools is less formal than the structure of a group captive.

Ability of a Finite Risk Plan to Meet Risk Financing Goals

Risk Financing Goal	How a Finite Risk Plan Meets the Goal
Pay for Losses	The plan can meet this goal because the insurer pays for losses as they become due. However, because of the limited risk transfer, the insured ultimately pays for almost all of its own losses.
Manage the Cost of Risk	The plan can meet this goal because the profit-sharing feature encourages and rewards successful risk control efforts and thereby reduces an organization's cost of risk.
Manage Cash Flow Variability	The plan can meet this goal because cash flows are smoothed over multiple periods; however, large premiums may be due at outset.
Maintain Appropriate Level of Liquidity	The plan cannot meet this goal because premium payments are usually paid upfront.
Comply With Legal Requirements	The plan can meet this goal because the insurer issues a policy guaranteeing that all covered claims will be paid.

[DA02702]

A pool operates like an insurer by collecting premiums, paying losses, purchasing excess insurance or reinsurance, and providing other services such as risk control consulting. Pools can be formed to cover various types of loss exposures and are well-suited for organizations that are too small to use a captive insurer.

For example, in the United States, workers compensation pools are common and are permitted in most states. The individual states regulate the formation and operation of these pools. Public entities are commonly members of workers compensation pools.

The pool achieves savings through economies of scale in administration, claim handling, and the purchase of excess insurance or reinsurance. Each pool member might realize a savings in premium compared with that for guaranteed cost insurance, yet still benefit from some risk transfer to the other pool members. A suitably designed pool can reduce an organization's cost of risk and keep the uncertainty of the cost associated with its retained losses at a tolerable level.

Before joining a pool, an organization should evaluate the pool's ability to meet the organization's risk financing goals. See the exhibit "Ability of a Pool to Meet Risk Financing Goals."

Retrospective Rating Plans

A **retrospective rating plan** is a risk financing plan under which an organization buys insurance subject to a rating plan that adjusts the premium rate after the end of the policy period based on a portion of the insured's actual losses during the policy period. See the exhibit "Comparison of Retrospective Rating and Experience Rating Plans."

Retrospective rating plans are used to finance low-to- medium-severity losses and are usually combined with other risk financing plans (such as excess liability insurance) to cover high-severity losses. An organization must have a substantial insurance premium, usually amounting to several hundred thousand dollars per year, to benefit from a retrospective rating plan.

Retrospective rating plan
A rating plan that adjusts the insured's premium for the current policy period based on the insured's loss experience during the current period; paid losses or incurred losses may be used to determine loss experience.

Design

At its inception, a retrospective rating plan appears to operate in the same way as a guaranteed cost insurance plan. The insured pays a premium (the deposit premium) at the beginning of the policy period and the insurer issues an insurance policy and agrees to pay covered losses up to the policy limit. However, in a retrospective rating plan, the insured's losses during the policy period are considered in calculating a major portion of the premium.

The insurer (using a rating formula agreed on at policy inception) adjusts the premium after the end of the policy period to include a portion of the insured's covered losses that occurred during the policy period. If the premium due is more than the original deposit premium, the insurer will collect additional premium from the insured.

Ability of a Pool to Meet Risk Financing Goals

Risk Financing Goal	How a Pool Meets the Goal
Pay for Losses	A pool can meet this goal because there is some risk transfer to other members of the pool. However, ultimately, the pool must pay for its own losses.
Manage the Cost of Risk	A pool can meet this goal through economies of scale in administration.
Manage Cash Flow Variability	A pool can meet this goal through risk sharing with the other members. This risk sharing can be a major benefit of a pool if it has enough loss exposures to benefit from the law of large numbers.
Maintain Appropriate Level of Liquidity	A pool can meet this goal if adequately funded and managed, reducing an organization's necessary level of liquidity.
Comply With Legal Requirements	A pool can meet this goal if organized and managed within state regulations.

[DA02704]

Comparison of Retrospective Rating and Experience Rating Plans

Retrospective rating is frequently confused with experience rating because both consider the insured's loss experience. Experience rating adjusts the premium for the current policy period to recognize the loss experience of the insured during past policy periods. In contrast, retrospective rating adjusts the premium for the current policy period to recognize the insured's loss experience during the *current* policy period.

[DA05019]

If the premium due is less than the deposit premium, the insurer will issue a refund to the insured. Because the premium is adjusted upward or downward based directly on a portion of covered losses, the insured is, in effect, retaining a portion of its own losses.

Loss Exposures

Organizations commonly use retrospective rating plans for losses arising from their liability loss exposures that are covered by workers compensation, auto liability, and general liability insurance policies. Organizations also use retrospective rating plans to finance auto physical damage and crime losses.

Loss Limit

Retrospective premiums are calculated using a **loss limit**. The loss limit can vary and is negotiated by the insurer and the insured.

For example, the loss limit under a retrospective rating plan might be $100,000 per occurrence. In this case, the first $100,000 of each covered loss occurrence is included in the retrospective premium, and the amount of each loss occurrence that exceeds $100,000 and is less than the policy limit is transferred to the insurer.

Loss limit
The level at which a loss occurrence is limited for the purpose of calculating a retrospectively rated premium.

Minimum and Maximum Premiums

The adjusted premium under a retrospective rating plan is subject to a maximum and a minimum amount, called the maximum premium and the minimum premium, respectively. For example, a retrospective rating plan might have a minimum premium of $200,000 and a maximum premium of $1 million. If the insured experiences no losses during the policy period, the minimum premium of $200,000 still applies. If, during the policy period, the insured experiences a total of $1.4 million in losses subject to the policy's loss limit, the premium is limited to the maximum premium of $1 million.

Because the premium for a retrospective rating plan includes a portion of the insured's covered losses during the policy period and is subject to maximum and minimum amounts, an insured retains a portion of its losses. If an insured incurs higher-than-average losses during a policy period, the final adjusted premium under a retrospective rating plan is higher than the premium that the insured would pay under a guaranteed cost insurance plan to cover the same losses.

The opposite is true if losses are lower than average. The portion of losses not retained is transferred to the insurer, which is compensated through risk transfer premium charges that are built into the retrospective rating plan premium. The retrospective rating plan premium also includes charges for other components, such as residual market loadings, premium taxes, and insurer overhead and profit. Such charges are also found in guaranteed cost insurance policies.

Administration

Retrospective rating plans require only a moderate amount of administration by the insured. The insured's responsibility is limited to making premium payments and arranging for any required security, such as a letter of credit, to guarantee future payments. The insurer is responsible for many of the administrative tasks, such as adjusting claims, making necessary filings with the states, and paying applicable premium taxes and fees. Because a portion of the premium includes the insured's covered losses, the insured should periodically audit the insurer's claim handling, loss payment, and loss reserving practices. Often, a broker or a risk management consultant performs this audit on the insured's behalf.

Cost Savings

An organization can save certain expenses by retaining a portion of losses under a retrospective rating plan instead of transferring all losses under a guaranteed cost insurance plan. One significant expense saved is insurer risk charges, which are extra charges that an insurer includes as part of its risk transfer premium to cover the chance that losses will be higher than expected.

Risk Control

Retrospective rating plans encourage risk control. With a retrospective rating plan, an organization that is able to prevent and/or reduce its losses quickly realizes a premium savings compared with what it would pay under a guaranteed cost insurance plan. This direct link between losses and premium is a major incentive for an insured to control its losses.

Financial Impact

If designed correctly, a retrospective rating plan also provides financial stability. If the loss limit and the maximum premium are set so as to reduce the uncertainty of the insured's premium adjustments to a level that it can tolerate, then the insured benefits from the relative stability that the retrospective rating plan provides for its earnings, net worth, and cash flow. If a retrospective rating plan covers more than one type of loss exposure, then the insured also benefits from the stability provided through diversification by retaining losses from different types of loss exposures under a single plan.

Risk Financing Goals

A retrospective rating plan can help an organization meet its risk financing goals by providing an appropriate balance between risk retention and risk transfer. Before adopting a retrospective rating plan, an organization should evaluate the plan's ability to meet the organization's risk financing goals. See the exhibit "Ability of a Retrospective Rating Plan to Meet Risk Financing Goals."

Hold-Harmless Agreements

Hold-harmless agreements are a noninsurance risk transfer measure. A hold-harmless agreement can be a stand-alone contract or a clause within a contract. An example of the latter would be the inclusion of the following hold-harmless agreement as part of a leasing arrangement: "To the fullest extent permitted by law, the lessee shall indemnify, defend, and hold harmless the lessor, agents, and employees of the lessor from and against all claims arising out of or resulting from the leased premises."

Hold-harmless agreements are commonly used to assign the responsibility for losses arising out of a particular relationship or activity. For example, it is common for manufacturers to enter into hold-harmless agreements with

Ability of a Retrospective Rating Plan to Meet Risk Financing Goals

Risk Financing Goal	How a Retrospective Rating Plan Meets the Goal
Pay for Losses	The plan can meet this goal because, as with any insurance plan, the insurer pays for losses as they become due.
Manage the Cost of Risk	The plan can meet this goal because it includes a significant amount of retention and can reduce an organization's cost of risk over the long run.
Manage Cash Flow Variability	The plan can meet this goal because it helps manage some cash flow uncertainty, but because of the retrospective nature of the premium, some cash flow uncertainty remains.
Maintain Appropriate Level of Liquidity	The plan can meet this goal if the loss limit and maximum premium are chosen carefully.
Comply With Legal Requirements	The plan can meet this goal because an insurer issues a policy guaranteeing that all covered claims will be paid.

[DA02705]

distributors whereby the manufacturer agrees to assume the liability losses the distributor suffers as a result of distributing the manufacturer's products. This type of hold-harmless agreement is a risk financing measure that transfers the financial responsibility for liability losses from the distributor to the manufacturer.

Before using a hold-harmless agreement as a risk financing measure, an organization should ascertain that the agreement is not affected by any statute that forbids certain types of hold-harmless agreements in the state where the agreement is made. If the hold-harmless agreement would be legally enforceable, the organization should then evaluate its ability to meet the organization's risk financing goals. See the exhibit "Ability of a Hold-Harmless Agreement to Meet Risk Financing Goals."

Capital Market Solutions

In a **capital market**, bonds and other financial assets having a maturity of more than one year are bought and sold. Recent innovative approaches to risk financing have used capital market products such as securitization, derivatives, and contingent capital arrangements as additional ART measures.

Capital market

A financial market in which long-term securities are traded.

Ability of a Hold-Harmless Agreement to Meet Risk Financing Goals

Risk Financing Goal	How a Hold-Harmless Agreement Meets the Goal
Pay for Losses	The agreement can meet this goal provided the loss exposures are covered by the agreement and the other party has the financial ability to pay losses subject to the agreement.
Manage the Cost of Risk	The agreement can meet this goal subject to any other contractual demands the other party requires before accepting the hold-harmless agreement.
Manage Cash Flow Variability	The agreement can meet this goal subject to the extent of the agreement.
Maintain Appropriate Level of Liquidity	The agreement can meet this goal because the organization requires less liquidity with a hold-harmless agreement compared with retention or other ART measures.
Comply With Legal Requirements	The agreement can meet this goal, especially regarding loss exposures that are required (by law or contractual obligation) to be transferred.

[DA02706]

Because these new capital market products involve significant time and expense to implement, only a few, large organizations (including insurers and reinsurers) have used them to finance risk. Nonetheless, these organizations have been able to use capital market products to finance a variety of organization- and industry-specific risks. For example, insurers have used capital market products mainly for catastrophe risks, such as the risk of large earthquake or hurricane losses. However, these products could also be used to finance any type of insurable risk, and some predict that the use of capital market products by insurers and reinsurers will expand rapidly.

Securitization

Securitization
The process of creating a marketable investment security based on a financial transaction's expected cash flows.

Securitization is the process of creating a marketable investment security based on a financial transaction's expected cash flows. For example, a bank might securitize its mortgage receivables and sell them through an intermediary (called a special purpose vehicle or SPV) to investors following this process:

1. The bank (mortgagee) lends money to both individuals and organizations (mortgagors) to purchase real property.
2. The mortgagors make a promise to repay the mortgage through periodic payments to the bank. These mortgage payments are mortgage receivables to the bank.
3. The bank, through an SPV, may sell a mortgage-backed security to investors.
4. The bank collects the money from the investors and transfers the mortgage receivables to the investors.

In this type of transaction, the bank is no longer exposed to any risk of non-payment by the mortgagors. That risk has been transferred from the bank to the investors through the mortgage-backed securities. These securities appeal to investors when they offer a sufficiently attractive return for the perceived risk of non-payment by the mortgagor. The bank exchanges one asset for another. It sells its mortgage receivables, which are subject to the possibility of default and other risks, and it receives the investors' money in exchange. Through securitization, the risk inherent in the mortgage receivables is transferred from the bank to the investors.

Insurance securitization is a unique form of securitization. The cash flows that arise from the transfer of insurable risks are similar to premium and loss payments under an insurance policy.

The most common insurance securitizations are catastrophe bonds. Insurers or reinsurers sell insurance policies that cover losses related to natural catastrophes.

For example, the insurance policies may cover property damage caused by hurricanes or earthquakes. Because of the catastrophic nature of the coverage, insurers and reinsurers may have difficulty using pooling and the law of large numbers to adequately mitigate the catastrophic risk. One solution is to transfer that risk to the capital markets where investors holding diversified portfolios have a larger pool of assets to absorb catastrophic losses.

Similar to mortgage-backed securities, insurers and reinsurers can purchase insurance from an SPV, which will use the premiums to sell a catastrophe bond to investors. The investor pays the principal to the SPV.

At the end of the bond term (typically one to three years), provided no covered catastrophe has occurred, the investor receives both the principal and interest payment from the SPV. If a catastrophe did occur, the investor receives less in return.

Depending on the terms of the bond issue, the investor may receive only the principal with no interest income, or may receive only a portion of the principal. The premiums paid by the insurer are used by the SPV to offset the cost

Insurance securitization

The process of creating a marketable insurance-linked security based on the cash flows that arise from the transfer of insurable risks.

of bond issue and to cover any interest payments (payment to the investor) promised by the bond.

The payoff on catastrophe bonds is linked to the occurrences of major catastrophes during the bond's term. For example, suppose an investor purchases a bond from an SPV that provides a rate of return higher than a similarly rated corporate bond or a U.S. Treasury bond of comparable maturity. The investor assumes the risk that a hurricane might occur during the bond's term in exchange for a higher rate of return.

If a hurricane does occur and causes losses that exceed a specified dollar threshold, the investor's return on the bond is reduced. If total property losses are high enough to trigger a reduced return on the bond, either the investor's interest income or the interest income and principal repayments on the bond may be lowered, depending on the terms of the bond and the extent of the losses.

The SPV uses the savings in interest and principal repayments to pay cash to the issuing insurer or reinsurer, which uses the cash to offset its hurricane losses. Through the process of insurance securitization, the risk of loss caused by a hurricane has been securitized by linking it with the returns provided to investors in a marketable security.

Securitization passes some of the catastrophe risk that an insurer has accumulated through its insurance policies on to investors, thereby reducing the insurer's overall risk. From the investor's perspective, insurance-linked securities help diversify the investor's portfolio because the insurable risk embedded in insurance-linked securities is not closely correlated with the risks normally involved in other investments.

Hedging

A financial transaction in which one asset is held to offset the risk associated with another asset.

Hedging

Hedging is the purchase or sale of one asset to offset the risks associated with another asset. The asset held to offset the risk is often a contract, such as an option or futures contract. Hedging as a risk financing measure is well suited to business risks created by price changes.

For example, commodities (such as energy, metal, or agricultural), foreign exchange rates or currencies, and interest rates are all frequently hedged. The risk transferred is the exposure to loss from declines or increases in an asset's market price. The asset concerned is one that the hedging party holds for an extended period as a normal part of doing business.

For example, suppose a manufacturer knows that it is going to require a substantial quantity of oil to support its manufacturing activities. If the manufacturer is concerned about the volatility in oil prices, it can hedge against changes in oil prices by entering a contract to buy the oil at a certain price and time at some point in the future. This type of hedging of speculative business risks allows an organization to protect itself against possible price-level losses by sacrificing possible price-level gains.

As another example, suppose that a soybean farmer is exposed to loss if the market price of soybean drops significantly between when he or she plants the crop and when he or she sells the harvest. Although the farmer is exposed to loss if the market price decreases, soybean consumers, such as a soy milk manufacturer, may profit from such a price decrease. If the market price were to rise, the farmer would profit but the manufacturer would be exposed to a loss.

To manage this market price risk, the farmer could enter into a soybean hedge with the manufacturer during the soybean growing season, locking in a future sales price via a futures contract before bringing the soybeans to market. Changes in market prices—whether increases or decreases—would no longer affect the farmer's anticipated revenue on a per-unit basis, just as they would no longer affect the manufacturer, because the price has already been agreed upon. Both manufacturer and farmer are insulated from gains or losses associated with market price changes.

Any price or other financial value that is uncertain in the future and that can be objectively measured, such as a stock market index, common stock price, commodity price, or consumer or industrial price index, can be the basis for a hedge. Those prices or financial values are called underlying assets. The hedging contracts that are based on those underlying assets are called **derivatives**.

Derivative
A financial contract that derives its value from the value of another asset.

For a derivative contract to be a successful hedging contract, two parties must be willing to hedge the underlying asset. For example, the soybean farmer (exposed to loss when prices decrease) would not be able to hedge the soybean prices for his or her harvest if there were no consumer (such as the soy milk manufacturer) who was exposed to loss when prices increase. There are several exchanges in which derivative contracts are traded that are easily accessible by organizations seeking to hedge.

One advantage of hedging is that hedging against possible net income losses from price changes can reduce an organization's business risk loss exposures. Consequently, an organization that uses hedging has a greater capacity to bear both business risks and hazard risks and at the same time reduces its dependence on traditional financial and insurance markets for its risk transfer needs.

A disadvantage of hedging is that it can destabilize not only an organization's general risk financing plans but also its entire financial structure. If an organization's retained earnings or capital are seriously jeopardized by unwise speculative investments in hedging instruments, the earnings or capital may no longer reliably pay for retained losses. Consequently, the financial security that they provide could be greatly impaired. The goal of reducing an organization's cost of risk for losses by generating high returns for loss reserves must be balanced against the goal of ensuring that funds will be available when needed to pay for losses.

Finally, the value of the derivative contract might not correspond exactly with organizations' losses. As hedging contracts are based on some general measure or index, if the general measure or index does not provide a payout that is highly correlated with an organization's losses, the risk financing measure does not provide the needed protection. As mentioned previously, these types of risk financing measures can expose an organization to basis risk.

Contingent Capital Arrangements

Contingent capital arrangement

An agreement, entered into before any losses occur, that enables an organization to raise cash by selling stock or issuing debt at prearranged terms after a loss occurs that exceeds a certain threshold.

A **contingent capital arrangement** is an agreement, entered into before any losses occur, that enables an organization to raise cash by selling stock or issuing debt on prearranged terms after a loss occurs that exceeds a certain threshold. The organization pays a capital commitment fee to the party that agrees in advance to purchase the debt or equity after the loss.

With a contingent capital arrangement, the organization does not transfer its risk of loss to investors. Instead, it receives a capital injection in the form of debt or equity after a loss occurs to help it pay for the loss. Because the terms are agreed to in advance, the organization generally receives more favorable terms than it would receive if it were to try to raise capital after a large loss, when it is likely to be in a weakened capital condition.

For example, a publicly traded pharmaceutical manufacturer may have a contingent capital arrangement with an investment bank that requires the investment bank to purchase a specified number of the manufacturer's shares at a predetermined price if the manufacturer suffers a significant property loss at its main manufacturing plant for which it was unable to acquire property insurance.

The manufacturer pays the investment bank a fee at the beginning of the agreement. If the loss occurs, the investment bank purchases the shares at the predetermined price, providing the manufacturer with the capital necessary to rebuild the plant. If no loss occurs, the agreement expires without any stock sale occurring. Similar agreements for bond issues have also been structured.

Ability of Capital Market Solutions to Meet Risk Financing Goals

Before using capital market solutions as risk financing measures, an organization should evaluate their ability to meet the organization's risk financing goals. See the exhibit "Ability of Capital Market Solutions to Meet Risk Financing Goals."

Combinations of Risk Financing Measures

Rather than using a single risk financing measure, individuals or organizations often combine two or more measures in order to meet their risk financing goals. Many combinations can be used, and frequently risk financing measures that transfer a substantial portion of risk are combined with retention and other risk financing measures that retain a significant portion of the risk.

Ability of Capital Market Solutions to Meet Risk Financing Goals

Risk Financing Goal	How Capital Market Solutions Meet the Goal
Pay for Losses	They can meet this goal because some of the financial consequences of the losses are transferred to investors.
Manage the Cost of Risk	They cannot typically meet this goal. Capital market solutions are expensive relative to other risk financing measures.
Manage Cash Flow Variability	They can meet this goal because some of the financial consequences of the losses are transferred to investors.
Maintain Appropriate Level of Liquidity	They can meet this goal because capital market solutions can reduce the necessary level of liquidity that an organization needs to maintain.
Comply With Legal Requirements	They can meet this goal if correctly structured.

[DA02708]

For example, an organization might self-insure its low-to-medium severity loss exposures and purchase guaranteed cost insurance for its high-severity loss exposures. Similarly, captives may be combined with guaranteed cost insurance or reinsurance or guaranteed cost insurance may be combined with contingent capital arrangements. Many possible combinations are available to meet an organization's risk financing goals. The combinations are limited only by the ingenuity of the organization, its broker, its risk management professional, and any participating transfer parties.

SUMMARY

Risk financing goals include these:

* Pay for losses—both paying for the actual losses or portions of losses that an organization retains and paying transfer costs, which are the costs paid in order to transfer responsibility for losses to another party

* Manage the cost of risk—including administrative, risk control, and risk financing costs

- Manage cash flow variability—requires determining the organization's maximum tolerance levels and arranging the risk management program within those parameters
- Maintain an appropriate level of liquidity—preserving a level of cash liquidity that is sufficient to pay for retained losses
- Comply with legal requirements—adhering to laws and regulations that either mandate risk financing measures or affect how risk financing measures are implemented

The four planned retention funding techniques are current expensing of losses, using an unfunded reserve, using a funded reserve, and borrowing funds. The advantages of using retention as a risk financing technique include cost savings, control of claims process, timing of cash flows, and incentives for risk control.

Most transfer methods limit the loss amounts that can be transferred, and the ultimate responsibility for paying losses remains with the transferor. The advantages of transfer include reducing the exposure to large losses, reducing cash flow variability, providing ancillary services, and avoiding adverse employee and public relations.

When selecting appropriate risk financing methods, one must evaluate the relative advantages of the available measures and their ability to meet risk financing goals. The main factors to consider are these:

1. The mix of retention and transfer needed to meet the goals
2. Characteristics of the loss exposures
3. Characteristics of the individual or organization

Various risk financing measures are available that enable an individual or organization to meet risk financing goals, including these:

- Guaranteed cost insurance
- Self-insurance
- Large deductible plans
- Captive insurers
- Finite risk insurance plans
- Pools
- Retrospective rating plans
- Hold-harmless agreements
- Capital market solutions

Direct Your Learning ▶▶

Enterprise-Wide Risk Management

Educational Objectives

After learning the content of this assignment, you should be able to:

▷ Contrast traditional risk management and enterprise-wide risk management (ERM).

▷ Explain how an organization can improve its strategic decision making by incorporating enterprise-wide risk management (ERM).

▷ Explain why enterprise-wide risk management (ERM) is an effective approach to use to face business uncertainties.

▷ Summarize the major risk management frameworks and standards.

Enterprise-Wide Risk Management

TRADITIONAL RISK MANAGEMENT VERSUS ERM

Traditional risk management (referred to as RM) considers only hazard and operational risks that can affect an organization. Enterprise-wide risk management (ERM) expands an organization's risk focus to include financial and strategic risks, allowing it to account for all eventualities that can affect its ability to achieve its goals.

There are four major differences between RM and ERM:

- Risk categories
- Strategic integration
- Performance metrics
- Organizational structure

Risk Categories

Both RM and ERM agree that, while risk can be quantified to some degree, it can only be estimated. The need to accurately measure risk in an effort to reduce uncertainty is common to all risk management frameworks, but beyond these points, the RM and ERM frameworks diverge.

Traditionally, risk can be classified as either pure risk or speculative risk, and further categorized as hazard risk, operational risk, financial risk, and strategic risk. See the exhibit "Traditional and Enterprise-Wide Risk Management."

Traditional risk management is concerned with pure risk, where there is no upside or positive outcome possible other than the status quo. An example of such risks would be hazard risks, which are pure risks that include damage to property from perils such as fire and explosion or losses stemming from accidents and injuries to employees or customers. Pure risks can also include operational risks that arise out of service, processing, or manufacturing activities.

Traditional risk management focuses on preventing or reducing potential losses and on compensation for losses that do occur. Preventive measures for hazard risks include the use of warning labels, process flow alterations, and other engineering considerations. Sprinkler systems, first aid training, and efficient product recall procedures are examples of pure risk loss mitigation strategies.

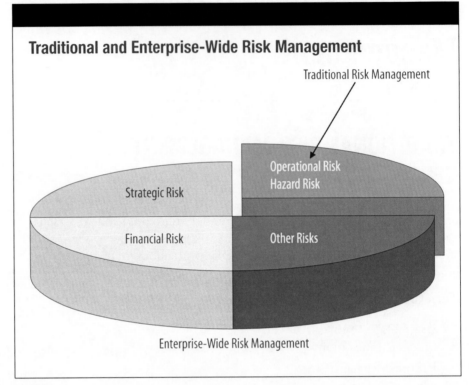

[DA03593]

In contrast, ERM considers all risks that an organization faces, regardless of their source or potential outcomes. Both pure risk and speculative risk, which can be commonly categorized as financial, strategic, and some operational risks, are included. Financial risks include interest rate risk, competitive risk, inflation, and market timing risks, among others. Strategic risks include management decisions regarding new products, emerging competitors, and planning issues. Examples of operational risks include supplier disruptions or periods of power loss during the failure or overload of the electrical grid. Another risk not normally considered by RM is risk to reputation.

ERM emphasizes the interrelationships between pure and speculative risk, while RM focuses only on pure risk. Then, ERM seeks to optimize risk taking in relationship to strategic goals, while RM seeks to prevent or reduce risks related only to losses.

ERM also considers "upside" risk—the risk that the organization will outperform its strategic goals. Examples of upside risks include situations in which a business venture experiences an unexpected increase in revenue or market share. What opportunities or threats does this variation from the expected present to the venture?

For example, the development of a new vaccine could present to a governmental health organization the upside risk of not having to spend its entire budget. It could use these funds to better promote wellness, fight other diseases, or even reinvest the funds in the general treasury for other purposes.

Strategic Integration

Traditional risk management is normally involved only in the elements of the organization's strategy that deal with pure risk and hazard risks. ERM, however, is integrated with the entire organization's strategy. By linking risk to the entire enterprise, the organization decouples its financial, strategic, operational, hazard, and other risks from individual operational silos and addresses them within strategy as a whole. Thus, ERM considers the global array of risks that affect the organization. See the exhibit "Strategic Integration—An Illustration."

Strategic Integration—An Illustration

LowCost, a regional airline, has three strategic objectives:

- Maintain its low-cost status

- Continuously improve its on-time arrival metrics

- Maintain its environmentally friendly reputation

Using a traditional risk management strategy, the airline would have given the fuel-hedging responsibility to the finance department and the management of risk at fuel storage facilities to the risk manager.

After adopting an ERM approach, LowCost challenged the organization to develop a hedging plan in relationship to the organization's strategy as a whole. Elements evaluated for LowCost included:

- The carrying, storage, and insurance costs of maintaining multiple storage facilities associated with the purchase of large amounts of fuel

- The adverse impact of a major fuel spill or fire in a metropolitan storage facility on its environmental reputation goal concomitantly with the cost of having to purchase more expensive fuel after the loss, which would affect its low-cost goal and, if layoffs are required, its on-time arrival goal

- The strategic implications for low-cost and on-time strategy if the hedging basis or timing risk is greater than expected

After assessing both the upside and downside risks of a hedging program within the strategic goals of the organization, LowCost adopted a hedging and fuel inventory risk management plan that optimized risk within and among the three enterprise strategic objectives. As a result, LowCost discovered that its previous traditional risk management plan, which considered risk independently in operational and financial risk silos, had underestimated the risk to the enterprise's low-cost and on-time arrival objectives.

[DA03595]

This global array can be represented by a three-dimensional depiction of attributes known as the exposure spaces model. The attributes are resources, events, and impacts. On the horizontal x-axis are the various resources of the enterprise that may change in value. The impacts—the actual consequences or changes in value of the resources—are shown on the vertical y-axis. The third dimension, the z-axis, shows the causes of the changes in value. ERM uses the exposure spaces model to consider the range of potential impact from positive to negative. Once this range is established, its estimated effect on resources can be contrasted against desired strategic changes in resource value so that appropriate risk treatment can be applied to minimize variation from the desired value. See the exhibit "Exposure Spaces Model."

Performance Metrics

Success in traditional risk management can be measured both as an activity and as a result. For example, a traditional risk management plan for an organization that employs a considerable amount of manual labor might include objectives for reducing worker injury costs and incidents in addition to an activity metric involving the number of safety meetings held. This approach assumes that reducing incidents will reduce the number of injuries. This reduction in injuries will affect product costs and duty of care to employees (result) over the long term. Also assumed is a direct link between the number of safety meetings and the extent of training (activity) and the number of worker injuries.

However, a certain amount of risk is unavoidable in business; eliminating all risk would be tantamount to terminating the organization's operations. ERM seeks to optimize risk taking in relationship to strategic goals. Optimization is both an eventuality and a process through which the organization searches for the equilibrium between risk and outcome in relationship to strategic goals. The enterprise then manages the organization toward that equilibrium. ERM asks, "How do risk management activities relate to the organization's strategic needs, and how should we measure success?"

Organizational Structure

The traditional risk manager generally reports to an organizational department such as finance, operations, or legal. Quite often, the responsibility for pure risk management may be localized within a risk management department, which then orchestrates the risk management plan as a central authority. While some responsibilities for risk management may be delegated to others, they are generally only those responsibilities involving pure risk. Thus, a local plant manager may be responsible for both hazard identification and conducting safety meetings in the facility. Conversely, in ERM, risk management responsibility is decentralized and integrated into all levels of the organization.

Chief risk officer
A generic term for the senior risk professional engaged in ERM in an enterprise; distinct from "Chief Risk Officer," a title given to some risk professionals who report to senior management.

Alternatively, the enterprise risk manager—often called a **chief risk officer**—may report to the chief executive officer (CEO) or the board of directors and act as a facilitator of and an educator about the ERM process and serve as a coach to other risk owners in the enterprise.

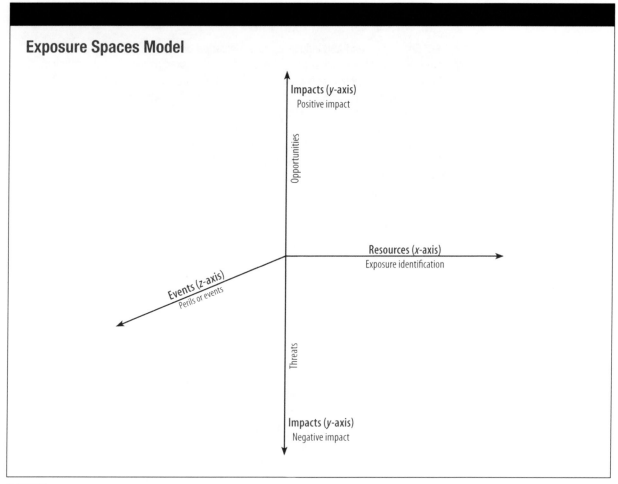

Exposure Spaces Model

Impacts (*y*-axis)
Positive impact

Opportunities

Resources (*x*-axis)
Exposure identification

Events (*z*-axis)
Perils or events

Threats

Impacts (*y*-axis)
Negative impact

[DA03599]

As facilitator, the chief risk officer engages the organization's management in a continuous conversation that establishes risk strategic goals in relationship to the organization's strengths, weaknesses, opportunities, and threats (SWOT). Unlike traditional risk management, ERM engages all the organization's stakeholders in the risk management process. Thus, the "enterprise" in ERM becomes the organization itself and its stakeholders, which include employees, management, board of directors, suppliers, customers, partners, community, and the government or regulators. The chief risk officer's responsibility in the strategic process is to help the organization develop tools that identify and manage events and perils that may cause variation from the achievement of specific strategic goals.

As an educator and coach, the chief risk officer helps the enterprise create a risk culture in which individual department heads and project managers are identified as "risk owners." Risk owners are then given tasks and responsibilities for identifying and managing variation from the achievement of organizational strategic goals. In the fully integrated ERM organization, attending to and addressing risk become part of every job description, every project, and every department. Successful risk management of strategic objectives becomes both an evaluation measurement and a success measurement.

RM Versus ERM: An Example

XYZ Enterprises and ABC Industries have similar problems. Management at XYZ, employing traditional risk management techniques, asked its risk manager to minimize the cost of a possible loss caused by pure risks. The traditional risk manager for XYZ Enterprises identified fire as a major peril that could affect the business by causing loss to property and business income over time. To combat the possibility of loss by fire, the traditional risk manager calculated the cost benefit of deploying fire-resistant structures, sprinkler systems, and less flammable processing chemicals in relationship to insurance and retention costs. In addition, the traditional risk manager considered a multiple-location strategy versus a one-location strategy as it related to the frequency and severity of fire loss and the entry of competitors to the market after a full shutdown in a single-plant strategy.

Engaging ERM, management at ABC considered not only how it would manage the pure risk of fire cost effectively, but also factored in the implications of operational efficiencies as they relate to span of control, the availability of workers, the ability of management to effect a continuous process improvement program, and the effect of competitive entry in a multi-location configuration as opposed to a single-plant operation.

XYZ's traditional risk management plan split the plant into five locations to minimize the pure risk associated with fire to no more than 20 percent of production capacity should one location burn. However, XYZ's traditional risk management process did not consider the effect of such measures on the process efficiency of the organization and the resulting cost increases that might make its products less competitive—the speculative risk. While XYZ's plan may prevent competitive entry following the sudden loss of all or most of its production, the cost inefficiencies of the five-location operation may lead to unanticipated entry by more efficient competitors regardless of fire losses.

ABC's ERM plan divided the operation into two plants and concluded that it could operate in shifts to generate lost capacity if one location burned. The plan produced operating efficiencies associated with larger plant structures to optimize ABC's need to reduce cost of production and to provide the spread of risk necessary to slow or prevent competitors' entry into the market brought about by a catastrophic event at a singular location.

Thus, while both the traditional risk management and ERM programs deployed spread of risk as a risk management strategy, the enterprise risk manager assessed the holistic impact on the organization from the perspective of both pure and speculative risk with a goal not simply of minimizing or eliminating risk but of optimizing risk in relationship to the organization's strategic goals of competitive advantage. In summary, ERM focuses on achieving strategic objectives for both pure and speculative risk, not just the operational need to compensate for expected losses.

An organization with a fully integrated ERM program develops a sophisticated but user-friendly communication matrix that moves information throughout the organization, laterally through peers and similar departments, and among internal and external stakeholders across the enterprise. Communications include dialogue and discussions that occur locally or among levels as a result of the development of personnel competencies that identify potential risks and communicate them to others.

The establishment of valid metrics and the continuous flow of cogent data are as important in this communication structure as the keen eyes of an observer trained to identify risk or its potential. These matrices and metrics are carefully woven into reporting structures that engage the entire organization—from individual risk owners to external stakeholders to senior management and the board—in an effort to identify emerging risk in relation to and in context with specific and aggregate strategic goals. They are also involved in quantifying the success of treatment of previously identified risks.

The process of ERM is both iterative and recursive—iterative in that the risk management process is engaged to identify and manage each discoverable risk, and recursive in that the risk management process is revisited regularly to maintain its optimization in relationship to strategic goals. As existing risks are successfully managed, new risks emerge that must be addressed. In other circumstances, existing risks evolve into something for which a previous treatment is no longer effective. When strategic goals change or evolve, entire risk management strategies may change as formerly important risks no longer exist and risks never before managed emerge to the forefront. See the exhibit "Beyond Traditional Risk Management."

Beyond Traditional Risk Management

	Traditional Risk Management	Enterprise-Wide Risk Management	
Risk Defined	Operational risk Pure risk—only loss, no gain Perils only Threats only Cost of risk containment	All risks. Risks that can produce positive or negative results.	Events Threats and opportunities Creating value while adhering to values
Risk Linked to Strategy	Rewards both activities and results	Links rewards to results and results to strategic needs. Risk management is aligned with strategy.	Optimize risk taking Preserving value; adding value
Enterprise-Wide	Considers only those parts of the organization affected by operational risk	Considers global risk, including: Supply chain Crisis management	Reputation Disturbances Involves all internal and external stakeholders Rating agencies
Common Language	Uses insurance industry terms and jargon	Uses a common language developed by standards-making organizations and government agencies.	
Elements of a Risk Culture	Traditional risk manager often without C-level authority or responsibility—not linked to corporate strategy other than operational risk	CRO—Interaction with board—C-level authority and responsibility that are linked directly to corporate strategy. Risk centers with risk owners. While ERM is a process, project management techniques can be used in the initial implementation of ERM.	Communication and consultation Building the business case within the organization Understanding and changing risk perception throughout enterprise Audit and self-assessment Portfolio approach to risk Stakeholder involvement in process
Exposure Spaces	Management of perils—pure risk—loss only	Exposure to any conceivable event or fact and resulting impact positively or negatively— variation from the expected.	
Information Systems	Risk Management Information System (RMIS)	Business intelligence (BI) systems integrate enterprise data flows and generate analytic information for risk management decision making, internal controls testing, and credit evaluation needs.	

[DA03604]

IMPROVING STRATEGIC DECISION MAKING WITH ERM

To be effective and improve an organization's likelihood for success, ERM must be intertwined with the way an organization is managed. Integrating ERM into strategic decision-making processes is key to its implementation. ERM is not exclusive to the corporate world. Sole proprietorships, partnerships, government and its institutions, not-for-profit organizations, non-governmental organizations (NGOs), and all other forms of enterprise have benefited from integrating ERM with strategy.

ERM can improve an organization's strategic decision making and enable it to become more strategically confident by allowing it to address threats to its existence and optimize opportunities. An organization can realize this improvement by readily integrating ERM into its strategic planning process and by addressing legal and regulatory issues related to ERM at a high level of planning.

Improving Strategic Decision Making

ERM improves an organization's strategic decision making by producing high-quality information that is essential to the organization's survival. ERM helps boards and executives make better decisions that can render their organizations less vulnerable to failure and better equipped to survive changes in the external environment.

Strategic planning is the process by which an organization's board and executives develop, refresh, and refine its strategies in line with its view of the future. The reason for developing a strategic plan is the recognition that an organization's current **business model** will not survive indefinitely. Risks to the business model can arise from changes in competition, technology, the market, and customers' demands. An organization that incorporates ERM with its strategic planning process improves its decision making in several ways, including these:

- It can address potentially devastating threats.
- It can exploit opportunities by incorporating them into its current business model or completely reinventing a new model that will successfully carry it into the future.
- It can use ERM as a process to manage unwanted variations from expectations.

Therefore, strategic planning that incorporates ERM can help ensure the continuation and success of the organization.

Business model

The core aspects of an organization, including its vision, mission, strategies, infrastructure, policies, offerings, and processes.

Integrating ERM and Strategic Planning

The ERM process framework requires an organization to establish its internal and external contexts, assess risks, choose appropriate treatments, and then monitor the treatment and the ERM plan. Within all steps of the process are the engagement of and communication with the organization's stakeholders. An organization that integrates ERM with its strategic planning process increases the likelihood that it will adequately address risks. To integrate ERM, an organization's board and executives can follow this process:

1. Develop ERM goals (establish the internal and external contexts)
2. Identify risks (risk assessment)
3. Analyze, evaluate, and prioritize critical risks (risk assessment)
4. Treat critical risks, considering priority (risk treatment)
5. Monitor critical risks (monitor and review)

The "identify risks" step in the risk assessment process should reveal many risks to the enterprise. The enterprise must evaluate these risks based on how critical they are to the organization's strategy or even its survival. Assessing, identifying, treating, evaluating, and monitoring critical risks is ERM's prime directive. An organization's determination of what it considers critical is part of the process of establishing its internal and external contexts. For example, a government institution may have zero tolerance for the risk of terrorist attacks on its infrastructure, leading to both an increase in intelligence and infrastructure hardening. A corporation may consider minor differences in the cost of raw materials as constituting a critical competitive risk that requires treatment in the form of hedging.

Over time, new risks emerge while others fade in importance. The enterprise must engage the ERM process continuously in order to maintain a current understanding of both the risks that can affect the organization and their potential for positively and negatively affecting expected outcomes. See the exhibit "ERM Process."

Develop ERM Goals (Establish the Internal and External Contexts)

The first step in integrating ERM with strategic planning is to consider goals for ERM as part of the organization's business model. Annually, the board and executive team develops or reviews the organization's vision statement, mission statement, strategic objectives, and financial projections. During this process, the board and executives should also develop the organization's ERM goals.

ERM Process

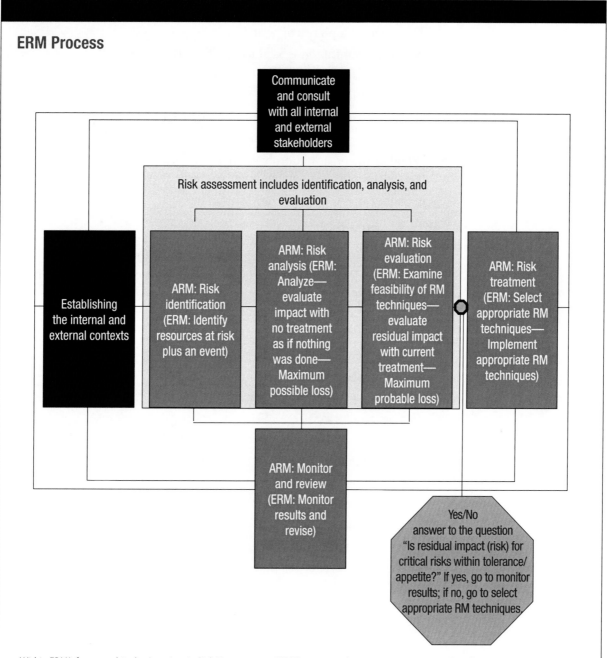

Within ERM's framework is the Associate in Risk Management (ARM) six-step risk management process: identify, analyze, examine feasibility of risk management techniques, select appropriate risk management techniques, implement selected risk management techniques, and monitor and review. However, ERM enhances the ARM six-step process in three ways: (1) ERM establishes internal and external contexts of the enterprise at the outset, (2) ERM requires communication and consultation with all stakeholders, and (3) ERM adds a decision step prior to risk treatment that asks the risk manager to determine whether residual impact is within risk tolerance/appetite. If within risk tolerance, the action is to monitor results. If not within risk tolerance, the action is to choose the appropriate risk management techniques (treatment).

An organization's ERM goals are based on several considerations:

- The organization's risk appetite
- Why the organization is establishing the ERM program
- The business or organizational need for an ERM program
- The intended scope of the ERM program
- How ERM will assist the organization in meeting its strategic goals
- How the organization defines ERM
- Whether the organization has a function- or department-focused culture or a collaborative culture and how that will affect ERM implementation

Sample ERM Goals

- Identify opportunities for and threats to achieving organizational goals
- Incorporate planning to take advantage of opportunities and mitigate threats to the organization
- Anticipate and reduce deviations from expected outcomes
- Anticipate and recognize emerging risks
- Improve business resiliency and sustainability
- Drive consistency in risk taking
- Optimize risk taking, considering appetite and tolerance
- Reduce earnings volatility
- Improve risk management competencies throughout the organization
- Encourage proactive management behavior in treating risks
- Achieve greater stakeholder consensus for risk management
- Increase management accountability and risk-based performance management
- Establish a consistent basis for risk-based decision making and planning
- Enhance the health and safety of employees, customers, and their communities
- Design and enhance appropriate management controls to more effectively and efficiently reduce defects and minimize loss
- Boost internal and external stakeholder confidence and trust
- Enable better-informed governance
- Improve external transparency and risk disclosure
- Comply with relevant legal and regulatory requirements and international norms
- Establish cross-functional and organizational awareness of risks posed in specific geographies

[DA03591]

An organization's ERM goals will guide the decisions that are made in the steps that follow and provide structures within the organization that support assessing, treating, and monitoring risks. See the exhibit "Sample ERM Goals."

Analyze, Evaluate, and Prioritize Critical Risks (Risk Assessment)

The board and executives next direct an examination of internal and external threats to the organization's mission, strategies, and goals. Such threats are identified by noting changes that can undermine the organization, as well as changes that present opportunities, in areas such as these:

- Competition
- Customer demographics or behaviors
- Technology
- Economy
- Politics and regulation
- The organization's ability to meet regulatory requirements

Asking "what if" questions is an effective method an organization may use to identify risks to strategies. For example, "What risks will result if. . ." could precede each of these items:

- Favorable exchange rates make our products more competitive in Europe?
- Frost in Florida decreases crop yield for our major competitors?
- A competitor emerges in our market that undercuts our prices?
- Regulations change that double the amount of time needed to develop our products?
- Technology changes make our leading product irrelevant?
- Consumers demand a "greener" product?
- Our company's unique manufacturing competencies are needed for an emerging product?

Each risk to strategy should be considered because it may affect the organization's success and sustainability. The impact of risk to strategy may manifest gradually rather than having immediate consequences. Therefore, identifying and evaluating trends is important in the assessment process.

After risks to strategy have been identified, the "criticality" of the risk to the organization is determined so that the organization can prioritize risks for treatment. There are many approaches to quantifying criticality, but most include measurements of impact upon the resources and goals of the enterprise and its stakeholders. Frequency combined with valuation is also a consideration, but a low-frequency/high-impact risk that cannot be completely avoided requires careful consideration. For each critical risk identified, potential triggers or warning signs should also be identified. At a minimum, an organization should identify its top five risks, consider their likelihood, and target them for treatment and monitoring.

Treat Critical Risks, Considering Priority (Risk Treatment)

Building answers to the "what if" questions from the assessment process is an effective way to initiate treatments to address the risks identified. Based on the likelihood (low, medium, or high) of the risk identified, the organization might initiate action to address a threat or to seize an opportunity. See the exhibit "Examples of Treating Risks to Strategies."

Practical techniques for treating risks to strategy can be placed into these categories:

- Avoid—Use alternative approaches that eliminate the cause of the risk or its consequences
- Accept—Accept the risk by planning for ways to deal with the uncertainty if it occurs
- Transfer—Assign the responsibility to manage the risk to a third party
- Mitigate—Initiate activities to reduce the probability, impact, or timing of a risk event to an acceptable risk tolerance
- Optimize/exploit—Develop actions to optimize positive consequences to achieve gains

Monitor Critical Risks (Monitor and Review)

Risks to strategy are periodically monitored by identifying trends, triggering events, and warning signs during the assessment phase for each risk identified. Reporting may be periodic or on an exception basis, depending on the likelihood of occurrence and the potential impact that the risk poses.

Monitoring risks to strategy is complex, because the triggering events must generally be identified from a variety of sources, including, for example, industry newsletters, regulatory announcements, and surveys. For risks that pose a potentially high severity and likelihood, an organization may foster relationships with key individuals in positions to know when changes are imminent that will trigger conditions that could result in an event. With such information, the organization can be prepared to launch treatments.

Emerging Legal and Regulatory Requirements Regarding ERM

Standards and guidelines regarding ERM as it is applied to strategic management are emerging. For example, rating agencies, specifically Standard & Poor's (S&P), view risk management in strategic decision making as an important keystone to an organization's planning and have expectations that focus on ERM's strategic applications. The international risk management framework ISO 31000:2009 includes guidelines regarding the risk management process.[1]

Examples of Treating Risks to Strategies

What risks will result if…	Likelihood	Treatment
A competitor emerges in our market that undercuts our prices?	*High*	Avoid—Lobby to prevent regulatory changes that will allow the competitor to enter the market
		Mitigate—If the competitor does enter the market, launch a marketing campaign that highlights our product's superior features
Regulations change that double the amount of time need to develop our products?	*Low*	Accept—If this occurs, address the time needed to develop products
Technology changes make our leading product irrelevant?	*Medium*	Mitigate—Initiate plans to diversify our products into distinctly different technological areas
Consumers demand a "greener" product?	*Low*	Mitigate—Study comparable "green" alternatives for our processes in case this becomes an issue
Our company's unique manufacturing competencies are needed for an emerging product?	*High*	Optimize/exploit—Contact the developers of the emerging product to seek a collaborative approach
Favorable exchange rates make our products more competitive in Europe?	*Medium (periodic fluctuations)*	Optimize/exploit—Increase marketing campaigns and direct as much inventory as practicable toward the European market
Frost in Florida decreases crop yield for our major competitors?	*High*	Optimize/exploit—In addition to capitalizing on inevitable higher prices, negotiate with competitors' supermarkets for increased shelf space for our product

[DA03592]

Standards, which define acceptable practices, methods, and processes, are not legal requirements in themselves. However, they may become mandatory when a government enacts them as legislation.

To ensure that emerging regulatory requirements are considered and documented when ERM is applied to strategic decision making, an organization's chief risk officer should search for requirements related to risk management in several areas:

- Management's view of the organization's most important risks, including the likelihood and potential severity or impact of such risks
- The frequency of key risks and the process used to identify key risks
- The influence of risk sensitivity on liability management and financing decisions
- The role of risk management in strategic decision making
- The culture of risk management in the organization as identified by communication systems, frameworks, roles, policies, and metrics applied

The organization's executives and board of directors should always consider that compliance with standards is not a substitute for sound risk management throughout the organization; rather, ERM can accomplish this.

ERM IN APPROACHING BUSINESS UNCERTAINTIES

In today's global, often volatile business climate, organizations must deal with business uncertainties in a thorough, systematic manner. They may do so by adopting an ERM approach, which transcends traditional risk management.

Traditional risk management focuses on hazard risks and long-established risk management techniques—avoidance, prevention, reduction, transfer, and retention. It restricts risk management to a middle-management function that is primarily responsible for purchasing insurance and making traditional risk management decisions.

An organization that has adopted an ERM approach monitors risks, threats, and opportunities that arise from many sources. This approach provides two important benefits:

- Enhanced decision making
- Improved risk communication

Enhanced Decision Making

Whether it is a profit-driven organization, a not-for-profit organization, a charity, or a governmental entity, an organization must manage competing interests to achieve its strategic goals. An ERM approach allows an organization to systematically explore new opportunities for economic efficiencies while it manages threats that stem from internal and external contexts. It does so by focusing on managing all of an organization's key or critical risks— its threats as well as its opportunities—in a manner that optimizes its value.

ERM provides a means for an organization to identify and select among alternative risk responses. Rather than consolidating risk management responsibility at the senior-management level (which slows the decision-making process and sacrifices potential corporate advantages to organizational gridlock), ERM enhances the organizational decision-making process by giving all decision makers in the organization access to its total risk picture.

When threats and opportunities are understood and risk taking is optimized strategically, managers may make better decisions, which in turn builds their confidence for decisions on future projects. This improved decision making enables an organization to quickly meet emerging marketplace challenges and provides several additional advantages:

- Increased profitability (or, for those organizations where profitability is not an issue, economic efficiency)
- Reduced volatility
- Improved ability to meet strategic goals
- Increased management accountability

Increased Profitability (Economic Efficiency)

An ERM approach increases an organization's profitability because strategic decisions involve more than preparing only for adverse outcomes. Properly implemented, ERM goes beyond evaluating insolvency at preset confidence levels. ERM allows organizations to engage in additional business opportunities by allocating resources through rational decision making at the local level. When an organization adopts an ERM approach, every strategic decision made at every level is sounder, which helps to further ensure economic efficiency. Therefore, over time, organizations with a sound ERM process in place will show higher earnings.

Historically, an organization's shareholders and the media tend to focus on quarterly profits and losses. An organization that adopts an ERM approach monitors systemic risks inherent in the organization that can adversely affect its long-term financial outlook. When an organization adopts an ERM approach, unexpected occurrences or variations cause much less disruption because the organization has already incorporated the possibility of such occurrences or variations into its decision-making process. Even natural disasters can be less disruptive to an organization that has built supply chain resilience into its operational model.

For example, an organization may have to decide whether it should continue to sell a product that is highly profitable but that also has the potential to produce a higher level of liability claims. In making this decision, the organization should consider that, ideally, business momentum in a unit that has an above average rate of return on risk should be increased, because the unit produces higher profits relative to units that may perform well but that generate liabilities. ERM is the framework that any organization could use in its decision-making process to aid in achieving increased profitability (economic efficiency) in all operating units.

Reduced Volatility

In addition to maintaining cash flows and balancing its budget, an organization must manage its cash flow to ensure an adequate pipeline of capital to meet challenges and to explore strategic growth opportunities. How organizations approach this aspect of risk management differs due to variations in internal characteristics such as the current environment, technology, competition, and regulatory climate. Organizations like the Red Cross, which rely heavily on their reputation to garner financial support, tend to be more risk averse than, for example, a pharmaceutical company that has extensive research and development expertise.

When an organization decides to embark on a new venture, the venture must be sufficiently capitalized to allow the organization to capitalize the increased cost of risk associated with it. For instance, the Red Cross may experience a decline in donations during a recession, posing a risk that it may not be able to provide needed services during a disaster and the risk that it could incur threats to its reputation in addition to the risks associated with having to take capital from its endowment to provide services. However, if the organization evaluates the risk only at the project level, it may miss the broader implications of that risk.

For example, suppose an apparel manufacturer outsourced the manufacture of one of its clothing lines to an offshore manufacturing site. The clothing line became enormously successful because the offshore site's lower labor costs made the clothes affordable. However, when the apparel manufacturer performed its initial cost/benefit analysis, it failed to consider the risks associated with outsourcing to the offshore site, which included significant use of child labor. When these child labor issues were made public, the clothing line was plagued by stinging press reviews, causing sales of the line and collateral lines of clothing to plunge.

In this situation, the manufacturer's cash flows would be significantly reduced, not just by sales attrition, but also by the funds expended for public relations damage control. The effects of these types of cash flow reductions could spiral through the organization, reducing the cash flow the organization has to embark on new ventures. If the organization had adopted an ERM approach, it would have incorporated the risks associated with the offshore site's use of child labor into its cost/benefit analysis of the venture.

ERM provides a systematic framework that allows organizations to deploy capital through organization-wide decision making, which ultimately results in stable earnings projections to fund future projects. If an organization focuses solely on risk avoidance or risk transfer, opportunities to use ERM to optimize economic efficiency through acquisition, mergers, exploring new product lines, or other avenues may be missed.

Improved Ability to Meet Strategic Goals

ERM provides for organization-wide involvement in the strategic formulation and decision-making process. This process examines factors in the internal and external environments to identify risks that would impede growth and achievement of established goals.

Factors considered when establishing strategic goals include competitors, the availability of substitute products, customers, and the supply chain. These considerations are especially important in today's increasingly global community, where a disruption in one system can cause widespread disruption to other organizations.

Consider the importance of supply acquisition. Organizations closely manage their vendor relationships to ensure a steady and inexpensive supply of raw materials or goods. However, they increasingly rely on single source vendors and vendors located abroad. Lean supply chains can drive down prices. However, supply-chain disruption can cause economic chaos for organizations that depend on the supply chain's competitive advantages. What happens if the main supplier faces problems of its own, such as a raw materials or labor shortage; cash-flow problems; or, in the case of foreign providers, political instability? ERM can help the organization uncover potential risks related to vendor relationships and establish contingency plans within the decision-making process. When used effectively, ERM can minimize variation through thorough risk identification and assessment, thus improving the organization's ability to meet its strategic goals.

Increased Management Accountability

While the ERM process is represented at the highest level of an organization with the appointment of a Chief Risk Officer (CRO), those closest to a particular risk are in the best position to evaluate and manage it. Therefore, the ERM approach must be embedded in corporate culture. When this occurs, the board and senior executives establish the organization's overall mission, vision, and strategic goals, but each manager is responsible and accountable for decision making about risks within his or her individual unit. The responsible manager is often called a risk owner, someone who is responsible for managing risks from a specific risk center or operation. Distributed responsibility and accountability for risk at the risk center level are features that distinguish ERM from traditional risk management. They also have contributed to the failure of some ERM implementations in which local risk owners were not permitted or would not accept responsibility and accountability for risks within their purview.

Consider the example of Société Générale, a large European financial services organization. Recently, a low-level futures trader who was experienced in back-end operations cost the company $7.2 billion when fictitious trades he engineered spiraled out of control—the largest banking fraud in history. As a result, the entire European banking industry and its risk management systems were suddenly in jeopardy. If Société Générale had adopted an ERM approach, it might have avoided this fraud. ERM increases management accountability, leading to improved corporate practices and greater managerial understanding of and consensus regarding corporate strategy.

Improved Risk Communication

ERM allows organizations to develop systems that drive information throughout the organization, eliminating the barriers created by "information silos," a term used to describe a situation in which access to critical knowledge about risks, corporate strategies, and the organizational framework is limited to a number of key personnel.

ERM also encourages an organization to widely communicate its risk management approach across all of its layers. This includes making all managers aware of the need to identify obstacles that could interfere with achievement of the organization's strategic goals. As part of the ERM approach, the organization establishes a method to gather information organization-wide and develops a framework for analyzing and communicating that information.

Improved organization-wide communication results in fewer surprises for managers who could otherwise be caught without adequate information or full knowledge of the gravity of risk. This communication relies on all employees operating in accordance with the same corporate values. Value-driven ERM must be instituted using an ethical philosophy that is embedded in the organization, guiding and monitoring all decision makers' actions throughout the organization.

Strong communication can also result in greater management consensus and improved acceptance by both internal and external stakeholders.

Management Consensus

ERM improves management consensus by creating a corporate culture that embraces risk as an additional component of each decision. By empowering all managers to consider risk optimization and the cost of risk, ERM provides them with complete information about the potential effects of a decision, including its downsides and upsides. Managers who can successfully gauge threats and opportunities act with confidence because they can appropriately evaluate the alternatives associated with any course of action. This builds a sense of management by consensus, as opposed to the traditional hierarchal model of management, in which a series of decisions is driven from the top down.

ERM most effectively improves management consensus if it has been integrated throughout the organization. For this to occur, upper management must lead the initiative and motivate all employees to embrace ERM. The organization also must include in its overall performance evaluation indicators of the quality of its risk management. These indicators include documentation of risk optimization activities as well contributions to the organization's total cost of risk. Such action encourages risk ownership through all levels of the organization.

Stakeholder Acceptance

An organization that has effectively incorporated ERM is also better able to gain the acceptance of both internal and external stakeholders.

ERM improves acceptance by internal stakeholders by building a spirit of cooperation among management, which subsequently instills confidence among all employees. Increasing the spirit of cooperation among management begins with managers' understanding that the way they manage risk will have a positive impact on the organization, which, in turn, will benefit them personally. Projecting the reduced cost of risk to the organization through ERM ensures that all managers are held to the same standards. As an organization begins working toward a unified view of risk and rewards, ERM becomes the vital link that guides the organization toward economic efficiency.

A strong ERM program also encourages the buy-in of an organization's external stakeholders by establishing management strategies that protect the organization's reputation and assets. Reputation management is critical in today's world of instant communication. Experts estimate that an organization's intangible, reputation-related assets may be worth several times more than its tangible assets. Therefore, an ERM approach encourages managers to take stock of more than dollars and cents and begin to benchmark behavioral metrics.

When crises occur, they tend to develop quickly. Therefore, organizations must have a crisis management approach in place to deal with adverse events, whether they are caused by natural forces or human error. Pre-event reputation-related risk exposures may be complex. Because the threat to an organization's reputation can come from diverse areas, organizations increasingly are outsourcing aspects of crisis management to public relations teams that help coordinate post-event communications. Protecting the organization's reputation and dealing effectively with crisis management are critical in maintaining the confidence of external stakeholders.

No risk management plan, however, is foolproof. An organization always will face some level of risk and must therefore evaluate the amount of risk it is willing to embrace. A key aspect of ERM is the conscious decision to accept or manage risk. See the exhibit "RM Versus ERM."

RM Versus ERM

Category	RM	ERM
Operational risk	Yes	Yes
Financial risk	No	Yes
Strategic risk	Limited to operational strategies	Yes
Strategic integration	Operational only or none—technical risk management	Enterprise-wide
Performance metrics	Activities and results	Metrics appropriate to the eventuality and risk
Organizational penetration	Limited integration: risk handled in silos; operational responsibilities delegated to departments or retained by risk manager	Systemic integration: risk owners at every level; job descriptions; all risks belong to all, not segregated in any one silo
Outcomes	Minimize; mitigate; eliminate risk	Optimize risk

[DA03605]

MAJOR RISK MANAGEMENT FRAMEWORKS AND STANDARDS

Some standards, such as ERM standards, are not compulsory or certifiable. Still, compliance with these standards demonstrates that an organization is following best practices. When an organization applies ERM frameworks and standards, it also can more effectively implement ERM and prepare for aspects of ERM that may become compulsory.

The risk management processes organizations apply have received increasing regulatory and private scrutiny because risk drives growth and opportunity as well as the potential downside of loss. ERM frameworks and standards provide an organization with approaches for identifying, analyzing, responding to, and monitoring risks (threats and opportunities) within the internal and external contexts in which it operates. Compliance with the assumed best practices represented by the frameworks and standards demonstrates that an organization is properly managing risk.

How an organization applies external frameworks and standards depends on its nature. Some risk management frameworks and standards (ISO 31000:2009, BS 31100, COSO II, AS/NZS 4360, and FERMA) are not compulsory unless a client or customer contractually requires them. They are, however, regarded as best practices for risk management implementation.

Other frameworks and standards are required. For example, United States public companies subject to securities laws and related matters must comply with the Sarbanes-Oxley Act of 2002 (SOX). Similarly, European banks are subject to Basel II, while European insurance companies are subject to Solvency II.

ISO 31000:2009

ISO 31000:2009 is a 2009 publication issued by the International Organization for Standardization, a body that establishes international standards in many areas of business. It includes guidelines and principles for implementing risk management and is supported by a glossary and documents that describe implementation methods.

ISO 31000:2009 provides an international standard for risk management as well as a generic approach to risk management applicable within any industry sector. It focuses on commonly accepted principles, such as meeting goals and the importance of risk communication. Overall, the standard emphasizes that risk management is integral to an organization's structures, strategies, and goals.

ISO 31000:2009 consists of three major parts: principles, a framework, and processes for managing risks. See the exhibit "ISO 31000:2009 Summary."

ISO 31000:2009 Summary

ISO 31000:2009 consists of three major parts: principles, framework, and processes for managing risks. Principles are rooted in risk management and are designed to generate value and continuously scan and react to the environment. The framework consists of elements based on program design, implementation, and monitoring. The processes necessary for risk management emphasize deliberative communication, context, risk evaluation and treatment, and follow-up.

[DA03606]

ISO 31000:2009 is a generic guidance document that must be supplemented with terminology, requirements, guidelines, and tools specific for an industry and/or a country. ISO/IEC Guide 73:2002 provides such terminology. The IPPC directive addresses environmental issues, while ISO 14001 covers information technology. Although ISO 31000:2009 is not certifiable, some of the other ISO standards are, such as ISO 14001.

BS 31100

In 2008, anticipating ISO 31000:2009, the British Standards Institution (BSI) published British Standard (BS) 31100 as a code of practice for risk management. The code establishes principles and terminology for risk management and provides recommendations for the model, framework, process, and implementation of risk management.

BS 31100 is intended to be a scalable standard that can be used by individuals responsible for risk management activity in organizations of all sectors and sizes as a basis for understanding, developing, implementing, and maintaining proportionate risk management. Application of the standards depends on the organization's context and complexity. The standard has four primary goals:

- Ensuring that an organization achieves its goals
- Ensuring that risks are managed in specific areas or activities
- Overseeing risk management in an organization
- Providing "reasonable assurance" on an organization's risk management

COSO II

The Committee of Sponsoring Organizations of the Treadway Commission (COSO) published the COSO Enterprise Risk Management—Integrated Framework (known as COSO II or COSO ERM) in 2004. COSO II defines ERM as a process driven from an organization's board of directors that establishes an organization-wide strategy to manage risk within its risk appetite.

COSO II provides an effective mechanism for initiating a dialogue with an organization's board and its senior executives about establishing ERM goals as part of the strategic management process. It does not delve into the details of risk management approaches and processes. Rather, it focuses on threats to the organization and application of controls. Therefore, COSO II's intended audience is an organization large enough to require examination of risk appetite and board direction of ERM strategies. See the exhibit "COSO II Summary."

AS/NZS 4360

Risk Management, a joint Australian/New Zealand Standard for ERM known as AS/NZS 4360, was published in 2004 as a generic framework for managing risk. AS/NZS 4360 is designed for directors, elected officials, chief executive officers, senior executives, line managers, and staff across a wide range of organizations:

- Public sector entities at national, regional, and local levels
- Commercial enterprises, including companies, joint ventures, firms, and franchises
- Partnerships and sole practices
- Nongovernment organizations
- Voluntary organizations such as charities, social groups, and sports clubs

COSO II Summary

Intended Audience	Organization of sufficient size to examine risk appetite at the board level
Concepts	ERM is: • A process, which is ongoing • Effected by people at all levels of an organization • Applied in strategy setting • Applied across the organization at every level and unit • Designed to identify potential events that will affect the organization within its risk appetite • Able to provide reasonable assurance to the organization's board of directors • Geared to the achievement of objectives in overlapping categories
Components	ERM has components integrated with the management process: • Internal environment • Objective setting • Event identification • Risk assessment • Risk response • Control activities • Information and communication • Monitoring
Objectives	ERM is geared to achieve these types of objectives: • Strategic—high-level goals, aligned with and supporting the organization's mission • Operations—effective and efficient use of resources • Reporting—reliability of operational and financial reporting • Compliance—compliance with applicable laws and regulations

Source: Committee of Sponsoring Organizations of the Treadway Commission. [DA03613]

This variety of organizations requires an adaptable risk management approach that is easy to understand and implement. Therefore, AS/NZS 4360 is intended to provide only a broad overview of risk management. Organizations are expected to interpret this guide in the context of their own environments and to develop their own specific ERM approaches.

AS/NZS 4360 builds consultation and communication into the ERM process and includes the entire organization in a collaborative environment. It thoroughly describes process steps with examples to facilitate implementation. It is accompanied by two documents that aid in its implementation:

- HB 436-2004—Risk Management Guidelines, Companion Guide AS/NZS 4360 helps implement the standard in an organization.

- HB 158-2006—Delivering Assurance, based on AS/NZS 4360 Risk Management, was developed jointly by risk managers and auditors to help auditors fulfill their obligation to audit risk management according to the standard.

The Standards Australia/Standards New Zealand Joint Technical Committee on Risk Management has approved the adoption of ISO 31000:2009 as AS/NZS/ISO 31000:2009 and the transition from AS/NZS 4360 when it becomes available. The only difference between the two documents is that the introductory section of AS/NZS/ISO 31000:2009 discusses the transition from 4360 to 31000.

Singapore, Austria, and Canada have their own frameworks, which liberally incorporate concepts and steps from existing frameworks. Other countries, states, or provinces are likely to adopt ERM over time. Individual jurisdictions will implement a modified version of an existing framework or closely imitate another country's framework. In France, for example, a noncompulsory implementation guide was to be published by Association Francaise de Normalisation (AFNOR), ISO's French affiliate, before the end of 2009.

FERMA

The Federation of European Risk Management Associations (FERMA) consists of national risk management associations, individual risk managers from Central European countries, and representatives from health organizations, educational sectors, and public sectors. FERMA adopted the Risk Management Standard, which was published in the United Kingdom in 2002. The standard has several elements:

- The establishment of consistent terminology
- A process by which risk management can be executed
- An organized risk management structure
- Risk management goals

The standard, which is intended for public and private organizations, recognizes that risk has both an upside and a downside. Its components allow organizations to report compliance with best practices.

Basel II and Solvency II

Basel II was issued by the Basel Committee on Banking Supervision[2] in 2004 to provide recommendations on banking laws and regulations. It established an international standard that banking regulators can use when creating regulations regarding the amount of capital banks need to keep in reserve to guard against the financial and operational risks they face. This standard is intended to protect the international financial system from problems that might arise if a major bank or a series of banks were to collapse.

Basel II establishes risk and capital management rules designed to ensure that a bank holds capital reserves appropriate to the risk the bank assumes through its lending and investment practices. The greater the volatility of the bank's portfolio, the greater the amount of capital the bank needs to hold to safeguard its solvency.

Solvency II, developed by the European Commission in 2007 (sometimes referred to as "Basel II for insurers"), consists of regulatory requirements for insurance firms that operate in the European Union. It facilitated the development of a single market in insurance services in Europe while providing adequate consumer protection. See the exhibit "Basel II and Solvency II Summary."

Sub-Frameworks

There are other frameworks that are not considered to be ERM frameworks but that provide specific industries and sectors with guidance. These sub-frameworks are likely to proliferate as governments and regulators grapple with systemic risk issues that could affect whole economies or specific sectors. Such sub-frameworks include these:

- Directive IPPC 96/61/CE, dated September 24, 1996 (Integrated Pollution Prevention and Control)—Imposes on all member countries of the European Union a common integrated approach to assessing the environmental impact of highly polluting industries
- ISO 14001:2004 (Environmental Management Systems Requirements with Guidance for Use)—Proposes a method to include environmental management within the overall management processes of an organization
- OSHAS 18001 (Occupational Health and Safety Assessment Series)—Proposes a certification and evaluation process for an organizational health and safety program compatible with other international management systems (including environment and quality)
- EN ISO 17776:2000 (Petroleum and Gas Industries—Offshore Production Installations)—Provides guidelines on tools and techniques for hazard identification and risk assessment
- ISO 17666:2003 (Space Systems Risk Management)—Proposes an integrated approach to managing risks associated with space projects and compatible with best practices for managing such projects

Basel II and Solvency II Summary

	Basel II	Solvency II
Intended Audience	Banks in the international market	Insurance companies in the European Union
Purpose	Basel II rules endeavor to: • Ensure that capital allocation is more risk sensitive • Separate operational risk from credit risk, and quantify both • Align economic and regulatory capital more closely to reduce the scope for regulatory arbitrage	Solvency II rules endeavor to: • Reduce the losses suffered by policyholders in the event that a firm is unable to meet all claims fully • Provide supervisors early warning so that they can intervene promptly if capital falls below the required level • Promote confidence in the financial stability of the insurance sector
Concepts	Basel II uses a "three pillars" concept: 1. Maintenance of minimum capital requirements based on credit risk, operational risk, and market risk 2. Supervisory review by regulators for the first pillar 3. Greater stability in the financial system through increased disclosures by banks	Solvency II uses a "three pillars" concept: 1. Quantitative requirements such as the minimum amount of capital an insurer should hold 2. Governance and risk management of insurers, as well as supervision of insurers 3. Disclosure and transparency requirements
	Source: Basel Committee on Banking Supervision	Source: European Commission

[DA03614]

- ISO 14971:2007 (Medical Devices—Application of Risk Management to Medical Devices)—Became EN ISO 14971:2009 when the European Centre for Normalization opted to make it a European standard for the managing of risk throughout the life cycle of medical devices
- ISO/EIC 27000 (InformationTechnology—Security Techniques—Information Security Management Systems—Overview and Vocabulary)—New information security standard published jointly by the ISO and the International Electrotechnical Commission

SUMMARY

Traditional risk management usually considers only operational risks that can affect an organization. ERM identifies the existence of hazard, operational, financial, strategic, and other risks such as risk to reputation; develops an understanding of their interrelationships; and then estimates variation over time to determine the potential effect on the enterprise. ERM seeks to optimize a risk management strategy that is integrated into the entire organization.

ERM improves an organization's strategic decision making by addressing risks essential to the organization's existence. Threats and opportunities are addressed in a process that integrates ERM with the strategic planning process. To integrate ERM, an organization's board and executives can follow this process:

1. Develop ERM goals (establish the internal and external contexts)
2. Identify risks (risk assessment)
3. Analyze, evaluate, and prioritize critical risks (risk assessment)
4. Treat critical risks, considering priority (risk treatment)
5. Monitor critical risks (monitor and review)

Emerging legal and regulatory issues related to ERM can be addressed at a high level of planning; however, compliance with standards should not be considered a substitute for an ERM policy.

ERM is a systemic approach to managing all of an organization's key business risks and opportunities in order to optimize shareholder value. In using an ERM approach to manage business uncertainties, organizations can enhance their decision making and improve communications.

ERM frameworks and standards establish best practices that demonstrate that an organization is properly managing risk and can fulfill risk management-related contractual obligations. Public companies that are subject to the securities laws apply particular frameworks and standards. Other frameworks and standards are not mandated unless a client or customer establishes the standards as a requirement in a contract, but are recognized as best practices for the implementation of risk management.

ASSIGNMENT NOTES

1.   International Organization for Standardization, *Editing Committee Draft, Pre-ISO/FDIS 31000* (Geneva, Switzerland: International Organization for Standardization, 2008).

2.   The Basel Committee on Banking Supervision is an institution created by the central bank governors of the Group of Ten (G10) nations (Belgium, Canada, France, Italy, Japan, the Netherlands, the United Kingdom, the United States, Germany, and Sweden).

Direct Your Learning ▶▶

Insurance as a Risk Management Technique

Educational Objectives

After learning the content of this assignment, you should be able to:

▹ Explain how insurance reduces risk through pooling.

▹ Explain how insurance benefits individuals, organizations, and society.

▹ Explain why each of the six characteristics of an ideally insurable loss exposure is important to the insurance mechanism.

▹ Explain how the six characteristics of an ideally insurable loss exposure apply to commercial loss exposures.

▹ Explain how the six characteristics of an ideally insurable loss exposure apply to personal loss exposures.

▹ Explain how state and federal governments are involved in the insurance market and the rationale for, and level of, their involvement.

Insurance as a Risk Management Technique

6

HOW INSURANCE REDUCES RISK

Pooling is a fundamental risk management concept that is essential to the operation of insurance. Understanding how insurance reduces risk through pooling helps risk management and insurance professionals evaluate the effectiveness of insurance relative to other risk management techniques.

In the context of risk financing, a pool is a financial arrangement that combines the loss exposures and financial resources of individuals or organizations within the group to share the losses experienced by members of the group. Although insurance is primarily a risk transfer technique, insurers use, and benefit from, pooling when they insure large numbers of loss exposures.

Pooling

Pooling is an arrangement that facilitates the grouping of loss exposures and the resources to pay for any losses that may occur. Pooling arrangements function best (reduce the most risk to the group) when the loss exposures being pooled are independent of (uncorrelated with) one another. Losses are independent when a loss at one loss exposure has no effect on the probability of a loss at another loss exposure.

For example, two warehouse properties, one in Hawaii and the other in Pennsylvania, would be independent loss exposures in terms of the possibility of loss by fire. A fire at one warehouse would not affect the frequency or severity of a fire at the other. However, two warehouses in Miami would not be independent loss exposures with respect to the windstorm cause of loss, because one hurricane could cause damage to both locations.

Loss exposures do not necessarily have to be independent to benefit from pooling. Correlated loss exposures (exposures that are not independent) can still benefit from pooling arrangements, provided that the loss exposures are not perfectly positively correlated (that is, if a loss happens to one exposure, it definitely happens to the other). However, although pooling correlated loss exposures can reduce risk to the pool members, the risk is not as effectively reduced as when the exposures are independent.

How Pooling Reduces Risk

To understand how pooling reduces risk (uncertainty), consider this example. Rachel owns a $100,000 home that is exposed to the possibility of loss in the coming year. Assume that a loss distribution for houses in Rachel's area is used to determine that, without any pooling arrangements, the expected loss for Rachel's house is $744, and the standard deviation of the loss is $9,121.

Suppose that Rachel agrees to enter a pooling arrangement with Keith, who owns the same type of house and faces the same loss distribution as Rachel. Also assume that the two houses are independent of one another and that Rachel and Keith agree to evenly split any losses that the two might incur. That is, they are pooling both their loss exposures and their resources to pay for any losses to those exposures.

The "Loss Distribution for Pools" exhibit shows that when there are two pool members (in this case, Rachel and Keith), the expected losses of the pool are twice the expected losses of one member (2 × $744 = $1,488). However, although the standard deviation of the pool has increased ($12,899 compared with $9,121), it has not doubled. The standard deviation of the pool is calculated using a formula that is beyond the scope of the educational objective.

The standard deviation of the pool will increase as the number of members increases. However, the standard deviation increases at a decreasing rate, which means that the standard deviation of losses on a per member basis actually decreases. See the exhibit "Loss Distribution for Pool."

Loss Distribution for Pool

Number of Members in Pool (n)	Expected Loss		Standard Deviation	
	Pool	Per Member	Pool	Per Member
1	$ 744	$744	$ 9,121	$ 9,121
2	$ 1,488	$744	$ 12,899	$ 6,450
10	$ 7,440	$744	$ 28,843	$ 2,884
100	$ 74,400	$744	$ 91,210	$ 912
1,000	$ 744,000	$744	$ 288,431	$ 288

[DA02743]

As shown in the exhibit, as the number of members in the pool increases, the expected losses and standard deviation of the pool both increase. However, on a per member basis, the expected value remains unchanged and the standard deviation decreases. This occurs because the extreme outcomes become less likely at the pool level.

For example, because Rachel's losses are independent of Keith's losses, the probability that neither individual will have a loss is simply the probability that Rachel does not have a loss multiplied by the probability that Keith does not have a loss. Assuming that the probability of each person's having no loss is .855, then the probability of neither one's having a loss is .855 × .855 = .731, or 73.1 percent.

Similarly, if the probability of each person's having a $100,000 loss is .005, then the probability of both of them having a total loss is .005 × .005 = .000025, or 0.0025 percent. Before the pooling arrangement, the chance of Rachel's not having any loss (and not having to pay anything) was 85.5 percent. With the pooling arrangement, the chance of Rachel's not having to pay anything has been reduced to 73.1 percent because Rachel has agreed to pay a part of Keith's losses as well as part of her own.

As far as losses are concerned, without the pooling arrangement Rachel had a 0.5 percent chance of having to pay $100,000 in losses. With the pooling arrangement, Rachel will have to pay $100,000 in losses only if both she and Keith suffer total losses, which will happen only 0.0025 percent of the time.

As this example demonstrates, the pooling arrangement does not change the frequency or severity of the individual loss exposures. It does change the probability distribution of losses facing each person simply because the sources of the loss exposures and resources to pay for losses have been combined. The expected value remains the same, but the uncertainty around that expected value (as measured by standard deviation) has decreased. Therefore, both Rachel's and Keith's risks are reduced by pooling.

The exhibit also shows that as the number of members of the pool increases, the standard deviation per member continues to decrease. This is a social benefit of pooling; it helps to reduce risk in society. As more members are added to the pool, it becomes more likely that the pool members will have to pay closer to the expected loss rather than an amount at the extremes of the original loss distribution.

In summary, the pooling arrangement does not change either person's expected cost, but it makes the actual cost more consistent and less variable, thereby reducing risk in society. Although pooling arrangements do not prevent losses or transfer risk, they reduce each individual's risk or uncertainty through sharing of losses and resources. See the exhibit "Pooling Arrangements With Correlated Losses."

How Insurance Uses Pooling

Insurers benefit from pooling, and, in fact, most insurers act as large, well-financed pools. However, although an insurer resembles a formal pooling mechanism, there are two key differences between pooling and insurance.

First, pooling is a risk-sharing mechanism, whereas insurance is primarily a risk transfer mechanism. With insurance, the insurance contract transfers the risk from the insured to the insurer in exchange for premiums. If premiums are not adequate to cover insureds' losses in a given year, the insurer cannot collect more from the insureds, as would happen in a pooling arrangement.

Pooling Arrangements With Correlated Losses

Pooling arrangements work best with loss exposures that are independent. However, most loss exposures are not independent. The occurrence of a loss is often the result of events that are common to many people or organizations. Catastrophes, such as hurricanes, tornadoes, wildfires, and earthquakes, cause property losses to many individuals at the same time. Consequently, property losses in certain geographic regions during a given period are positively correlated. Pooling arrangements still work when loss exposures are correlated, provided they are not perfectly positively correlated. With independent loss exposures, there is a high probability that one person's large losses will be offset by other participants' small losses. Therefore, the average loss becomes more predictable. When losses are positively correlated, similar losses are incurred by more participants; therefore, one person's large losses are less likely to be offset by other participants' small losses.

From the "Loss Distribution for Pools" exhibit, if Rachel and Keith's houses were close together, their loss exposures would be positively correlated. Their proximity would determine how highly correlated. Therefore, although the expected loss would remain unchanged ($1,488 for the two of them), the standard deviation for the two of them would be higher. For example, the standard deviation for the two of them may be $15,000 rather than $12,899 if they were on the same street, or $17,000 if they were next-door neighbors. Therefore, although pooling would still reduce the risk to both Rachel and Keith if they were next-door neighbors, and the standard deviation would drop from $9,121 per member to $8,500 ($17,000 ÷ 2), it would not reduce as much risk as it would have had their loss exposures been uncorrelated.

[DA02744]

Even with insurance products that are loss sensitive, such as retrospective rating plans, the risk sharing occurs between the insurer and the insured, not the insured and other insureds. In a retrospective rating plan, if the insured's losses were higher than expected, the insurer can adjust the premium amount. However, the insurer would not adjust all insureds' premiums because one insured's losses were higher. The insurer simply has to pay the additional losses from its policyholders' surplus.

With a pool, losses are shared among all pool members, not transferred to the pool. If the losses of the pool were greater than expected, each member of the pool would have to commit additional resources to pay for losses. Because there is no cost certainty, pools are risk-sharing mechanisms rather than risk transfer mechanisms.

Second, the insurer has additional financial resources that enable it to provide a stronger guarantee that sufficient funds will be available in the event of a loss, further reducing risk. Such additional financial resources are primarily derived from these sources:

- Initial capital from investors—The initial capital is the money that investors provide to establish an insurer. The minimum amount of initial capitalization is established by law in the state where the insurer is chartered. This startup fund might be provided by stockholders, who expect a return on their investment, or by insureds, who want to establish an insurer that will provide a market for their particular insurance needs.

- Retained earnings—Retained earnings are derived from premiums in excess of amounts used to pay claims and expenses, and from earnings on invested money. Each premium should be sufficient to cover that insured's fair share of claims and expenses—and to provide a profit for the insurer. The premium might also include an amount to cover contingencies (known as a risk loading) to pay claims when aggregate loss experience is worse than expected without impairing the insurer's solvency.

Because the premiums charged are greater than the expected average loss costs and expenses, and because the insurer begins with an initial capitalization, the insurer can be comfortable agreeing to accept the transfer of risks from its insureds—provided the risks it accepts are within its capacity.

The "Pooling and Capital Requirements" exhibit demonstrates the limitations on the financial resources of an insurer. The loss distribution is the same as that shown in the "Loss Distribution for Pools" exhibit. In the "Pooling and Capital Requirements" exhibit, assume the insurer has been funded by investors with $1 million in initial capital. If the insurer sells one policy to Rachel, the insurer assumes the risk that loss amounts will be greater than the premium it charged. See the exhibit "Pooling and Capital Requirements."

Pooling and Capital Requirements

Insurer's initial capital = $1,000,000.

Number in Pool	Expected Loss		Standard Deviation		Resources Needed to Pay Losses Two Standard Deviations From the Expected	Additional Resources per Policy
	Pool	Per Member	Pool	Per Member		
1	$ 744	$744	$ 9,121	$9,121	$ 18,986	$ 0
10	$ 7,440	$744	$ 28,843	$2,884	$ 65,126	$ 0
1,000	$744,000	$744	$288,431	$ 288	$1,320,862	$321

[DA02746]

Suppose that the insurer wants to ensure that it can pay losses that are two standard deviations above the expected loss. In this case, that means the insurer must have at least $18,986 to pay for losses to Rachel's policy (calculated as $744 + [2 × $9,121]). With $1 million in initial capital and only one policy sold, the insurer has more than enough capacity to pay any loss that Rachel may suffer. Therefore, the insurer does not need any significant additional resources beyond the premium on the policy.

If the insurer sells ten identical policies to ten independent insureds, the resources needed to pay losses that are two standard deviations above the expected loss of $7,440 are $65,126 (calculated as $7,440 + [2 × $28,843]). With ten policies, the initial capital still provides more than enough capacity. However, if the insurer sold 1,000 policies, it would need $1,320,862 (same calculation method) to be able to pay losses two standard deviations above the expected losses of $744,000. In this case, the initial investment of $1 million does not provide enough capacity. Therefore, the insurer would need to charge an extra $321 per policy to cover its desired contingencies.

Every insurer's capacity is limited by its financial resources, and its ability to fulfill its obligations is based on remaining solvent. Just as insurance buyers transfer risks that they are unwilling to retain to insurers, insurers can transfer risks that they are unwilling to retain to reinsurers. Through reinsurance, primary insurers pool or transfer risks, thereby staying within capacity constraints and helping to ensure their solvency. Reinsurance helps to reduce risk for insurers that accept risks transferred by insurance buyers. Therefore, reinsurance also contributes to the social function of insurance by assisting insurers in reducing risk for society.

BENEFITS OF INSURANCE

Insurance is a prominent risk management technique, and several risk financing measures involve the use of insurance to some degree. It is therefore important for risk management and insurance professionals to consider the benefits of insurance when selecting the most appropriate techniques for meeting risk management goals.

When used as a risk financing measure, insurance can help an individual or organization achieve risk financing goals such as paying for losses, managing cash flow uncertainty, and complying with legal requirements. Insurance also provides benefits to individuals, organizations, and society as a whole by promoting insureds' loss control activities, enabling insureds to use resources efficiently, providing support for insureds' credit, providing insurers with a source of investment funds, and reducing social burdens.

Paying for Losses

The primary role of insurance is to indemnify individuals and organizations for covered losses. This benefit is consistent with the risk financing goal of paying for losses. Provided that the loss is to a covered loss exposure and a covered cause of loss, insurance will indemnify the insured, subject to any applicable deductibles and policy limits.

Managing Cash Flow Uncertainty

Insurance also enables an individual or organization to meet the risk financing goal of managing cash flow uncertainty. Insurance provides the insured with some degree of financial security and stability. The insured can be confident that as long as a loss is covered, the financial effect on the insured's cash flow is reduced to any deductible payments and any loss amounts that exceed the policy limits. The remainder of the loss will be paid by the insurer, reducing the variation in the insured's cash flows.

Meeting Legal Requirements

The final risk financing goal that insurance meets is the goal of meeting legal requirements. Insurance is often used or required to satisfy both statutory requirements and contractual requirements that arise from business relationships.

For example, all states have laws that require employers to pay for the job-related injuries or illnesses of their employees. Employers generally purchase workers compensation insurance to meet this financial obligation. In addition, certain business relationships require proof of insurance. For example, building contractors are usually required to provide evidence of liability insurance before a construction contract is granted.

Promoting Risk Control

A major benefit of insurance is the promotion of risk control. Insurance often provides the insured with the incentive to undertake cost-effective risk control measures. Insurers provide this incentive through risk-sharing mechanisms such as deductibles, premium credit incentives, and contractual requirements.

Because these incentives can lead to a reduction in losses paid by the insurer and therefore lower premiums, they benefit not only the individual insured but also all other insureds. Furthermore, risk control measures can save not only financial resources but also the lives of individuals or employees. Therefore, society as a whole benefits.

Enabling Efficient Use of Resources

People and businesses that face an uncertain future often set aside funds to pay for future losses. However, insurance makes it unnecessary to set aside a large amount of money to pay for the financial consequences of loss exposures that can be insured. In exchange for a relatively small premium, individuals and organizations can free up additional funds. As a result, the money that would otherwise be set aside to pay for possible losses can be used to improve an individual's quality of life or to contribute to the growth of an organization.

Providing Support for Insured's Credit

Insurance can also provide support for an insured's credit. Before making a loan, a lender wants assurance that the money will be repaid. For example, when loaning money to a borrower to purchase property, the lender usually acquires a legal interest in that property. This legal interest enables the lender to take actions such as repossessing a car or foreclosing a home mortgage if the loan is not repaid. Without this ability to recover the loan amount, the lender would be less likely to make the loan. Insurance facilitates loans to individuals and organizations by guaranteeing that the lender will be paid if the collateral for the loan (such as a house or a commercial building) is destroyed or damaged by an insured event, thereby reducing the lender's uncertainty.

Providing Source of Investment Funds

Insurance provides a source of investment funds for both insureds and insurers:

- Insureds are not required to set aside large retention funds to pay for losses that are covered by insurance.
- The premiums collected by insurers are invested until needed to pay claims. Such investments can provide money for projects such as new construction, research, and technology advancements.

Insurers also invest in social projects, such as cultural events, education, and economic development projects. Investment funds promote economic growth and job creation that, in turn, benefit individuals, organizations, and society. Also, because investment brings additional funding to insurers in the form of interest, this additional income helps keep insurance premiums at a reasonable level.

Reducing Social Burdens

Finally, insurance can help reduce social burdens. For example, the social costs of natural disasters, such as Hurricanes Katrina and Rita in 2005, are increased by uninsured losses suffered by individuals and organizations that can amount to billions of dollars. Without other assistance, the victims of natural disasters would rely on the state or federal government. Insurance helps to reduce this burden by providing compensation to the affected parties.

Compulsory auto insurance is another example, because it provides compensation to auto accident victims who might otherwise be unable to afford proper medical care or who might be unable to work because of the accident. Without insurance, victims of job-related or auto accidents might become a burden to society and need some form of state welfare. See the exhibit "Benefits of Insurance."

Benefits of Insurance

Benefit	Explanation
Pay for losses	The primary role of insurance is to indemnify (restore to pre-loss status) individuals and organizations for covered losses.
Manage cash flow uncertainty	Insurance provides financial compensation when covered losses occur. Therefore, insurance greatly reduces the uncertainty created by many loss exposures.
Comply with legal requirements	Insurance can be used both to meet the statutory and contractual requirements of insurance coverage and to provide evidence of financial resources.
Promote risk control activity	Insurance policies may provide insureds with incentives to undertake risk control activities as a result of policy requirements or premium savings incentives.
Efficient use of insured's resources	Insurance makes it unnecessary to set aside a large amount of money to pay for the financial consequences of loss exposures that can be insured. This allows that money to be used more efficiently.
Support for insured's credit	Insurance facilitates loans to individuals and organizations by guaranteeing that the lender will be paid if the collateral for the loan (such as a house or a commercial building) is destroyed or damaged by an insured event, thereby reducing the lender's uncertainty.
Source of investment funds	The timing of insurer's cash flows, premiums collected up front, and claims paid at a later date enable insurers to invest funds in a variety of investment vehicles.
Reduce social burden	Insurance helps to reduce the burden to society of uncompensated accident victims.

[DA02722]

CHARACTERISTICS OF AN IDEALLY INSURABLE LOSS EXPOSURE

Private insurers insure some, but not all, loss exposures. Insurable loss exposures ideally have certain characteristics. Although most insured loss exposures do not completely meet all of these criteria, the criteria can be useful to an insurer when deciding whether to offer new coverages or whether to continue offering existing coverages.

The six characteristics of an ideally insurable loss exposure are summarized in the exhibit. See the exhibit "Six Characteristics of an Ideally Insurable Loss Exposure."

Six Characteristics of an Ideally Insurable Loss Exposure

1. Pure risk—Involves pure risk, not speculative risk

2. Fortuitous losses—Subject to fortuitous loss from the insured's standpoint

3. Definite and measurable—Subject to losses that are definite in time, cause, and location and that are measurable

4. Large number of similar exposure units—One of a large number of similar exposure units

5. Independent and not catastrophic—Not subject to a loss that would simultaneously affect many other similar loss exposures; not catastrophic

6. Affordable—Premiums are economically feasible

[DA02747]

Pure Risk

The first ideal characteristic of an insurable loss exposure is that the loss exposure should be associated with pure risk, not speculative risk. Unlike many other risk financing measures, such as hedging, insurance is not designed to finance speculative risks. See the exhibit "Industry Language—What Does Private Mean?."

Industry Language—What Does Private Mean?

Insurance organizations that are not owned or operated by federal or state governments are generally referred to as private insurers. The insurance products they sell are sold in the private insurance market. The term "private" may be confusing because some insurers are publicly traded stock organizations (owned by the public), not privately owned. Furthermore, the markets they compete in are open to all consumers, not restricted to certain parties. When federal or state governments compete with private insurers, they compete in the private insurance market. When federal or state governments are the only source of an insurance product, then no private market exists.

[DA02748]

One purpose of insurance is to indemnify the insured for the loss, not to enable the insured to profit from the loss. Indemnification is the process of restoring an individual or organization to a pre-loss financial condition. If the loss exposure has the possibility of gain, the insurance premium the insurer would need to charge would offset the potential gain. See the exhibit "Industry Language: What Does Insurability Mean?."

For example, assume a gambling opportunity involves a roulette wheel that has only red and black numbers (50 percent red and 50 percent black; no

Industry Language: What Does Insurability Mean?

Although a particular loss exposure has the characteristics of a commercially insurable loss exposure, an insurer still may prefer not to sell an insurance policy for it. This may be the result of externally or internally imposed constraints placed on the insurer or simply because the insurer prefers not to cover those types of exposures. Internal constraints may be a lack of expertise or resources to offer insurance coverages in that particular line of business. External constraints include state regulation.

State laws regulate the types of insurance that can be written in each state and prescribe the minimum capital and surplus an admitted insurer must have to transact business. Some financial requirements are so high that an insurer might forgo writing a type of business it would otherwise prefer to include in its portfolio. In addition, state insurance departments regulate forms and rates for some types of coverage, which could involve substantial paperwork, making it relatively unattractive for an insurer to offer those coverages. Finally, regulatory approval is often a slow process that constrains insurers' ability to provide new products and services because various marketing practices are also regulated, and some activities are prohibited.

[DA02749]

green), a mandatory $5 bet, and an insurer that is willing to insure a red number outcome. Consider two scenarios:

- The insurer does not charge a premium—If a roulette player can place a bet on black, knowing that if the result is black, he or she will win $5.00, and if the result is red, an insurer will refund the bet, the player can gain without any risk of loss. This is arbitrage (or risk-free) profits. The roulette player would win $5 with a black number and $0 with a red number (the $5 bet is refunded by the insurer). In the long run, the roulette player can expect to win $2.50 ([$5 × .50] + [$0 × .50] = $2.50) every spin of the roulette wheel, without ever losing.

- The insurer charges an appropriate premium—The insurer can expect to lose $2.50 every spin of the roulette wheel. If the outcome is a black number (which happens 50 percent of the time), the insurer loses nothing and if the outcome is a red number, the insurer loses $5.00. This gives an expected value of a loss of $2.50 ([$5 × .50] + [$0 × .50] = $2.50). If the insurer has no expenses, makes no profit, and has no risk charges, then the premium it would charge would be $2.50 per spin (the expected loss). Therefore, the minimum premium an insurer would have to charge offsets any potential gain the insured could have earned from the speculative risk.

Although this example is not realistic, it demonstrates that to insure the downside in a speculative risk, an insurer would have to charge a premium that removed all the expected profits for the insured. In addition, to cover an insurer's expenses, risk charges, and profitability, the minimum premium an insurer would have to charge more than offsets any expected profits. This in turn removes the incentive for the insured to buy the insurance.

Furthermore, limiting insurance coverage only to pure risks helps reduce the complexity of the loss exposures insured by the policy and therefore reduces the difficulty in analyzing the loss exposures during the underwriting process. Insuring speculative risks would require the underwriter to calculate all the possible bad outcomes that would involve the claims against the insurer in order to accurately price the insurance policy. The additional work required in the underwriting process would add to the cost of insurance for all policyholders.

Fortuitous

Fortuitous loss
A loss that is accidental and unexpected.

The second characteristic of an ideally insurable loss exposure is that the loss associated with the loss exposure should be a **fortuitous loss** from the insured's standpoint.

Some causes of loss may be fortuitous only from one point of view. For example, vandalism and theft are intentional (and therefore not fortuitous) acts from the perspective of the individual or organization committing the acts. However, they are fortuitous (and insurable) from the victim's standpoint because they were not intended or expected by the victim.

Other causes of loss are fortuitous regardless of the perspective from which they are examined. For example, naturally occurring events such as windstorms, hail, or lightning are fortuitous events whether one is the insurer, the insured, or any third party associated with the loss exposure.

If the insured has some control over whether or when a loss will occur, the insurer is at a disadvantage because the insured might have an incentive to cause a loss (moral hazard). Also, if losses are not fortuitous, the insurer cannot calculate an appropriate premium because the chance of loss could increase as soon as the policy is issued.

Ideally, private insurance is suitable for situations in which there is reasonable uncertainty about the probability or timing of a loss without the threat of a moral or morale hazard. If policyholders were compensated for losses they cause, they may be encouraged to generate losses for property they no longer wish to own. This could undermine the pricing structure for insurance and increase insurance premiums for all policyholders.

Definite and Measurable

The third characteristic of an ideally insurable loss exposure is that the loss exposure is subject to losses that are definite in time, cause, and location and that are measurable.

Definite

For a loss exposure to be definite in time, cause, and location, the insurer must be able to determine the event (or series of events) that led up to the loss, when that event or series of events occurred, and where it occurred.

All insurance policies have a policy period that specifies the precise dates and times of coverage. A typical property-casualty policy has a policy period ranging from six months to one year. Although other periods may be specified, shorter or longer policy periods are not as common. As an example, the policy period for a homeowners policy is shown in the exhibit. In this policy, the policy period appears in the declarations. See the exhibit "Homeowners Policy Declarations."

Homeowners Policy Declarations

Homeowners Policy Declarations

POLICYHOLDER: (Named Insured)	David M. and Joan G. Smith 216 Brookside Drive Anytown, USA 40000	**POLICY NUMBER:**	296 H 578661
POLICY PERIOD:	**Inception:** March 30, 20X1 **Expiration:** March 30, 20X2	Policy period begins 12:01 A.M. standard time at the residence premises.	

The insurer usually needs to be able to determine that the event occurred during the policy period. For some events, this may be a difficult process; insurers are reluctant to insure such events. For example, suppose an insurer was considering insuring a gas station against environmental pollution. A definite loss would be a fire that ruptured an underground gas tank if the gasoline that was in the tank leaked into the surrounding soil and caused a large environmental pollution loss.

A less definite loss might be an inspector's discovery of a high concentration of gasoline in the soil of an adjacent property that has been caused by a leaking underground gas tank. It is impossible to pinpoint the exact date or the cause of the leak. The leak could have been occurring for months or even years. Therefore, it may be impossible to determine a precise cause of loss or whether the event occurred during the policy period. Because they are not definite, these types of loss exposures are not ideally insurable.

Measurable

As well as being definite, the loss needs to be measurable in order to be ideally insurable. Insurers cannot determine an appropriate premium if they cannot measure the frequency or severity of the potential losses. As discussed, when evaluating a loss exposure, an insurance professional needs to be able to quantify both the frequency and severity of potential losses to determine what future losses may be.

The fact that the future losses may be immeasurable creates a substantial amount of uncertainty for the insured and the insurer. Insurers are reluctant to insure losses that are highly uncertain without receiving substantial compensation (high premiums) from the insured. In summary, if a loss cannot be defined in time or measured, it would be extremely difficult for an insurer to write a policy that specifies what claims to pay and how much to pay for them.

If multiple insurance policies issued by different insurers were issued to cover the loss exposure at various renewals, it would be difficult to determine which policy applied and which insurer was responsible for the loss. At a minimum, the costs of adjusting losses would increase and the likelihood of litigation would be greatly increased.

Large Number of Similar Exposure Units

The fourth characteristic of an ideally insurable loss exposure is that the loss exposure is one of a large number of similar exposure units. Some common loss exposures that satisfy this requirement include homes, offices, and automobiles. There are two risk transfer functions that insurance can provide—cross-sectional and intertemporal risk transfer. See the exhibit "Industry Language—Loss Exposure, Exposure Units, Exposures."

Cross-Sectional Risk Transfer

The most common risk transfer function that insurance provides is the spreading of risk across a large number of similar exposure units within the same period. This is commonly referred to as cross-sectional risk transfer, and it requires a large number of similar loss exposures. Cross-sectional risk transfer is achieved through pooling, which takes advantage of the law of large numbers. The law of large numbers has three criteria:

- The events have occurred in the past under substantially identical conditions and have resulted from unchanging, basic causal forces.
- The events can be expected to occur in the future under the same unchanging conditions.
- The events have been, and will continue to be, independent and sufficiently numerous.

The third criterion ensures that the loss exposures are numerous enough for the insurer to pool a large number of exposure units. This large pool enables

> ## Industry Language—Loss Exposure, Exposure Units, Exposures
>
> The term "loss exposure" can be defined as any condition or situation that presents a possibility of loss, whether or not an actual loss occurs. An exposure unit is defined as a fundamental measure of the loss exposure assumed by an insurer. The terms "exposure" and "exposure unit" are often used interchangeably by insurance professionals. However, this practice can lead to confusion as to whether the individual is referring to loss exposures or exposure units.
>
> A loss exposure may be made up of multiple exposure units. For example, Henry may own a $300,000 house (a property loss exposure). Similarly, Alison may own a $500,000 house (also a property loss exposure). From each insured's point of view, these are single loss exposures. To the insurer, they are not identical exposure units, because one house is more valuable than the other. The insurer may use $100,000 as a single exposure unit. Therefore, Henry's house is equivalent to three exposure units, and Alison's house is equivalent to five exposure units. The three exposure units that Henry's house comprises are not independent exposure units, but those three exposure units are independent of the five exposure units that Alison's house comprises. The insurer can increase the number of independent exposure units ($100,000 units) it insures by increasing the number of independent loss exposures (houses) it insures.

[DA02751]

the insurer to more accurately project losses and determine appropriate premiums because loss statistics can be maintained over time and losses for similar exposure units can be projected with a higher degree of accuracy.

Intertemporal Risk Transfer

Another risk transfer function insurance can provide is the spreading of risk through time, known as intertemporal risk transfer. This function does not require a large number of similar exposure units; therefore, insurers are willing to insure unique loss exposures where there is little or no pooling of similar exposure units.

Independent and Not Catastrophic

The fifth characteristic of an ideally insurable loss exposure is that the loss exposure is not subject to a loss that would simultaneously affect many other similar loss exposures (that is, the loss exposure would be independent) and that the loss exposure would not be catastrophic to the insurer. This characteristic is similar to the characteristic of a large number of similar exposure units in that they are both tied to the third criterion of the law of large numbers. The difference is that this characteristic focuses on the independence of the loss exposures, not their number and similarity.

Independent

For insurers to utilize pooling most effectively, the insured exposure units need to be independent. Although pooling will work to some degree if the exposure units are correlated (not independent), it will not be as effective. An example of correlated loss exposures would be two adjacent houses. Given the proximity of the houses to each other, certain causes of loss, such as a tornado, hurricane, or fire, could affect both houses at the same time. The fact that one of the houses is on fire does not mean the other house will catch fire, but the probability of the second house catching fire is much higher. Therefore, these two loss exposures are correlated.

Not Catastrophic

Insurance operates economically because many insureds pay premiums that are small relative to the cost of the potential losses they could each incur. The cost can stay relatively small because insurers project that they will incur far fewer losses than they have loss exposures. However, if a large number of insureds who are covered for the same type of loss were to incur losses at the same time, the insurance mechanism would not operate economically and losses to the insurer could be catastrophic.

Following Hurricane Andrew in 1992 (and reinforced by Hurricane Katrina in 2005), property-casualty insurers are much more aware of the catastrophic risk that a correlated portfolio of insured loss exposures presents. Geographic diversification, line of business diversification, and reinsurance can help insurers both to improve the independence of their insured loss exposures and to minimize their catastrophic exposure.

In addition to correlated losses, single events or a series of events can also present catastrophic risk to an insurer. Consequently, an insurer should not insure any single loss exposure that would pose a serious financial hardship if a loss occurred.

For example, a small insurer should not insure a multimillion dollar property, such as an oil refinery. Although the loss exposure may be independent of the other properties the insurer has chosen to insure, a loss at such a single location may cause the insurer severe financial difficulty.

Economically Feasible Premium

The final characteristic of an ideally insurable loss exposure is that the insurer is able to charge an economically feasible premium—one that the insured can afford to pay. Of all the characteristics of an ideally insurable loss exposure, this is probably the most important. Supply and demand of insurance demonstrate that if an insurer cannot provide the insurance product at a reasonable premium, there will be no demand. The first five characteristics are designed to ensure that the insurer can provide insurance at a reasonable premium.

Loss exposures involving only small losses, as well as those involving a high probability of loss, are generally considered uninsurable. Providing insurance to cover small losses may not make economic sense when its expense exceeds the amount of potential losses. It also may not make economic sense to insure losses that are almost certain to occur. The expense of providing insurance increases with the frequency of claims because insurers incur some of their largest expenses settling insured claims. In such a situation, the premium would probably be as high as or higher than the potential loss. To maintain the balance of supply and demand, it is important that the insurance mechanism establish a pricing structure that adequately supports the expenses for providing coverage at a price (premium) appropriate for the purchaser when compared with the potential loss.

INSURABILITY OF COMMERCIAL LOSS EXPOSURES

Evaluating a sampling of commercial loss exposures against the six characteristics of an ideally insurable loss exposure demonstrates why insurers may choose to insure some loss exposures and not others. The same method of analyzing insurability can be applied to any other loss exposures.

The commercial loss exposures examined are property (caused by fire, windstorm, and flood), liability (caused by premises and operations liability and products liability), personnel (caused by death and retirement), and net income (caused by property and liability losses).

Property

All organizations have property loss exposures related to their business operations. Some organizations may rely more on real property and others may rely more on personal property, but all rely on property to some extent. This section focuses on a real property loss exposure—the building that houses an organization's main operations—and on three different causes of loss: fire, windstorm, and flood.

A review of how and why the property loss exposure generally meets the ideally insurable criteria reveals that this widely insured loss exposure may not always meet these criteria. The exhibit summarizes whether the building that houses an organization's main operations meets the six ideally insurable characteristics for fire, windstorm, and flood. See the exhibit "Ideally Insurable Characteristics: Commercial Property Loss Exposures."

Fire

For most property loss exposures, the main underwriting criteria focus on the threat of loss by fire. As shown in the exhibit, commercial property loss exposures associated with fire generally meet all six characteristics.

Ideally Insurable Characteristics: Commercial Property Loss Exposures

	Fire	Windstorm	Flood
Pure risk	Yes (except arson-for-profit)	Yes	Yes
Fortuitous	Yes (except for arson-for-profit)	Yes	Yes
Definite and measurable	Yes	Yes	Yes
Large number of similar exposure units	Depends on property location, property type, and use	Depends on property location, property type, and use	Depends on property location, property type, and use
Independent and not catastrophic	Yes	Can be catastrophic	Can be catastrophic
Premiums are economically feasible	Yes	Depends on location	Depends on location

[DA02753]

Fire loss to a building is a pure risk rather than a speculative risk because it generally involves only the possibility of loss and no possibility of gain. An exception would be arson-for-profit. For example, an organization might own an obsolete, run-down building in a prime location whose land is worth more without the building.

In an arson-for-profit, the organization would deliberately burn down the building, both to claim on the insurance and to increase the value of the land. Insurance underwriters guard against knowingly providing insurance for such obviously potential moral hazards. Moreover, insurers use claim investigation techniques to detect arson-for-profit claims so that such claims can be lawfully denied. Insurance policies can be modified to limit losses for these exceptions.

An accidental fire loss would be fortuitous from the perspective of both parties. However, not all fires are accidents. Again, arson committed by the insured (arson-for-profit) is the exception because it is intentional.

Similarly, other intentional fires may not be started by the insured, such as fires resulting from riots or civil commotion. As long as the intentional fire is not started by the insured, it is fortuitous from the perspective of both the insurer and insured.

An insurer can project aggregate claims from fortuitous fire losses with reasonable confidence, based on past experience. However, it is not as easy to project the number and extent of claims that are not fortuitous. So although fires generally meet the fortuitous criteria, the fact that they can be deliberately set detracts from their being considered an ideally insurable loss exposure.

Property fires are typically definite and measurable. Occasionally, pinpointing the time of an unobserved property fire is difficult, such as when the fire that destroys an office building occurs over a weekend. Because fire insurance is usually written for a one-year policy period, loss timing becomes critical only if the loss occurs near the policy's expiration date and a question exists about whether the loss occurred during the policy period. In some cases, continuous coverage exists (such as a renewal policy), but the question remains as to which policy was in force at the time of the loss.

Knowing the value of a building or its contents is critical in measuring the amount of a fire loss. Such value can be measured in different ways. It is often necessary to specify—before a loss occurs—whether the insured loss will be the amount necessary to repair or replace the loss with like kind and quality, or whether the insured loss will be a depreciated actual cash value.

Some insurance provides coverage for additional living expenses, fair rental value, or other financial losses resulting from a building that cannot be used. These losses are somewhat more difficult to measure because they depend on an estimate of what an insured's financial position would have been had the event not occurred.

Therefore, with respect to being definite and measurable, fire loss exposures are usually ideally insurable because a fire's occurrence typically is obvious. However, uncertainty about the timing of a fire's occurrence or the value of the property at the time of the loss may make insuring such a fire loss less than ideal.

Many properties present a large number of similar loss exposures for an insurer. For example, many retail organizations are located in malls, which tend to be rather homogenous. However, many organizations have unique locations, or perform a unique function at their locations, making pooling by the insurer very difficult. Whether a specific commercial property location meets this ideally insurable criterion depends on the location, type, and usage of the property.

The characteristic of being independent and not catastrophic applies to the insurer's perspective, based on its portfolio of insurance policies. The insurer needs to consider whether a loss exposure under consideration for insurance coverage could be subject to a loss that would simultaneously affect many other similar insured loss exposures.

For example, a retail shop in an enclosed mall would not be an independent loss exposure if its insurer covered other retail shops in the same mall. A large fire at the mall could simultaneously affect all of the shops, which could be catastrophic if a single insurer had insured most or all of the shops. If an insurer is insuring only one retail shop in the mall, the loss exposure would be independent of the other loss exposures it has chosen to insure and a fire loss would not be catastrophic.

Fires at an organization's main location tend to be low-frequency, high-severity (from the insured's perspective) events that insureds could not usually recover from financially without insurance. Although the frequency of fire loss to any one specific building is usually too small for insurers to project with confidence, aggregate fire losses generate credible statistical information on which insurance rates can be based. Because fires tend to be low-frequency events, and because a fire loss exposure typically exhibits most or all of the first five ideally insurable characteristics, this cause of loss is usually economically feasible to insure.

Windstorm

As shown in the previous exhibit, many of the ideally insurable characteristics that are met by fire are also met by windstorm. Windstorm damage to commercial property loss exposures is generally a pure risk subject to fortuitous losses that are definite and measurable. However, it may not meet the last three ideally insurable characteristics. This drastically changes how some insurers view the insurability of windstorm loss.

As with fire, windstorm can be insured on many similar buildings. However, identical buildings at different locations can face substantially different windstorm exposure. With fire, property type and use are significant factors in determining if there are a large number of similar exposure units. With windstorm, those factors are still important, but not as important as location.

Hurricanes and tornadoes, the most common windstorms, are geographically concentrated, making pooling a large number of similar, yet independent loss exposures more difficult. The exhibit shows the geographic regions of the United States that have the highest exposure to hurricane activity. See the exhibit "Hurricane Risk Map."

Different buildings in the same geographic area are not independently exposed to windstorm loss. Unlike fire, a single windstorm is likely to damage many buildings; for example, hurricanes generally affect a widespread geographic area. Although tornadoes are more concentrated, they can still cause catastrophic damage to all property in a limited area, sometimes wiping out an entire community.

For small insurers in geographic locations that are exposed to hurricane or tornado activity, windstorm can therefore be catastrophic. Adverse selection (when high-risk individuals or organizations are more likely to demand insurance than low-risk individuals or organizations) is present because property owners in windstorm-prone areas are more likely to demand insurance.

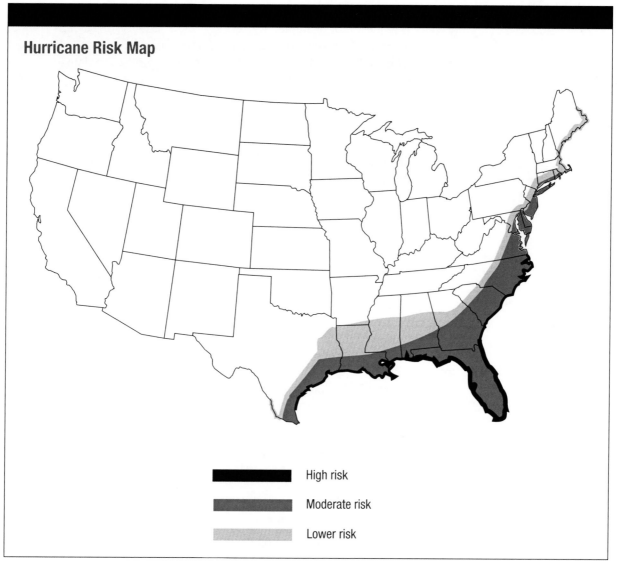

Hurricane Risk Map

High risk

Moderate risk

Lower risk

[DA02754]

The catastrophic nature of some windstorms—notably hurricanes—makes windstorm insurance difficult to underwrite, especially for insurers with a high volume of business in a limited geographic area. Appropriate rating is complicated by the fact that premium and loss calculations are performed in one-year periods, whereas weather cycles are much longer.

Advances in catastrophe modeling have increased the accuracy of predicting storm damage. These models indicate that, in high-risk areas, higher premiums are typically necessary to offset the insurer's predicted losses.

As catastrophe modeling improves, it may lead to economically infeasible premiums for some insureds. Windstorm does not meet as many of the ideal characteristics of an insurable loss exposure as does fire. Although common commercial property insurance policies have previously tended to cover windstorm, this has been changing in states where the probability of hurricane activity is highest. For example, insurers in some coastal states such as Florida, Texas, and South Carolina are able to sell homeowners insurance policies in the highest-risk coastal regions that do not cover windstorm damage. Homeowners can obtain coverage for windstorm damage through state-run windstorm pools.

Flood

Flood damage to property at fixed locations has traditionally been considered uninsurable by private insurers, even for property that was insured against fire and windstorm losses. In contrast, flood insurance is readily available for autos and other personal property that can easily be moved in order to avoid damage.

Similar to windstorm, flood generally involves pure risk and losses that are fortuitous, definite, and measurable. Whether property is part of a large number of similar loss exposures suitable for pooling depends on the location, property type, and use.

The main issue is that the flood cause of loss is geographically concentrated, so loss exposures tend not to be independent, and losses could be catastrophic from the insurer's perspective. As a result of the potentially catastrophic losses resulting from floods, flood loss premiums are high and flood can be economically unfeasible to insure for some organizations.

Although some uncertainty exists about whether a flood will occur at a particular location in a particular year, in many areas the long-term probability of flood can be forecast. Property located within a 10-year, 20-year, or 100-year flood plain is almost certainly exposed to loss. Although that does not mean a flood occurs at specified intervals (a 100-year flood could occur in two consecutive years), on average, a flood can be expected with certain regularity.

Premiums in these flood zones would be too high for most insureds to pay without government assistance. Flood insurance is now available under the National Flood Insurance Program (NFIP). The federal government has also devoted engineering resources to evaluating flood zones, and these evaluations have facilitated underwriting flood insurance by private insurers. Some private insurers are willing to insure commercial properties against flood loss if they are located outside flood-prone areas as determined by the federal government. See the exhibit "Hurricane Damage: Windstorm or Flood?."

Liability

The second category of loss exposures is liability loss exposures. The frequency and severity of liability losses associated with these exposures vary widely, depending on factors such as the organizations' operations and product lines and on the legal environment in which the organizations operate. This section focuses on commercial liability loss exposures stemming from two sources

Hurricane Damage: Windstorm or Flood?

For commercial properties with windstorm coverage, distinguishing between covered windstorm damage and not-covered flood damage can be difficult because a storm may produce both causes of loss. For example, hurricanes produce a phenomenon known as storm surge, in which ocean waves are larger and ocean levels rise. Flooding caused by storm surge is not covered by property insurance policies that exclude flood coverage. Damage caused by flood must then be covered by separate policies sold by the National Flood Insurance Program. Ongoing litigation in those states severely affected by Hurricane Katrina in 2005 is challenging the validity of the flood exclusion in many property policies where it has been difficult to discern the cause of loss because of the extent of the damage. For example, consider the properties for which all that remained of a structure was a concrete slab. Was it wind or flood that caused the complete destruction of the building and contents?

[DA02755]

of risk faced by many organizations—premises and operations liability and products liability. The exhibit summarizes how well these two categories of liability loss exposures meet the six characteristics of an ideally insurable loss exposure. See the exhibit "Ideally Insurable Characteristics: Commercial Liability Loss Exposures."

Ideally Insurable Characteristics: Commercial Liability Loss Exposures

	Premises and Operations Liability	Products Liability
Pure risk	Yes	Yes
Fortuitous	Yes	Yes
Definite and measurable	Yes	Depends on product
Large number of similar exposure units	Yes	Depends on product
Independent and not catastrophic	Yes	Can be catastrophic
Premiums are economically feasible	Yes	Depends on product

[DA02757]

Premises and Operations Liability

The premises and operations liability loss exposure is the possibility that an organization will be held liable because of injury or damage from either of two causes:

- An accident occurring on premises owned or rented by the organization
- An accident occurring away from such premises, but only if it arises out of the organization's ongoing operations

Examples of accidents that would be classified as premises or operations liability loss exposures include these:

- A customer's bodily injury resulting from a slip-and-fall in ice, snow, or wet conditions at the insured's premises
- A visitor's bodily injury or property damage resulting from the insured's failure to provide sufficient premises security

Premises and operations liability loss exposures often exhibit all the characteristics of an ideally insurable loss exposure. The loss exposures involve pure risk and generate fortuitous losses that are definite in time, cause, and location and are measurable. Some organizations are more exposed to premises and operations liability loss exposures than others.

For example, retail stores have a large volume of customers visiting their premises relative to other types of organizations, such as manufacturers. Therefore, retail stores are more likely to see a higher frequency of liability claims from customers.

Given the large number of retail stores in the U.S., the premises and operations liability loss exposure is one of a large number of similar exposures. Each loss would be independent and not catastrophic, and premiums should be economically feasible because all the other five characteristics are met.

Products Liability

Products liability loss exposures arise out of injury or damage that results from defective or inherently dangerous products. Unlike premises and operations liability loss exposures, not all products liability loss exposures exhibit all the characteristics of an ideally insurable loss exposure. Although they involve pure risk and fortuitous losses, the losses are not necessarily definite in cause.

For example, the cause of a person's injury is not always definite. There could be several potential causes, only one of which is the insured's product. The loss may also not be measurable. For example, it may be difficult to measure the monetary value of an injury. If the product has been widely distributed, then the loss may simultaneously affect many individuals or organizations. Therefore, the loss could be catastrophic in terms of the number of claims. As a result, some products may not be economically feasible to insure.

Personnel

The third category of loss exposures is personnel loss exposures. A personnel loss exposure is a condition that presents the possibility of loss caused by a key person's death, disability, retirement, or resignation that deprives an organization of that person's special skill or knowledge that cannot be readily replaced. The frequency and severity of personnel losses vary widely by organization and industry. In general, personnel losses are fairly infrequent, but their severity will depend on the personnel involved.

The more valuable the key person is to the organization, the more severe the loss. Unlike property, liability, and net income loss exposures, personnel loss exposures are generally not insured through property-casualty insurers. Personnel loss exposures resulting from the death of a key person can be insured by employer-owned life insurance policies, but the remaining causes of loss are often uninsurable. This section focuses on two causes of personnel losses—death and retirement. The exhibit summarizes how well personnel loss exposures associated with these two causes of loss meet the six characteristics of an ideally insurable loss exposure. See the exhibit "Ideally Insurable Characteristics: Commercial Personnel Loss Exposures."

Ideally Insurable Characteristics: Commercial Personnel Loss Exposures

	Death	Retirement
Pure risk	Yes	Yes
Fortuitous	Yes	Depends on circumstances and personnel involved
Definite and measurable	Depends on personnel involved	Depends on personnel involved
Large number of similar exposure units	Depends on personnel involved	Depends on personnel involved
Independent and not catastrophic	Yes	Yes
Premiums are economically feasible	Yes	N/A

[DA02758]

Death

Unless a disaster occurs, an organization's losses from death are of low frequency, with the loss severity depending on the employee's value to the organization. Because of the low frequency of employee deaths in many organizations, it is difficult to predict their number over a given period with much accuracy.

Personnel loss exposures associated with death generally exhibit the six characteristics of an ideally insurable loss exposure. The loss exposure involves pure risk that is fortuitous, independent, and not catastrophic, and that is usually economically feasible to insure. The two characteristics that death may not meet are that losses are definite and measurable and that they are among a large number of similar exposure units. Although the death of a key employee is typically definite in time, cause, and location, it may be difficult to measure the actual loss to the organization.

Personnel losses are often difficult to quantify because a single employee's value to an organization may be incalculable. Many organizations have hundreds or thousands of employees. This can make it difficult to quantify their number of key employees. In some industries, qualified employees are difficult to find and replace. For example, very few individuals in the world are experts in oil location and extraction. In these cases, there are not a large number of similar exposure units to create an ideally insurable loss exposure.

Retirement

Although death often occurs suddenly, retirement is usually planned. Therefore, most personnel losses resulting from retirement can be handled with proper planning by the organization. However, sudden retirements can cause severe personnel losses. The personnel loss exposures associated with retirement involve pure risk; are definite in time, cause, and location (although they may be hard to measure); may not be one of a large number of similar loss exposures; and are generally independent and not catastrophic. The characteristics that retirement does not meet are that the loss may not be fortuitous and it may not be economically feasible to insure.

Organizations can influence key employees' retirement decisions through a variety of methods. For example, benefits such as early retirement packages may induce key employees to retire. Alternatively, organizations may lose key employees to retirement because of poor work conditions or poor compensation packages. Therefore, a personnel loss resulting from a key employee's retirement may not be fortuitous from the organization's perspective.

Because it is not possible to purchase retirement insurance on key employees to compensate the organization if they retire, it is impossible to determine whether premiums are economically feasible. Given that a loss may not be fortuitous, premiums for such a product would have to account for the moral hazard and adverse selection that would exist in the market, making premiums less likely to be affordable.

Net Income

The fourth category of loss exposures is net income loss exposures. Net income is the difference between an organization's total revenues and its total expenses (including taxes). In a broad sense, a net income loss could involve any decrease in net income an organization incurs, for whatever reason. Net income can be higher or lower than expected as a result of either the business environment or fortuitous events (such as property, liability, or personnel losses).

Net income losses caused by the business environment clearly do not meet the first characteristic of the loss exposure involving pure risk. The remainder of this section therefore focuses on net income loss exposures associated with two causes of loss that are pure risks—property losses and liability losses. The exhibit summarizes how well net income loss exposures associated with property and liability causes of loss exhibit the six characteristics of an ideally insurable loss exposure. See the exhibit "Ideally Insurable Characteristics: Commercial Net Income Loss Exposures."

Ideally Insurable Characteristics: Commercial Net Income Loss Exposures

	Net income loss associated with property losses	Net income loss associated with liability losses
Pure risk	Yes	Yes
Fortuitous	Yes	Yes
Definite and measurable	Yes	May not be definite
Large number of similar exposure units	Yes	Yes
Independent and not catastrophic	May be catastrophic	Yes
Premiums are economically feasible	Yes	N/A

[DA02759]

Net Income Loss Associated With Property Losses

Net income losses stemming from property losses result from physical damage to property (either property the organization owns or property of others on which the organization depends) that either prevents the organization from operating or that reduces its capacity to operate. Net income losses associated with property losses are insured by a variety of business income insurance coverages.

Net income loss exposures associated with property losses exhibit almost all the characteristics of an ideally insurable loss exposure. The net income loss exposure associated with the property cause of loss involves pure risk, with losses that are fortuitous, definite and measurable, one of a large number of similar exposure units, and economically feasible to insure.

Net income losses may not be independent and can be catastrophic if the property losses they are associated with were caused by catastrophic causes of loss such as a windstorm. A substantial portion of insured losses following hurricanes, such as Hurricane Katrina in 2005, are business income losses stemming from the property damage done to businesses in the affected areas.

Net Income Loss Associated With Liability Losses

Unlike the net income losses associated with property losses, there are no standardized insurance products that provide first-party coverage for net income losses stemming from liability losses.[1] The major difference between net income losses stemming from property losses and those stemming from liability losses involves the determination of the time of the loss. For net income losses associated with property losses, insurance coverage is provided until the property has been restored or should have been restored (plus some additional time to return to normal operations). The restoration of the property provides a definite end to the payment of benefits by the insurance policy.

There is no similar end point for net income losses that are associated with liability losses. For example, a restaurant could suffer a net income loss because customers stop frequenting it after it is found liable in a food poisoning case. There is no definite end point in such a case, because there is no definite time when customers will return.

INSURABILITY OF PERSONAL LOSS EXPOSURES

Evaluating a sampling of personal loss exposures against the six characteristics of an ideally insurable loss exposure demonstrates why insurers may choose to insure some loss exposures and decline to insure others.

In general, many of the loss exposures faced by organizations are also faced by individuals. For individuals, these loss exposures can be divided into property, liability, and net income loss exposures. Although individuals do not typically have personnel loss exposures, they do have life, health, and retirement loss exposures that organizations do not face.

Property

An individual's key property loss exposure is typically a residence. Therefore, this section focuses on how the fire, windstorm, and flood causes of loss affect the insurability of that residence. Although all homes are different, they generally can be grouped into classes that face essentially the same loss potential. Individual homes are easier to group together than commercial property exposures, mainly because individual homes all serve the same function. See the exhibit "Ideally Insurable Characteristics: Personal Property Loss Exposures."

Ideally Insurable Characteristics: Personal Property Loss Exposures

	Fire	Windstorm	Flood
Pure risk	Yes (except for arson-for-profit)	Yes	Yes
Fortuitous	Yes (except for arson-for-profit)	Yes	Yes
Definite and measurable	Yes	Yes	Yes
Large number of similar exposure units	Yes	Yes	Yes
Independent and not catastrophic	Yes	Can be catastrophic	Can be catastrophic
Premiums are economically feasible	Yes	Depends on location	Depends on location

[DA02760]

Insurers still must identify buildings with higher-than-normal hazards, guard against arson-for-profit, avoid excessive concentration of loss exposure, ensure adequate diversification of exposures, and carefully establish the insurable value of property subject to loss. The exhibit summarizes whether an individual's residence meets the six ideally insurable characteristics for fire, windstorm, and flood.

The property loss exposures associated with fire are ideally suited to insurability because the loss exposure involves a pure risk, a large number of similar, yet independent exposure units, and losses that are fortuitous, definite, measurable, and not catastrophic. These characteristics make premiums economically feasible. However, windstorm and flood losses can be catastrophic and, depending on the location of the residence, may not be economically feasible to insure.

Liability

The exhibit titled "Ideally Insurable Characteristics: Personal Liability Loss Exposures" focuses on liability loss exposures stemming from two common sources of risk faced by many individuals: real property ownership (premises) liability loss exposures and automobile liability loss exposures. The exhibit summarizes how well these two categories of liability loss exposures meet the six characteristics of an ideally insurable loss exposure. See the exhibit "Ideally Insurable Characteristics: Personal Liability Loss Exposures."

Ideally Insurable Characteristics: Personal Liability Loss Exposures

	Premises liability	Automobile liability
Pure risk	Yes	Yes
Fortuitous	Yes	Yes
Definite and measurable	Yes	Yes
Large number of similar exposure units	Yes	Yes
Independent and not catastrophic	Yes	Yes
Premiums are economically feasible	Yes	Yes

[DA02761]

The exhibit shows that both premises and automobile liability loss exposures display all six of the characteristics of an ideally insurable loss exposure. Premises liability loss exposures are generally covered by the variety of homeowners insurance policies available, and the automobile liability loss exposures are covered by a personal auto policy.

Net Income

A net income loss could involve any decrease in net income, regardless of the reason. Revenues (such as salary) and expenses (such as housing) can be higher or lower than expected as a result of either the economic environment or fortuitous events such as a property or liability loss.

Net income losses caused by the economic environment clearly do not meet the first characteristic of the loss exposure involving pure risk. For example, rising gas and oil prices would cause an individual's expenses to increase, resulting in a net income loss. However, falling gas and oil prices would result in a net income gain.

Net income losses caused by fortuitous events, such as a fire to an individual's residence, would involve pure risk because there is no potential for the individual to gain.

Life, Health, and Retirement

In addition to the property, liability, and net income loss exposures, individuals and families can face financial difficulty resulting from life, health, and retirement loss exposures. These loss exposures are generally managed through life and health insurance products and also through government programs. See the exhibit "Ideally Insurable Characteristics: Personal Life, Health, and Retirement Loss Exposures."

Ideally Insurable Characteristics: Personal Life, Health, and Retirement Loss Exposures

	Life loss exposures	Health loss exposures	Retirement loss exposures
Pure risk	Yes	Yes	Yes
Fortuitous	Yes (except for suicide)	Depends on cause of loss	Not usually, but may be forced retirement
Definite and measurable	Yes	Depends on cause of loss	Yes
Large number of similar exposure units	Yes	Yes	Yes
Independent and not catastrophic	Yes	Yes	Yes
Premiums are economically feasible	Usually	Usually	N/A

[DA02763]

A variety of causes of loss contribute to the life, health, and retirement personal loss exposures. Although some of these causes of loss are fortuitous, others are under the control of the person involved and therefore make life, health, and retirement causes of loss subject to moral and morale hazards. The exhibit shows how life, health, and retirement causes of loss meet the characteristics of an ideally insurable loss exposure.

Life Loss Exposures

Although life is not generally considered a loss exposure, the loss of life to premature death is. Premature death is a term used to refer to the death of a person with outstanding financial obligations. These financial obligations, such as children to support or mortgage payments, can result in financial difficulty for the family that depended on the deceased's earnings if they are unable to generate replacement income from other sources.

There are individual circumstances, such as health conditions or hazardous occupations, that may prevent insurers from offering an economically feasible premium. However, for most individuals, life loss exposures satisfy all six of the ideally insurable characteristics.

Health Loss Exposures

Poor health is another personal loss exposure that can create serious financial problems for individuals and families. First, an individual might incur significant medical bills. Without health insurance or significant personal savings, these expenses can cause financial distress or bankruptcy. Second, if a person is unable to work because of poor health or disability, earnings can also be lost, again resulting in financial difficulties.

Similar to the life loss exposures, widely available health insurance appears to indicate that health loss exposures have the ideally insurable characteristics. However, health insurance is subject to adverse selection as well as moral and morale hazard.

Unlike life loss exposures, for which most causes of loss are fortuitous, many causes of loss to health are under some control of the individual involved. Smoking and obesity are examples of health-related causes of loss over which an individual may have some control. These factors have contributed to some of the issues in the health insurance market. The two major issues are availability and affordability of health insurance.

Whereas most Americans obtain health insurance through their employer, those who need to purchase coverage individually often have difficulty obtaining coverage, or obtaining coverage at an economically feasible premium. Furthermore, pre-existing health conditions exacerbate the problem for those shopping for coverage individually. The affordability issue exists for employers as well. Rising healthcare costs are a major concern for both small and large organizations.

Retirement Loss Exposure

The possibility of insufficient income during retirement is another important loss exposure faced by individuals. Although workers are not typically forced to retire, most retire by age sixty-five. If the replacement income generated by Social Security, private retirement plans, and personal savings is not sufficient to cover expenses, financial hardship may result. This situation is compounded by increasing life expectancy, which lengthens the retirement period. If the individual has underestimated the number of years that could be spent in retirement, his or her savings may not be adequate.

Retirement does not usually exhibit the fortuitous characteristic of ideally insurable loss exposures because the individual has control over savings and choice of retirement dates. Consequently, individuals are not able to purchase retirement insurance.

GOVERNMENT INSURANCE PROGRAMS

In some cases, property-casualty insurance for certain loss exposures can be obtained only through government insurance programs. It is therefore important for insurance and risk management professionals to know why government insurance programs exist, how they are structured, and why some are run at the state level while others are federal programs.

Government insurance programs exist to fill unmet needs in the private insurance market, to facilitate compulsory insurance purchases, to provide efficiency in the marketplace, and to accomplish social goals. Government can participate in such programs as an exclusive insurer, as a partner with private insurers, or as a competitor to private insurers. Whether a program involves federal or state government is often a politically motivated decision, but other motivating factors can exist.

Rationale for Government Involvement

The United States, like most developed countries, has a mature private property-casualty insurance market that provides a mechanism for consumers and insurers to interact in the demand and supply of insurance products. Although much of the market is heavily regulated and behaves in a somewhat cyclical manner, in general it functions properly. That is, consumers are able to purchase insurance products they desire for a price determined by the market, and insurers can earn an appropriate rate of return on their capital. In a perfectly functioning market, there is no need for state or federal governments to supply insurance products.

However, private insurance markets do not always function perfectly. Occasionally, insurers are unable or unwilling to supply an insurance product to consumers at a mutually acceptable price. In addition to market failures, other reasons for government involvement in insurance include these:

• To fill insurance needs unmet by private insurers
• To compel people to buy a particular type of insurance
• To obtain greater efficiency and/or provide convenience to insurance buyers
• To achieve collateral social purposes

Fill Unmet Needs

When private insurers are unable or unwilling to satisfy certain insurance needs, government programs can provide insurance to meet legitimate public demands. By doing this, the government provides protection against loss that would otherwise not be provided.

An example of a government insurance program formed to fulfill an unmet need in the private insurance market is the Terrorism Risk Insurance Program (TRIP), formed by the Terrorism Risk Insurance Act of 2002 (TRIA). The program was intended as a temporary provider of reinsurance for losses caused by terrorism and was designed to run until the end of 2005, when it was assumed that the private insurance market would have developed its own terrorism insurance products.

In December 2005, Congress extended TRIP for two more years, and in December 2007, Congress extended it for seven more years. Although the private market role was increased and the federal share of compensation for losses insured under TRIP was decreased, the private market for terrorism insurance and reinsurance has not been deemed adequate to let TRIA expire as originally anticipated.

Compel Insurance Purchase

Another reason federal and state governments are involved in insurance is to facilitate compulsory insurance purchases. For example, workers compensation insurance has proven to efficiently manage workplace injuries. However, it is possible that some employers would not purchase workers compensation insurance if they were not required to do so.

Because states require employers to purchase this insurance (or provide proof of self-insurance), they must have a mechanism to ensure that workers compensation insurance is available at a reasonable cost. Another example is personal automobile liability insurance. As auto liability coverage is required in almost all states, each state has some type of mechanism in place to provide insurance for those drivers who cannot obtain coverage at a reasonable price in the private market. In the workers compensation and auto liability insurance markets, most consumers obtain coverage through private insurers.

Government programs are necessary to fulfill the needs of those who cannot obtain the required coverage in the private market; they are not required to insure all consumers.

Obtain Efficiency and Provide Convenience

Two related rationales for government involvement in insurance are providing efficiency in the market and convenience to insureds. In economic terms, these two rationales are essentially the same. Providing convenience to insureds, by reducing either the time or the resources they need to expend to obtain the desired insurance coverage, adds to the efficiency of the market.

Legislators often find it is more straightforward to establish government insurance plans for particular purposes than to invite and analyze bids from private insurers and then supervise and regulate the resulting plans. When insurance provided by the government is compulsory, spending money on marketing or paying sales commissions (two large expenses for insurers) is unnecessary. Governments sometimes try to avoid sales costs by setting up their own distribution channels. Alternatively, as is the case with the National Flood Insurance Program (NFIP), they market through established insurance producers who also market other insurance.

Achieve Collateral Social Purpose

The government may participate in insurance to accomplish social goals because insurance is often seen as a social good. By making use of the pooling mechanism, insurance can reduce risk to society. This is beneficial both to society and to the overall economy. In economic terms, these benefits are often referred to as positive externalities.

An issue arises when individuals do not have an incentive to purchase insurance, even though it would benefit society. Individuals and organizations make decisions that are in their best interest. If, for example, an organization conducted a cost-benefit analysis and determined that workers compensation insurance was too expensive, it would not want to purchase the insurance.

However, workers compensation laws encourage injury prevention and injured workers' rehabilitation, a positive externality. Therefore, it falls to the government to provide incentives for the purchase of insurance. It does this through a combination of regulation and provision of insurance at a reasonable price.

Organizations respond to these measures by purchasing insurance, which, as well as benefiting the organization, benefits society. Similarly, the NFIP provides strong incentives to amend and enforce building codes and otherwise reduce the loss exposure of new construction to floods. Without the involvement of the federal government in providing flood insurance, these incentives would be lacking.

Level of Government Involvement

The level of government involvement varies widely and depends on many factors, such as the rationale for government involvement, the availability and willingness of private insurers to partner with the government program, and the level of competition in the market. There are three levels at which the government can participate:

- Exclusive insurer
- Partner with private insurers
- Competitor to private insurers

Exclusive Insurer

The government can be an exclusive insurer either because of law or because no private insurer offers a competing plan. A federal or state government can function as a primary insurer by collecting premiums, providing coverage, and paying all claims and expenses (with the backing of government funds if necessary).

Examples include some state government-run workers compensation programs. Alternatively, the government can function as a reinsurer, either by providing 100 percent reinsurance to private insurers writing a particular coverage (an exclusive reinsurer), or by reinsuring part of the risk in excess of the private insurer's retention. If the government is reinsuring only part of the risk, the program is essentially a partnership with private insurers.

Partner With Private Insurers

Government partnerships with private insurers can develop when private insurers are no longer able to adequately provide coverages they had typically offered previously. Two examples of such partnerships are TRIP and NFIP.

TRIP is an example of a partnership under which the government operates a reinsurance plan, providing reinsurance on specific loss exposures for which private insurers retain only part of the loss. The NFIP is an example of a partnership under which the federal government underwrites the insurance policy but private insurers and insurance producers deliver the policies to consumers. The private insurers take a percentage of the premium as a sales commission and pass the remainder of the premium on to the NFIP.

Both terrorism and flood coverage had previously been offered by private insurers, but the nature of the loss exposures indicated that the insurance industry was not well suited to providing coverage alone. In addition to the TRIP and NFIP partnership structures, other partnerships use a wide variety of structures.

Competitor to Private Insurers

Government involvement may also take the form of operating an insurance plan in direct competition with private insurers. This type of involvement often evolves when the private insurance market has not failed, but is not operating as efficiently as regulators would like. In these instances, the government performs essentially the same marketing, underwriting, actuarial, and claim functions as a private insurer. Examples include the competitive workers compensation funds offered in some states.

Federal Compared With State Programs

The final distinction among government property-casualty insurance programs is whether a state government or the federal government is involved

with the program. Because federal government involvement in these types
of issues is often a politically motivated decision, predicting what factors will
influence federal government involvement is difficult. One motivating factor
may be that if the rationale for government involvement extends beyond
state boundaries or would affect interstate commerce, the federal government should be running the insurance program. See the exhibit "Examples of
Property-Liability Insurance Offered by the Federal Government."

Examples of Property-Liability Insurance Offered by the Federal Government

Plan	Characteristics of Government Plan	Relationship to Private Insurance
National Flood Insurance Program	• Meets previously unmet needs for flood insurance. • Serves the social purposes of amending and enforcing building codes and reducing new construction in flood zones.	• Federal government can act as primary insurer. • Federal government can partner with private insurers. Private insurers sell the insurance and pay claims; government reimburses insurers for losses not covered by premiums and investment income.
Terrorism Risk Insurance Program	• Designed to temporarily meet the unmet needs for a backstop to insured terrorism losses. • Serves the social purpose of preventing economic disruptions that market failures in terrorism coverage could have caused.	• Private insurers act as the primary insurer for terrorism coverages. • Federal government temporarily acts as reinsurer for terrorism coverage.
Federal Crop Insurance	• Provides crop insurance at affordable rates to reduce losses that result from unavoidable crop failures. • Covers most crops for perils such as drought, disease, insects, excess rain, and hail.	• Federal government subsidizes and reinsures private insurers; private insurers sell and service the federal crop insurance. • Private insurers also independently offer crop insurance for certain perils.

[DA02764]

This may explain why the federal government is involved with the NFIP and
Federal Crop Insurance. However, it would not explain why windstorm and
beach plans are state government-run insurance programs. Hurricanes often
cause damage in multiple states. Although hurricane risk is regional, the same
can be said for flood risk. In fact, when taking into account storm surge, hurricane risk and flood risk often go together. The first exhibit contains examples
of property-casualty insurance plans that involve the federal government,
and the second exhibit contains examples of property-casualty insurance
plans that involve state governments. See the exhibit "Examples of Property-
Causality Insurance Offered by State Governments."

Examples of Property-Causality Insurance Offered by State Governments

Plan	Characteristics of Government Plan	Relationship to Private Insurance
Fair Access to Insurance Requirements (FAIR) Plans	• Make basic property insurance available to property owners who are otherwise unable to obtain insurance because of their property's location or any other reason.	• Organization varies by state. Typically it is an insurance pool through which private insurers collectively address an unmet need for property insurance on urban properties. • Does not replace normal channels of insurance; is only for consumers who could not obtain coverage in the private market.
Workers Compensation Insurance	• Helps employers meet their obligations under state statutes to injured workers.	• Private insurers provide workers compensation insurance. • State government can operate as an exclusive insurer, as a competitor to private insurers, or as a residual market.
Beach and Windstorm Plans	• Make property insurance against the windstorm cause of loss available to property owners who are otherwise unable to obtain insurance because of their property's location.	• Organization varies by state: some states are insurance pools of private insurers; other states are ultimately guaranteed with taxpayer funds. • Does not replace normal channels of insurance; is only for consumers who could not obtain coverage in the private market.
Residual Auto Plans	• Make compulsory automobile liability coverage available to high-risk drivers who have difficulty purchasing coverage at a reasonable rate in the private market.	• Organization varies by state. Typically it is an insurance pool through which private insurers collectively address an unmet need for compulsory auto liability coverage. • Does not replace normal channels of insurance; is only for consumers who could not obtain coverage in the private market.

[DA02765]

SUMMARY

Pooling is an arrangement that facilitates the grouping of loss exposures and resources. Insurance works as a pooling mechanism to reduce risk (uncertainty) for individuals, organizations, and ultimately society.

The benefits of insurance include paying for losses, managing cash flow uncertainty, complying with the law, promoting risk control, allowing efficient use of the insured's resources, providing support for the insured's credit, providing a source of investment funds, and reducing social burdens.

The six characteristics of an ideally insurable loss exposure include these:

1. Pure risk—involves pure risk, not speculative risk

2. Fortuitous losses—subject to fortuitous loss from the insured's standpoint

3. Definite and measurable—subject to losses that are definite in time, cause, and location, and that are measurable

4. Large number of similar exposure units—one of a large number of similar exposure units

5. Independent and not catastrophic—not subject to a loss that would simultaneously affect many other similar loss exposures; loss would not be catastrophic

6. Affordable—premiums are economically feasible

Applying the six characteristics of an ideally insurable loss exposure can help an insurer to decide whether to insure commercial loss exposures that are under consideration.

Applying the six characteristics of an ideally insurable loss exposure can help an insurer to decide whether to insure personal loss exposures that are under consideration.

Government insurance programs may provide insurance coverage when insurers are unwilling or unable to insure loss exposures that do not exhibit ideally insurable characteristics. These government programs vary based on their purpose or rationale, the level of government involvement, and whether the program is run at the state or federal level.

ASSIGNMENT NOTE

1. Various liability policies cover their insureds against third-party claims for property damage, including resulting loss of use, which encompasses net income loss caused by damage to tangible property.

Direct Your Learning ▶▶

Insurance Policy Analysis

Educational Objectives

After learning the content of this assignment, you should be able to:

▷ Describe the following characteristics of insurance policies, including common exceptions to these characteristics:

- Indemnity
- Utmost good faith
- Fortuitous losses
- Contract of adhesion
- Exchange of unequal amounts
- Conditional
- Nontransferable

▷ Describe these approaches to insurance policy structure and how they can affect policy analysis:

- Self-contained and modular policies
- Preprinted and manuscript policies
- Standard and nonstandard forms
- Endorsements and other related documents

▷ Describe the purpose(s) and characteristics of each of these types of policy provisions in a property-casualty insurance policy:

- Declarations
- Definitions
- Insuring agreements
- Exclusions
- Conditions
- Miscellaneous provisions

▷ Describe the primary methods of insurance policy analysis.

Insurance Policy Analysis

DISTINGUISHING CHARACTERISTICS OF INSURANCE POLICIES

An insurance policy is a formal written contract by which an insurer provides protection if an insured suffers specified losses. Insurance policies display certain distinguishing characteristics not often found in other types of contracts. Some of the distinguishing characteristics that apply to insurance policies are also called insurance principles because they adhere to the economic theory behind the business of insurance. Understanding these characteristics assists insurance and risk management professionals in analyzing insurance policies.

The distinguishing characteristics of insurance policies are these:

- Indemnity
- Utmost good faith
- Fortuitous losses
- Contract of adhesion
- Exchange of unequal amounts
- Conditional
- Nontransferable

Although these characteristics are unique to insurance policies, not all insurance policies exhibit every one of these characteristics.

Indemnity

The goal of an insurance policy is to indemnify (make whole) the insured who has suffered a covered loss. An insurance policy adheres to the **principle of indemnity**; the policyholder should not profit from insurance. This adherence to the principle of indemnity means that an insurance policy is a **contract of indemnity**.

In practice, an insurance policy does not necessarily pay the full amount necessary to restore an insured who has suffered a covered loss. Most insurance policies contain a dollar limit, a deductible, or other provisions or limitations that result in the insured's being paid less than the entire loss amount. Furthermore, insurance policies do not always indemnify the insured for the inconvenience, time, and other nonfinancial expenses involved in recovering from an insured loss. The valuation method used to value the loss is also a

Principle of indemnity

The principle that insurance policies should provide a benefit no greater than the loss suffered by an insured.

Contract of indemnity

A contract in which the insurer agrees, in the event of a covered loss, to pay an amount directly related to the amount of the loss.

major factor in determining the level of indemnity the insured receives from the insurance policy.

Some insurance policies violate the principle of indemnity. For example, certain insurance policies are valued policies, not contracts of indemnity. Under the terms of a valued policy, the insurer agrees to pay a pre-established dollar amount in the event of an insured total loss. That dollar amount may be more or less than the value of the insured loss. For example, rare objects of art are often insured with a valued policy. If the artwork is destroyed, the policy pays the dollar value specified, regardless of the value of the artwork at the time of the loss.

Despite the fact that some policies do not adhere to the principle of indemnity, in order to reduce or avoid moral hazards, insurance policies should not do either of these:

• Overindemnify the insured
• Indemnify insureds more than once per loss

Insurance Should Not Overindemnify

Insureds should be compensated, but not overcompensated (overindemnified), for a loss. Ideally, the insured should be restored to approximately the same financial position that he or she was in before the loss. The principle of indemnity implies that an insured should not profit from an insured loss.

The potential for overindemnification can constitute a moral hazard. For example, a rundown building that is insured for more than its value might be a tempting arson target for an insured owner who could use the insurance money to build a better building on that site. Insurers can reduce moral hazard (and thereby reduce the potential for overindemnification) by clearly defining the extent of a covered loss in the policy provisions and by carefully setting policy limits.

Insureds Should Not Be Indemnified More Than Once per Loss

Ideally, a loss exposure should be the subject of only one insurance policy and only one portion of that insurance policy. Multiple sources of recovery (payment from many policies or more than one portion of the same policy) could result in the insured's overindemnification. To limit overindemnification, most property and liability insurance policies contain clauses called "other insurance provisions" that limit multiple sources of recovery.

However, sometimes duplicate recovery is both available and justifiable. For example, people can be insureds under more than one policy when they carry multiple policies, such as auto and health insurance. If an insured who has overlapping coverage has been charged an actuarially fair premium for the duplicate portion of coverage, it may be unfair for an insurer to deny coverage simply because the insured has more than one policy. In some instances, prohibiting duplicate recovery for an insured could unfairly absolve the responsible parties from bearing the financial consequences of the loss.

To illustrate, if a person (the plaintiff) sues another (the defendant) for injuries suffered as a result of the defendant's negligence and the court finds in favor of the plaintiff, it is not acceptable for the negligent party to avoid paying some or all of those damages because the plaintiff can also recover money under his or her own insurance policies. This is known as the **collateral source rule**.

Utmost Good Faith

An insurance policy is generally more vulnerable to abuses such as misrepresentation or opportunism than other contracts, for two reasons: information asymmetry and costly verification.

Information asymmetry exists when one party to a contract has information important to the contract that the other party does not. For example, a homeowner may know that an insured home is in a state of disrepair that makes a loss more likely. If the insurer does not know this, then information asymmetry exists.

To reduce information asymmetry, the insurer attempts to gather as much relevant information as possible during the underwriting process. For example, the insurer could conduct an inspection to verify the condition of the property. If the property is in disrepair, the insurer may charge a higher premium or require a higher deductible than it would have charged had the house been in good condition. However, verification of information is often time consuming and expensive (costly verification). The more difficult or more costly it is to verify information provided by the insured, the less likely it is that the insurer will expend the resources to verify information, and the information asymmetry will remain.

Information asymmetry can lead to adverse selection; that is, the insurer may improperly price insurance policies by charging a higher-risk insured a lower than actuarially fair premium. Similarly, it may lead to the insurer's issuing a policy on a loss exposure that it may not want to insure at all. Such situations can be prevented if all parties exercise the utmost good faith in the insurance transaction.

Utmost good faith is an obligation to act with complete honesty and to disclose all relevant facts. The characteristic of utmost good faith has its roots in early marine insurance transactions, when underwriters could not verify the condition of ships and their cargoes. Therefore, insurance policies became agreements founded in the utmost good faith that the statements made by both the insured and insurer could be relied upon as accurate fact. Although the principle of utmost good faith has been eroded somewhat by court deci-

Collateral source rule
A legal doctrine that provides that the damages owed to a victim should not be reduced because the victim is entitled to recover money from other sources, such as an insurance policy.

sions, the doctrines of misrepresentation, fraud, and concealment in insurance policies are based on utmost good faith.

The most common violations of the concept of utmost good faith in insurance policies involve fraud and/or buildup in insurance claims filed by insureds. Fraud is the misrepresentation of key facts of a claim, and buildup is the intentional inflation of an otherwise legitimate claim. For example, filing a claim for an auto accident that never occurred would be fraud. Overstating the extent of injuries suffered in a legitimate auto accident would be buildup.

Fortuitous Losses

Fortuitous losses are losses that happen accidentally or unexpectedly. For a loss to be fortuitous, reasonable uncertainty must exist about its probability or timing. For insurance purposes, the loss must be fortuitous from the insured's standpoint. For example, although robbery is an intentional act from the perpetrator's standpoint, it is a fortuitous loss from the victim's standpoint.

If an insured knows in advance that a loss will occur and the insurer does not, the insured has an information advantage over the insurer. This information asymmetry, if acted on by the insured (the insured purchases an insurance policy covering the known loss), promotes adverse selection, thereby changing the loss distribution in the pool the insurer insures. Therefore, the premium the insurer charges the pool is no longer actuarially fair, because the loss distribution on which the premium was based has changed. Underwriting is designed to minimize the effect that adverse selection can have on the insurer's loss distribution. One method of avoiding adverse selection is precluding coverage for losses that are not fortuitous.

Fortuitous losses are not necessarily covered by insurance. Many losses happen fortuitously but are not covered. For example, earthquake is a fortuitous cause of loss that is excluded by most property insurance policies.

Many finite risk insurance contracts cover losses that have occurred but have not been settled. In such cases, some uncertainty remains about the final settlement values. For example, an auto manufacturer may have recalled a model because of a faulty part that was responsible for fifty accidents that involved bodily injury and property damage. Although all the accidents have been reported, none of the claims have been settled. Both the auto manufacturer and insurer would have an estimate of the ultimate claims settlement amounts; however, there is still some uncertainty regarding both the timing and the amount of the settlements. The insurer may be willing to provide liability insurance coverage to the auto manufacturer for these fifty accidents after the fact for a very high premium because the insurer believes that it will be able to negotiate settlements that would make the transaction profitable.

Contract of Adhesion

The amount of negotiation required to formulate a contract varies widely. Some contracts are the result of extensive negotiation between parties, in which every clause is discussed before agreement is reached. Other contracts involve little or no negotiation. Between these two extremes are contracts that contain some standard clauses, leaving the remainder of the contract to be negotiated.

Insurance policies typically involve little or no negotiation (except for unique loss exposures that require special underwriting consideration, such as a highly valued property). An insurer generally chooses the exact wording in the policies it offers (or uses the wording developed by an insurance advisory organization), and the insured generally has little choice but to accept it.

A basic insurance policy might be altered by endorsements, but the insurer or advisory organization also typically develops these endorsements. Consequently, a party who wants to purchase an insurance policy usually has to accept and adhere to the standard policy forms the insurer or advisory organization drafts. The typical insurance policy is, therefore, a **contract of adhesion**.

Courts have ruled that any ambiguities or uncertainties in contracts are to be construed against the party who drafted the agreement because that party had the opportunity to express its intent clearly and unequivocally in the agreement. Therefore, unless the insured drafted the policy (which is rare), ambiguities in an insurance policy are interpreted in the insured's favor. The insurer has a good-faith obligation to draft a policy that clearly expresses what it intends to cover. Any policy provision that can reasonably be interpreted more than one way can be considered ambiguous.

Standard insurance policies are sometimes constructed with acceptable ambiguities. If an insurance policy can be interpreted in two different ways and the insurer is satisfied with either interpretation, no expansion of the policy is necessary to make it more precise.

An important consideration affecting the interpretation of a contract's ambiguity is the level of sophistication of the parties to the contract. In cases concerning insurance policies, the level of sophistication of the insured has had these effects on court decisions:

- Unsophisticated insured—Usually, the insurer has drafted a ready-made policy, and the insured has little or no control over the policy's wording. This is true of most homeowners and personal auto insurance policies. Ambiguities in these cases are typically interpreted against the insurer. This is the case for most personal insurance consumers.

- Sophisticated insured—In a minority of cases, the insured (or its representatives) drafts all or part of the insurance policy. Alternatively, the insurer and a sophisticated insured negotiate the policy wording. In these cases, the contract of adhesion doctrine may not apply. Courts do not necessar-

Contract of adhesion
Any contract in which one party must either accept the agreement as written by the other party or reject it.

ily interpret any ambiguity in the insured's favor if the insured had some understanding and ability to alter the policy wording before entering the agreement. Sophisticated insureds include many medium to large organizations with dedicated risk management functions.

The courts consider several factors when determining whether an insured can be considered sophisticated. These factors include the size of the insured organization, the size of the insured organization's risk management department, use of an insurance broker or legal counsel with expertise in insurance policies, and the relative bargaining power of the insured in relation to the insurer.

The most common examples of insurance policies that are not contracts of adhesion are manuscript policies or policies that contain manuscript forms. When the insured contributes to the precise wording of the contract, courts generally do not apply the standards that are common under contracts of adhesion.

Reasonable expectations doctrine
A legal doctrine that provides for an ambiguous insurance policy clause to be interpreted in the way that an insured would reasonably expect.

An extension of the contract of adhesion doctrine is the **reasonable expectations doctrine**, which is a legal doctrine that provides for an ambiguous insurance policy clause to be interpreted in the way that an insured would reasonably expect. For example, the reasonable expectations doctrine is sometimes applied to the renewal of insurance policies that contain a change from the original policy. Unless an oral or a written notification and explanation accompanies the renewal policy, the insured can reasonably expect that the renewal policy is the same as the expiring policy.

The reasonable expectations doctrine is an important extension of the contract of adhesion doctrine because it accounts for the fact that most insureds are not practiced in policy interpretation. However, insureds should not rely on the reasonable expectations doctrine because not all courts recognize it.

Exchange of Unequal Amounts

Consideration
Something of value or bargained for and exchanged by the parties to a contract.

Consideration is an element of any enforceable contract. For insurance policies, the consideration offered by the insured is the premium; the consideration offered by the insurer is the promise to indemnify the insured in the event of a covered loss. There is no requirement that the amounts exchanged be equal in value. In most insurance policies, the tangible amounts exchanged, the premium from the insured, and any payments made by the insurer, will be unequal.

For example, consider an insurer that charges a $1,500 premium to insure a property valued at $500,000. An infinite number of potential losses could occur. However, the potential losses fall into the following four categories:

- The insured does not suffer a loss during the policy period. The insured paid the $1,500 premium, and the insurer pays nothing to the insured.

- The insured suffers losses of less than $1,500 during the policy period. The insured pays the $1,500 premium and the insurer reimburses the insured for the loss amount (ignoring any deductible).

- The insured suffers losses exactly equal to $1,500 during the policy period.

- The insured suffers losses of more than $1,500 during the policy period.

It is impossible to predict which of the four possible situations will occur, but it is highly unlikely that the tangible amounts exchanged between the insurer and insured will be equal. The four situations consider only the exchange of tangible values—the premium paid by the insured and the recovery of losses paid by the insurer (if any)—not the intangible value of the insurance promise.

It is difficult to explicitly value the reduction in volatility of losses and the reduction in the maximum amount at risk that insurance policies provide for an insured because they vary based on the insured's level of risk aversion. However, when both the tangible and intangible values are jointly considered, the values exchanged between the insurer and the insured are closer in value.

Although the tangible values exchanged between an insurer and insured may not be equal, in general they are equitable—that is, the premium the insurer charges the insured is directly proportional to the insured's expected losses on an actuarially sound basis. This is often called the equitable distribution of risk costs. That is, the insured's premium should be commensurate with the risk it presents to the insurer. By charging the appropriate premium, the insurer can ensure that the tangible consideration offered by the insured is equitable compared with the intangible consideration offered by the insurer.

Finite risk insurance policies involve an exchange of amounts closer in value than other types of policies, because their premiums are often close to the present value of the limit stated on the policy. Finite risk insurance involves little or no actual risk transfer and often functions as a loan.

Conditional

Insurance policies are **conditional contracts** because the insurer is obligated to pay for losses incurred by the insured only if the insured has fulfilled all of the policy conditions. For example, under a property insurance policy, an insured must allow the insurer to inspect the damaged property after a covered cause of loss, such as a fire. The insurer is not obligated to fulfill the insurance policy (pay for any covered losses) unless the insured meets this condition. If the

Conditional contract

A contract that one or more parties must perform only under certain conditions.

property is not available for inspection, the insurer has the right to deny the claim because the insurer was unable to verify that the loss actually occurred.

The most common exception to "the conditional nature of an insurance policy" occurs when the insurer is willing to waive some of the conditions of the insurance policy. This often occurs in practice. For example, an insurer may be willing to pay a claim without making an inspection, thereby waiving the condition that the insured make damaged property available for inspection.

Nontransferable

Insurance policies are sometimes referred to as "personal contracts" to indicate their nontransferable or nonassignable nature. An insurance policy is a contract between two parties; most property and liability policies contain a condition stating that the insured cannot assign (transfer) the policy to a third party without the insurer's written consent. For example, although property, such as a residence or a business, can be sold to a third party, the insurance policy that covers the property cannot be sold with it unless the insurer approves the transfer in writing.

Insurers sometimes transfer policies to other insurers. Insureds are notified of the transfer or assignment, but their written approval is not required. For example, if an insurer wants to exit from a line of business or geographic area, the insurer can sell its entire portfolio for that business or area to another insurer. Alternatively, an insurer can transfer all of its business if it is acquired by another insurer, or a state regulator can assign insurance policies from an insolvent insurer to other insurers that are licensed in that state.

Insurance policies typically do not contain any condition prohibiting the insurer from transferring or assigning the policy to a third party without the insured's written consent. If insureds are not receptive to the transfer or assignment by the insurer, they essentially have two choices. First, they may cancel their policies and purchase policies from other insurers. Second, they may pursue claims through the courts based on the notion that the consideration offered by the transferee (new insurer) is lower than the consideration offered by the transferor (original insurer).

In essence, the insured would be claiming that the transferee's claim-paying ability is not equal to the transferor's. However, typically the consideration offered by the new insurer is equal to or greater than that of the original insured, improving the insured's position. When a policy is transferred from an insolvent insurer, insureds' coverage is more secure.

Some policies contain exceptions to the usual assignment condition in order to help insureds manage situations that arise in normal commercial operations. For example, ocean marine hull insurance policies typically contain a change of ownership clause, which states that the policy will terminate automatically with a change in the insured vessel's ownership. However, this clause usually has an exception stating that the policy does not terminate if a change in ownership occurs while the insured vessel is at sea.

For example, a vessel is transporting cargo across the Atlantic Ocean when its owner sells the vessel to another company. The hull policy covering the vessel would remain in force for the new owner without the written consent of the insurer. This exception to the change of ownership clause is designed to ensure that coverage remains in force, given that the change in ownership would have little or no effect on the risk of loss to the insured vessel while at sea. Once the vessel reaches the final port of discharge, the hull policy will automatically terminate, and the new owner must obtain its own insurance on the vessel.

STRUCTURE OF INSURANCE POLICIES

Understanding the various ways in which insurance policies can be structured helps insurance and risk management professionals analyze and interpret any particular policy.

The structure of an insurance policy can be either self-contained or modular. The form or forms used to make up a policy can be either preprinted or manuscript, and either standard or nonstandard. In addition to forms, related documents of various types can be incorporated in a policy.

Self-Contained and Modular Policies

The basic structure of every property-casualty insurance policy can be classified as either self-contained or modular.

A **self-contained policy** contains, within one document, all the provisions needed to make up a complete insurance policy. Endorsements can be added to a self-contained policy to provide additional, optional coverages or to exclude unnecessary coverages. An endorsement is a document that amends an insurance policy.

Self-contained policy
A single document that contains all the agreements between the insured and the insurer and that forms a complete insurance policy.

A self-contained policy is appropriate for insuring loss exposures that are similar among many insureds. For example, private passenger auto insurance is typically provided in a self-contained policy (such as the ISO Personal Auto Policy). Such a policy is used for each of an insurer's individual auto policyholders throughout a state—and potentially in several different states. Endorsements, such as the Towing and Labor Costs Coverage endorsement or the Customizing Equipment Coverage endorsement, can be added as needed.

A self-contained policy can be either a **monoline policy** or a **package policy**. An example of a self-contained monoline policy is an insurance agent's errors and omissions liability policy. An example of a self-contained package policy is a homeowners policy, which provides both property and liability coverages.

Monoline policy
Policy that covers only one line of business.

Package policy
Policy that covers two or more lines of business.

Modular policy

An insurance policy that consists of several different documents, none of which by itself forms a complete policy.

A **modular policy** is created by combining a set of individual components, such as one or more coverage forms, one or more causes of loss forms, and one or more conditions forms. The modular approach is often used in commercial insurance because the insured's loss exposures are typically unique and require more customization of the insurance policy than is the case with other lines of insurance.

A modular policy can be either a monoline policy or a package policy. An example of a modular monoline policy is a commercial property policy that consists of a commercial property coverage form, a causes of loss form, a commercial property conditions form, and a common policy conditions form. An example of a modular package policy is a commercial package policy that consists of multiple forms for providing commercial property coverage, commercial general liability coverage, commercial auto coverage, and commercial crime coverage.

The insured has the option of purchasing multiple standalone policies or a single package policy to cover the same loss exposures. However, relative to self-contained policies, modular policies have these advantages:

- Carefully designed and coordinated provisions in the various forms minimize the possibility of gaps and overlaps that might exist when several monoline policies are used.
- Consistent terminology, definitions, and policy language make coverage interpretation easier for the insured.
- Fewer forms are required to meet a wide range of needs.
- Underwriting is simplified because much of the basic information that must be analyzed applies to all lines of insurance.
- Adverse selection problems can be reduced when the same insurer provides several lines of insurance for an individual insured.
- Insurers often give a package discount when several coverages are included in the same policy.

Minimal coverage gaps, consistent terminology, and fewer forms are important advantages to insurance and risk management professionals conducting policy analysis. Analyzing multiple self-contained policies is usually more difficult than analyzing a modular policy.

Multiple self-contained policies will often use inconsistent terminology and have gaps and overlaps in coverage, making policy analysis more difficult. Well-coordinated modular policies typically offer a better framework for policy analysis than multiple self-contained policies.

Preprinted and Manuscript Forms

The forms used to make up insurance policies can be classified as either preprinted forms or manuscript forms.

Most insurance policies are assembled from one or more preprinted forms and endorsements. Preprinted forms are developed for use with many different insureds. Therefore, they refer to the insured in general terms (such as "the insured" or "you") so that the forms can be used in multiple insurance policies without customization. The declarations page then adds the specific information about the insured that customizes the insurance policy.

Using preprinted forms significantly reduces the paperwork necessary for an insurance policy. When the policy is issued, insurers send the insured the generic preprinted policy and the customized declarations page. The declarations page indicates the form number or numbers and edition dates of the insurer's form or forms that apply to the insurance policy. When insureds update (for example, change deductibles) or renew their policies, the insurer can simply send the insureds new declarations pages without having to resend entire new policies containing copies of the preprinted forms (provided the preprinted forms have not been changed).

Furthermore, if they are using preprinted forms, the insurer and its producer do not have to keep a complete duplicate of each insured's entire policy in their files. All that needs to be filed is the declarations page, either on paper or as an electronic file. Details of specific coverage can be obtained by examining copies of the preprinted forms referenced in the declarations page. See the exhibit "Preprinted Forms as Electronic Forms."

Preprinted Forms as Electronic Forms

Although they are still referred to as preprinted forms in the insurance industry, printing technology has reduced the need for producers and insurers to maintain a supply of actual preprinted forms. Producers and insurers can now quickly print the electronic copies of all the forms and endorsements as needed.

[DA05792]

Preprinted forms typically are interpreted as contracts of adhesion. The wording of preprinted forms and endorsements is carefully chosen by the insurer (or developed by an advisory organization and then adopted by the insurer). Courts tend to interpret any ambiguities in policy language in favor of the insured, because the insured did not have an opportunity to choose the policy wording.

In contrast to preprinted forms, **manuscript forms** are custom forms developed for one specific insured—or for a small group of insureds—with unique coverage needs.

If an insurance policy includes a manuscript form, it is often referred to as a manuscript policy. A manuscript form can be specifically drafted or selected to cover a unique loss exposure or to customize regular coverage to meet an insured's particular specifications.

Manuscript form

An insurance form that is drafted according to terms negotiated between a specific insured (or group of insureds) and an insurer.

Because the insurer and the insured develop policy language together, manuscript policies are not generally considered to be contracts of adhesion. Therefore, courts do not automatically interpret ambiguous policy provisions in the insured's favor. Manuscript forms are the most difficult to interpret during policy analysis. These forms, because they often contain unique wording, can vary widely in their interpretation.

Manuscript forms do not have the same history of court interpretations for insurance and risk management professionals to rely on during policy analysis. This fact can lead to differences between how an insurance or a risk management professional interprets a manuscript form and how the insured or courts will interpret the same form. Consequently, substantial delays in claim adjusting or strained relations between the insurer and insured can occur. To reduce the likelihood of such problems, most manuscript forms are not individually composed but are adapted from wording previously developed and used in standard forms or other insurance policies.

Standard and Nonstandard Forms

An insurer may use the standard forms that are also used by other insurers, or it may develop its own nonstandard forms. A nonstandard form drafted or adapted by one insurer is sometimes called a company-specific or proprietary form.

Insurance service and advisory organizations, such as Insurance Services Office, Inc. (ISO) and the American Association of Insurance Services (AAIS), have developed standard insurance forms for use by individual insurers. These standard forms are accompanied by portfolios of coordinated endorsements that apply necessary state variations or customize coverage. Because they are widely used, standard forms provide benchmarks against which nonstandard forms can be evaluated.

Standard forms are typically easier than nonstandard forms for insurance and risk management professionals to evaluate during policy analysis. Standard forms are widely used and usually have been more consistently interpreted by the courts than other forms. Furthermore, most professionals have more experience working with standard forms than with nonstandard forms.

Many insurers have developed their own company-specific preprinted forms, especially for high-volume lines of insurance (such as auto or homeowners) or for coverages in which the insurer specializes (such as recreational vehicle insurance). Other insurers use manuscript forms to provide nonstandard policy wordings for either individual customers or small groups of customers. By their very nature, all manuscript forms are nonstandard forms. Nonstandard forms (whether preprinted or manuscript) include provisions that vary from standard-form provisions and often contain coverage enhancements not found in standard forms.

Similar to preprinted standard forms, preprinted nonstandard forms are typically easier than manuscript forms for insurance or risk management professionals to evaluate during policy analysis. Although these preprinted forms are referred to as nonstandard, many of them are widely used by some of the largest insurers.

Endorsements and Other Related Documents

Documents other than insurance forms can become part of an insurance policy, either by being physically attached to or by being referenced within the policy. Subject to statutory and regulatory constraints, an insurance policy may incorporate a wide range of documents in addition to policy forms. Examples include endorsements, the completed insurance application, and various other documents.

Endorsements, if added to the policy, form part of the policy. An endorsement may be a preprinted, computer-printed, typewritten, or handwritten line, sentence, paragraph, or set of paragraphs on one or more pages attached to the policy. In rare cases, an endorsement may take the form of a handwritten note in the margin of the policy and be dated and initialed by an insured and the insurer's authorized representative.

Because endorsements are usually intended to modify a basic policy form, the endorsement provisions often differ from basic policy provisions. This difference can lead to questions of policy interpretation. These two general rules of policy interpretation apply to endorsements:

- An endorsement takes precedence over any conflicting terms in the policy to which it is attached.
- A handwritten endorsement supersedes a computer-printed or typewritten one. Handwritten alterations tend to reflect true intent more accurately than do preprinted policy terms.

In several lines of business, policies are issued with what many practitioners call "standard" endorsements included in the policy. These are endorsements that are included with most of the policies written in that line. Because they are so common, they essentially become part of the basic policy form. In addition, certain states require state-specific endorsements to be included with every policy sold in that state. This results in most policies' having multiple endorsements attached.

An insurance application is the documented request for coverage, whether given orally, in writing, or electronically (over the Internet). The application contains information about the insured and the loss exposures presented to the insurer. Underwriters use the information provided on the application to decide whether to provide the requested insurance and, if so, to price the policy. Although the declarations page often contains much of the same information as the application, the insurer usually keeps the completed application to preserve the representations made by the insured. The application can be used, if necessary, to provide evidence of misleading or false material information supplied by the insured. In some jurisdictions, statutes explicitly require that any written application be made part of the policy for certain lines of insurance.

In certain circumstances, the insurer's bylaws are incorporated into an insurance policy. For example, the policyholders of mutual and reciprocal insurers typically have some rights and duties associated with managing the insurer's operations, and these rights and duties are specified in the policy.

Insurance policies sometimes incorporate the insurer's rating manual (or the insurer's rules and rates, whether found in the manual or elsewhere) by referring to it in the policy language. Although the rules and rates themselves do not appear in the policy, reference to them makes them part of the policy.

Other documents incorporated in insurance policies include premium notes (promissory notes that are accepted by the insurer in lieu of a cash premium payment), inspection reports, and specification sheets or operating manuals relating to safety equipment or procedures. If, for example, an insurer and an applicant agree that the coverage provided by a particular property or liability insurance policy is conditional on the use of certain procedures or safety equipment, then a set of operating instructions or a manual of specifications can be incorporated into the policy by reference and then used to define the agreed-upon procedures or equipment.

Any of these related documents can alter the forms that are included in a policy. Therefore, related documents make policy analysis more difficult for insurance professionals because they add to the volume and complexity of forms that must be evaluated. As the number of related documents grows, so does the likelihood that one or more of the documents may contradict, exclude, or expand provisions in the basic forms.

POLICY PROVISIONS

Every insurance policy is composed of numerous policy provisions. A policy provision is a contractual term included in an insurance policy that specifies requirements or clarifies intended meaning. Despite wide variation in property-casualty insurance policy provisions, each provision can typically be placed into one of six categories, depending on the purpose it serves. Comprehending the purpose(s) and characteristics of each of these categories of policy provisions assists insurance and risk management professionals in analyzing and interpreting insurance policies.

The exhibit lists the six categories of policy provisions, briefly describes each category, and summarizes the effect that policy provisions in each category may have on coverage. Each of the policy provisions must be examined during policy analysis to determine its exact effect on coverage. See the exhibit "Property-Casualty Insurance Policy Provisions."

Property-Casualty Insurance Policy Provisions

Policy Provision Category	Description	Effect on Coverage
Declarations	Unique information on the insured; list of forms included in policy	Outline who or what is covered, and where and when coverage applies
Definitions	Words with special meanings in policy	May limit or expand coverage based on definitions of terms
Insuring Agreements	Promise to make payment	Outline circumstances under which the insurer agrees to pay
Conditions	Qualifications on promise to make payment	Outline steps insured needs to take to enforce policy
Exclusions	Limitations on promise to make payment	Limit insurer's payments based on excluded persons, places, things, or actions
Miscellaneous Provisions	Wide variety of provisions that may alter policy	Deal with the relationship between the insured and the insurer or establish procedures for implementing the policy

[DA03052]

Declarations

Insurance policy declarations typically contain not only the standard information that has been "declared" by both the insured and the insurer but also information unique to the particular policy. The declarations (commonly referred to as the **declarations page**, or simply dec page) may be only one page or several pages in length and typically appear in the front of an insurance policy. The declarations state important facts about the particular policy, such as these:

- Policy or policy number
- Policy inception and expiration dates (policy period)
- Name of the insurer
- Name of the insurance agent
- Name of the insured(s)
- Names of persons or organizations whose additional interests are covered (for example, a mortgagee, a loss payee, or an additional insured)
- Mailing address of the insured
- Physical address and description of the covered property or operations
- Numbers and edition dates of all attached forms and endorsements
- Dollar amounts of applicable policy limits
- Dollar amounts of applicable deductibles
- Rating information and the policy premium

Declarations page (declarations, or dec.)

An insurance policy information page or pages providing specific details about the insured and the subject of the insurance.

Sometimes endorsements also contain information similar to that contained in the declarations. For example, an endorsement to a homeowners policy may contain a "schedule" listing descriptions and limits of coverage for valuable pieces of personal property that need special insurance treatment.

Definitions

Most insurance policies or forms include a section that contains definitions of certain terms used throughout the entire policy or form. Boldface type or quotation marks are typically used in the body of the policy to distinguish words and phrases that are defined in the definitions section.

Many of the definitions that appear in insurance policies are there because of real or perceived ambiguity that has arisen regarding the use of those terms in previous policies.

Most insurance policies refer to the insurer as "we" and the named insured as "you." These and other related pronouns, such as "us," "our," and "your," are often defined in an untitled preamble to the policy rather than in a definitions section.

Words and phrases defined within an insurance policy are interpreted according to their definitions in the policy. Undefined words and phrases are interpreted according to these rules of policy interpretation:

- Everyday words are given their ordinary meanings.
- Technical words are given their technical meanings.
- Words with an established legal meaning are given their legal meanings.
- Consideration is also given to the local, cultural, and trade-usage meanings of words, if applicable.

Insuring Agreements

Insuring agreement

A statement in an insurance policy that the insurer will, under described circumstances, make a loss payment or provide a service.

Following the declarations, and possibly preceded by a section containing definitions, the body of most insurance policies begins with an **insuring agreement**.

Policies typically contain an insuring agreement for each coverage they provide. Consequently, package policies contain multiple insuring agreements. For example, the Personal Auto Policy of Insurance Services Office, Inc. (ISO) contains a separate insuring agreement for each of these four parts of the policy:

- Part A—Liability Coverage
- Part B—Medical Payments Coverage
- Part C—Uninsured Motorists Coverage
- Part D—Coverage for Damage to Your Auto

The term "insuring agreement" is usually applied to statements that introduce a policy's coverage section. However, "insuring agreement" can also be used to describe statements introducing coverage extensions, additional coverages, supplementary payments, and so on.

Insuring agreements can be classified into two broad categories: comprehensive and limited. Whether comprehensive or limited, insuring agreements state the insurer's obligations in relatively broad terms. The full scope of coverage cannot be determined without examining the rest of the policy because the insurer's obligations are clarified or modified by other policy provisions.

Comprehensive insuring agreements provide an extremely broad grant of unrestricted coverage that is both clarified and narrowed by exclusions, definitions, and other policy provisions.

In commercial property insurance, a comprehensive insuring agreement is called special-form coverage (or open perils coverage), and a limited insuring agreement is called either basic-form or broad-form coverage (or named perils coverage).

The special-form coverage provides protection against causes of loss that are not specifically excluded. This comprehensive approach covers all the named causes of loss included in the basic- or broad-form coverage, as well as additional causes of loss that are not otherwise excluded.

Limited insuring agreements restrict coverage to certain causes of loss or to certain situations. Exclusions, definitions, and other policy provisions serve to clarify and narrow coverage but may also broaden the coverage.

The limited insuring agreements in commercial property insurance are the named perils, specified perils, or specified causes of loss coverage, referred to as the basic-form or broad-form coverages. The basic-form coverage protects against a list of named causes of loss, and the broad-form coverage protects against the named causes of loss in the basic form plus some additional named causes of loss.

In liability insurance, a limited or single-purpose insuring agreement (which uses specific policy language to define the policy terms) applies to a limited number of incidents. In contrast, comprehensive liability insuring agreements are much broader and do not limit coverage to a particular location, operation, or activity. Additional policy provisions, such as exclusions, limit the coverage of these policies.

Many insurance policies include secondary or supplemental coverages in addition to the main coverage in the insuring agreement. These coverages are described by terms such as "coverage extensions," "additional coverages," or "supplementary payments." The terms "coverage extensions" and "additional coverages" are often used in property coverages. "Supplementary payments" clarify the extent of coverage for certain expenses in liability insurance. The provisions that express these secondary or supplemental coverages are considered insuring agreements.

Exclusions

Exclusion

A policy provision that eliminates coverage for specified exposures.

Exclusions state what the insurer does not intend to cover. The word "intend" here is important; the primary function of exclusions is not only to limit coverage but also to clarify the coverages granted by the insurer. Specifying what the insurer does not intend to cover is a way of clarifying what aspects the insurer does intend to cover. An exclusion can serve one or more of six basic purposes:

• Eliminate coverage for uninsurable loss exposures

• Assist in managing moral and morale hazards

• Reduce likelihood of coverage duplications

• Eliminate coverages not needed by the typical insured

• Eliminate coverages requiring special treatment

• Assist in keeping premiums reasonable

Eliminate Coverage for Uninsurable Loss Exposures

Some loss exposures possess few, if any, of the ideal characteristics of an insurable loss exposure. The first purpose of exclusions is to eliminate coverage for loss exposures that are considered uninsurable by private insurers. For example, most property and liability insurance policies exclude coverage for loss exposures relating to war. (The main exception is the "war risks coverage" often available in ocean marine insurance policies covering vessels or cargoes, even those that might pass through war zones. Insurers charge appropriately higher rates for such coverage.)

In addition to war, examples of loss exposures that most private insurers consider to be uninsurable, and therefore widely exclude, are criminal acts committed by the insured and normal wear and tear of property. Each of these excluded loss exposures is lacking one or more of the characteristics of an ideally insurable loss exposure. For example, war involves an incalculable catastrophe potential, and the other examples involve losses that are not fortuitous from the insured's standpoint.

Assist in Managing Moral and Morale Hazards

The second purpose of exclusions is to assist in managing moral and morale hazards. Both moral and morale hazards can cause individuals and organizations to behave differently when they are insured because they do not have to assume the entire cost of a loss.

Exclusions help insurers minimize these hazards because they ensure that the individual or organization remains responsible for certain types of loss. For example, to manage moral hazards, the property section of the ISO Homeowners 3—Special Form excludes "any loss arising out of any act an 'insured' commits or conspires to commit with the intent to cause a loss."[1]

This exclusion reduces moral hazard incentives by eliminating coverage for intentional loss caused by an insured.

Some exclusions assist in managing morale hazards by making insureds themselves bear the losses that result from their own carelessness. For example, the Neglect exclusion in ISO homeowners forms eliminates coverage for property loss caused by "neglect of an 'insured' to use all reasonable means to save and preserve property at and after the time of a loss."[2]

Reduce Likelihood of Coverage Duplications

The third purpose of exclusions is to reduce the likelihood of coverage duplications. Having two insurance policies covering the same loss is usually unnecessary and inefficient. It is unnecessary because coverage under one policy is all that is needed to indemnify the insured (unless policy restrictions or limits of insurance preclude full recovery).

It is inefficient because, at least in theory, each policy providing coverage for certain types of losses includes a related premium charge. Therefore, an insured with duplicated coverage is paying higher premiums than is necessary. Exclusions ensure that multiple policies can work together to provide complementary, not duplicate, coverage and that insureds are not paying duplicate premiums.

For example, assume Karim has both a personal auto policy and a homeowners policy. If Karim leaves his laptop computer in his car and the car is stolen, he can submit a claim for the laptop under his homeowners insurance. Therefore, the loss of the laptop does not need to be covered under his personal auto policy. If it were covered under his auto policy, Karim would likely be paying more than necessary for his auto insurance. Excluding the laptop under the auto insurance avoids duplication of coverage.

Eliminate Coverages Not Needed by the Typical Insured

The fourth purpose of exclusions is to eliminate coverages that are not needed by the typical purchaser of a given line of insurance. Elimination of such coverages avoids the situation of all insureds having to share the costs of covering loss exposures that relatively few insureds have.

For example, the typical auto owner or homeowner does not own or operate private aircraft or rent portions of the family home for storage of others' business property. Therefore, homeowners policies typically exclude coverage for such loss exposures. People who do have these loss exposures may be able to obtain coverage separately through endorsements to their policies (for an additional premium) or by purchasing separate insurance policies.

Insurers are not always permitted to exclude coverage for loss exposures not faced by the typical insurance purchaser. For example, insurers may want to exclude auto liability coverage for drivers who have accidents while driving under the influence of alcohol. However, state insurance regulators are unlikely to approve such an exclusion because it tends to eliminate a source of recovery for the victims of drunken drivers. The effect is that auto policyholders who never drink and drive are required to share the costs of accidents caused by those who do.

Eliminate Coverages Requiring Special Treatment

The fifth purpose of exclusions is to eliminate coverages requiring special treatment. Such special treatment may entail underwriting, risk control, or reinsurance that is substantially different from what is normally required for the policy containing the exclusion. For example, commercial general liability policies issued to professionals are usually endorsed to exclude their professional liability loss exposures. These insureds can purchase separate professional liability insurance to cover claims alleging that they made errors or omissions in providing their professional services.

Assist in Keeping Premiums Reasonable

The sixth purpose of exclusions is to assist in keeping premiums at a level that a sufficiently large number of insurance buyers will consider reasonable. All exclusions serve this purpose to some extent. However, for some exclusions it is the primary or sole purpose, whereas for others it is simply one of the effects.

Excluded losses are not necessarily uninsurable. In many cases, few people are willing to pay the premiums necessary to include coverage for losses that ordinarily are excluded. For example, auto physical damage coverage typically excludes loss due and confined to mechanical breakdown or road damage to tires. These loss exposures are not uninsurable. In fact, many auto dealers, tire shops, and various other organizations offer insurance-like service warranties covering such loss exposures.

An insurance policy could probably be priced to reflect the expected costs of mechanical breakdowns or tire losses, but the insured would be paying the projected costs of maintenance plus the insurer's expenses in administering insurance to cover the maintenance costs. The additional premium might exceed the typical costs associated with these losses.

Conditions

Policy condition

Any provision that qualifies an otherwise enforceable promise made in the policy.

Some **policy conditions** are found in a section of the policy titled "Conditions," while others are found in other sections of the forms, endorsements, or other documents that constitute the policy. For example, a standard homeowners insurance policy has three major sections in which conditions are listed: Section I Conditions, Section II Conditions, and Sections I and II Conditions.

In a policy's insuring agreement, the insurer promises to pay to the insured, to pay on behalf of the insured, to defend the insured, and/or to provide various additional services. However, the insurer's promises are enforceable only if an insured event occurs and only if the insured has fulfilled its contractual duties as specified in the policy conditions.

Examples of policy conditions include the insured's obligation to pay premiums, report losses promptly, provide appropriate documentation for losses, cooperate with the insurer in any legal proceedings, and refrain from jeopardizing an insurer's rights to recover from third parties responsible for causing covered losses. If the insured does not comply with these conditions, then the insurer may be released from any obligation to perform some or all of its otherwise enforceable promises.

Miscellaneous Provisions

In addition to declarations, definitions, insuring agreements, exclusions, and conditions, insurance policies often contain miscellaneous provisions that deal with the relationship between the insured and the insurer or help to establish working procedures for implementing the policy. However, such provisions do not have the force of conditions. Consequently, even if the insured does not follow the procedures specified in the miscellaneous provisions, the insurer may still be required to fulfill its contractual promises.

Miscellaneous provisions often are unique to particular types of insurers, as in these examples:

- A policy issued by a mutual insurer is likely to describe each insured's right to vote in the election of the board of directors.
- A policy issued by a reciprocal insurer is likely to specify the attorney-in-fact's authority to implement its powers on the insured's behalf.

POLICY ANALYSIS

Each pre-loss question posed or post-loss claim filed by an insured is a unique situation that may require a review of policy provisions.

Insurance professionals should conduct pre-loss policy analysis to prepare themselves to answer an insured's coverage questions and to ensure that the policy being sold is appropriate for the insured's loss exposures. Insureds should conduct pre-loss policy analysis to verify that the policy they're purchasing adequately addresses their loss exposures. After a loss, the insurer must analyze the policy to determine whether it covers the loss and, if necessary, the extent of coverage the policy provides.

Pre-Loss Policy Analysis

Pre-loss policy analysis almost exclusively relies on scenario analysis to determine the extent of coverage (if any) the policy provides for the losses generated by a given scenario. For insureds, the primary source of information for generating scenarios for analysis is their past loss experience. Particularly if the insured has never suffered a loss that triggered insurance coverage, friends, neighbors, co-workers, and family members can also provide information about their experiences with losses and the claim process. Such information can help an insured formulate scenarios for pre-loss policy analysis.

Another source of information for the insured's scenario analysis is the insurance producer or customer service representative consulted in the insurance transaction. Such insurance professionals need to be able to accurately interpret coverage questions raised. Producers may have specialized knowledge of the loss exposures covered under the policy. They also understand the alternative ways insurance policies may describe the same coverage and may be aware of any policy provisions that depart from customary wording. For example, homeowners who have read news articles about toxic mold may consult their insurance producers to determine whether their homeowners insurance policy covers mold, fungus, or wet rot.

One of the limitations of scenario analysis is that, because the number of possible loss scenarios is theoretically infinite, it is impossible to account for every possibility. For example, most insurance professionals or insureds would not have envisioned the terrorist attacks of September 11, 2001. Alternatively, the insured or insurance professional may recognize the possibility of an event but underestimate the extent of potential loss. For example, the damage Hurricane Andrew caused in 1992 was unprecedented, as was the extent of flooding New Orleans experienced following Hurricane Katrina in 2005. These events prompted insurers to fundamentally change the methods used to evaluate these types of risks.

Post-Loss Policy Analysis

When an insured reports a loss, the insurer must determine whether the loss triggers coverage and, if so, the extent of that coverage. The primary method of post-loss policy analysis is the DICE (an acronym representing the policy provision categories: declarations, insuring agreements, conditions, and exclusions) method, which is a systematic review of all the categories of property-casualty policy provisions. See the exhibit "DICE Decision Tree."

The DICE method entails following four steps to determine whether a policy provides coverage. The first step is an examination of the declarations page to determine whether the information provided by the insured precludes coverage. For example, an insured may report to the property insurer that a fire occurred at the insured premises on May 5. The declarations page contains both the policy inception and expiration dates (delineating the policy period). If the policy period ended on April 30, then the policy would not provide coverage for this loss.

If nothing in the declarations precludes coverage, the insurance professional would move to the second step in the DICE method, an analysis of the insuring agreement. For example, in the homeowners policy, the insurer agrees to provide coverage in exchange for the insured's payment of the premium.

DICE Decision Tree

To determine whether a policy covers a loss, many insurance professionals apply the DICE method. ("DICE" is an acronym for categories of policy provisions: declarations, insuring agreement, conditions, and exclusions.) The DICE method has four steps:

1. Review of the declarations page to determine whether it covers the person or the property at the time of the loss
2. Review of the insuring agreement to determine whether it covers the loss
3. Review of policy conditions to determine compliance
4. Review of policy exclusions to determine whether they preclude coverage of the loss

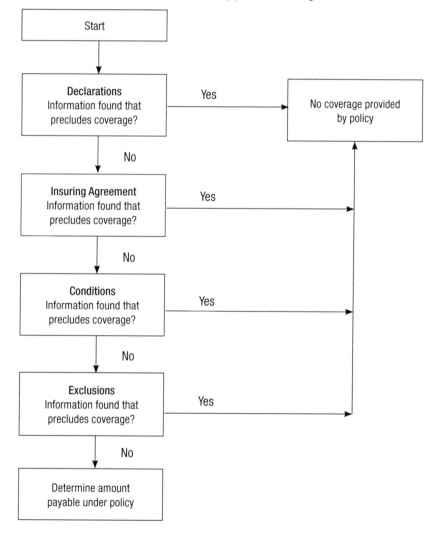

Each of these four steps is used in every case. Other categories of policy provisions should be examined. For example, endorsements and terms defined in the policy should be reviewed in relation to the declarations, insuring agreement, exclusions, and conditions.

If the premium is not paid, the policy would not cover the claim. The insuring agreement or agreements often contain policy provisions regarding the covered property or events, covered causes of loss, and coverage territories. If these provisions contain specially defined terms, those definitions should be analyzed. If a provision in an insuring agreement precludes coverage, the claim will be denied.

If nothing in the insuring agreement precludes coverage, the insurance professional proceeds to the third step of the DICE method, analyzing conditions. Policy conditions specify the duties of the insurer and the insured. Examples of common policy provisions include the insured's obligation to report losses promptly, provide appropriate documentation for losses, and cooperate with the insurer in any legal proceedings. Violating a condition can change the coverage on an otherwise-covered claim. Examining the policy conditions can help the insurance professional clarify these important points:

- Whether fulfillment of certain conditions, such as premium payment conditions, is required for there to be an enforceable policy
- Whether coverage will be denied if an insured party breaches a policy condition
- Whether coverage triggers and coverage territory restrictions affect the loss
- Whether conditions concerning the rights and duties of both parties to maintain the insurance policy apply (for example, the insurer's right to inspect covered premises, the rights of either or both parties to cancel the policy, and the insurer's right to make coverage modifications)
- Whether the post-loss duties of the insured and the insurer affect coverage
- Whether conditions have been or need to be adhered to regarding claim disputes
- Whether subrogation and salvage rights and conditions must be considered

One breach of a condition that can occur under a homeowners policy is the concealment of a material fact. For example, assume an insured has a primary business running a furniture refinishing operation in his home. If he fails to disclose this fact when obtaining his homeowners coverage, in violation of one of the policy's coverage conditions, the policy would not cover a fire caused by flammable rags used to polish furniture.

If the insured has complied with all of the policy's conditions, the insurance professional performs the final step of the DICE method, analyzing policy exclusions and any other policy provisions not already analyzed, including endorsements and miscellaneous provisions. This is the fourth and final step of the DICE method. Exclusions, which can appear anywhere in the policy, state what the insurer does not intend to cover. The primary function of exclusions is not only to limit coverage but also to clarify the coverages granted by the insurer. They also eliminate coverage for uninsurable loss exposures (such as intentional acts) and can be used to reduce the likelihood of coverage duplications, eliminate coverages not needed by the typical insured, eliminate coverages requiring special treatment, or assist in keeping premiums reasonable. For example, an exclusion in a homeowners policy precludes coverage for claims resulting from earth movement caused by an earthquake, landslide, or subsidence that damages a dwelling or its contents.

After using the DICE method to determine whether the claim is covered, the insurer must then determine how much is payable under that insurance policy. The amount payable under a given insurance policy can be affected not only by the value of the loss but also by policy limits and deductibles, or self-insured retentions. For property insurance, the amount payable is affected by several factors. The valuation provision indicates how the property will be valued for claim purposes, which could be on the basis of its replacement cost, its depreciated actual cash value, or some other valuation method. The amount payable is also affected by applicable policy limits and can be limited by a coinsurance provision or other insurance-to-value provisions. Some policies designate a deductible to be subtracted from the amount otherwise payable. For liability insurance, the valuation of a covered loss is established by the courts or, more commonly, by a negotiated settlement. The amounts payable for both property and liability insurance losses can also be affected by other insurance.

SUMMARY

These are the distinguishing characteristics of insurance policies:

- Indemnity
- Utmost good faith
- Fortuitous losses
- Contract of adhesion
- Exchange of unequal amounts
- Conditional
- Nontransferable

The physical structure of an insurance policy can be that of a self-contained policy or that of a modular policy. The forms of which a policy is composed may be preprinted forms or manuscript forms, and standard forms or nonstandard forms. In addition to forms, endorsements and other related documents may be incorporated in a policy. All of these approaches to policy structure affect policy analysis.

Every insurance policy is composed of numerous policy provisions. Each provision can be placed into one of six categories, depending on the purpose it serves:

• Declarations
• Definitions
• Insuring agreements
• Exclusions
• Conditions
• Miscellaneous provisions

Being able to classify policy provisions into these categories is an important part of analyzing an insurance policy.

Insureds and insurers should analyze an insurance policy before a loss occurs in order to ensure that the policy adequately covers the loss exposures it is intended to address. The primary method of pre-loss policy analysis is scenario analysis. After a loss occurs, an insurer uses the DICE method to determine whether the insurance policy provides coverage.

ASSIGNMENT NOTES

1. Copyrighted material of Insurance Services Office, Inc., with its permission. Copyright, ISO Properties, Inc., 1999.
2. Copyrighted material of Insurance Services Office, Inc., with its permission. Copyright, ISO Properties, Inc., 1999.

Direct Your Learning ▶▶

Common Policy Concepts

Educational Objectives

After learning the content of this assignment, you should be able to:

▸ Given a case, evaluate one or more entities' insurable interests.

▸ Explain why insurance to value is important to property insurers, how insurers encourage insurance to value, and what insureds can do to address the problems associated with maintaining insurance to value.

▸ Explain how property is valued under each of the following valuation methods in property insurance policies:

- Actual cash value
- Replacement cost
- Agreed value
- Functional valuation

▸ Explain how the amount payable for a claim covered under a liability insurance policy is determined.

▸ Explain how deductibles in property insurance benefit the insured.

▸ Explain why deductibles are not commonly used in some liability policies but are commonly used in other liability policies, and how a self-insured retention differs from a deductible.

▸ Describe the multiple sources of recovery that may be available to an insurance policyholder for a covered loss.

Common Policy Concepts

8

INSURABLE INTEREST

When determining whether a loss is covered under a property insurance policy, a professional must determine whether the insured, who is claiming a financial loss, has an insurable interest in the property that was damaged or destroyed. The analysis must determine two things: whether the claimant is an insured under the policy and, if so, whether the insured has an insurable interest in the property.

An insured under a property policy must have an insurable interest in property that is damaged or destroyed in order to have a legitimate claim. Several legal bases can be established for an insurable interest. In some situations, multiple parties can have an insurable interest in the same property; for example, spouses who have tenancy in the same property both have an insurable interest in it. An examination of when and why insurable interest is required, along with the descriptions of the legal bases for insurable interest and the multiple parties that can have an insurable interest, will help insurance and risk management professionals determine whether the insurable interest requirement is met when an insured submits a property claim.

When and Why Insurable Interest Is Required

An **insurable interest** arises as the result of a relationship with a person or a right with respect to property. Whether an insurable interest exists depends on the relationship between the claiming party and the property, person, or event that is the subject of the insurance policy. For example, to make a claim under a property insurance policy, the claimant must stand to suffer a financial loss if the insured property is damaged or destroyed.

The requirement for an insurable interest is a matter of law and exists even in the absence of policy provisions specifically addressing insurable interest. However, policies often include provisions that limit insureds' right of recovery to no more than their interest in the covered property at the time of the loss.

The requirement for insurable interest is different in property-casualty insurance than in life insurance. In life insurance, the beneficiary must have an insurable interest in the life of the insured when the policy is purchased, but not necessarily at the time of the insured's death. For example, Mary is the beneficiary on her husband's life insurance policy. If the couple divorces, Mary may no longer have an insurable interest in her ex-husband's life, but she

Insurable interest
An interest in the subject of an insurance policy that is not unduly remote and that would cause the interested party to suffer financial loss if an insured event occurred.

would not be prevented from collecting under the policy in the event of his death.

In contrast, insurable interest in property-casualty insurance must be present at the time of the loss. For example, if Jacob sold his home but did not cancel his homeowners insurance, he could not present a valid claim under that policy if the property were subsequently damaged because he would have no insurable interest in the home at the time of the loss.

Insurance policies have an insurable interest requirement for these three reasons:

- It supports the principle of indemnity.
- It prevents the use of insurance as a wagering mechanism.
- It reduces the moral hazard incentive that insurance may create for the insured.

Insurable interest supports the principle of indemnity by ensuring that only those parties who suffer financial loss are indemnified, and then only to the extent of their loss. Requiring an insurable interest prevents individuals or organizations from wagering (gambling) by insuring an event from which they would not suffer a loss and then profiting when that event occurs. In addition, because the insurable interest requirement limits insureds' ability to profit from insurance, the incentive to cause losses intentionally (moral hazard incentive) is reduced.

Legal Bases for Insurable Interest

Insurable interest can arise from a legal relationship between the party filing the claim and the subject of insurance. The legal bases for insurable interest include these:

- Ownership interest in property
- Contractual obligations
- Exposure to legal liability
- Factual expectancy
- Representation of another party

Ownership Interest in Property

Ownership of property creates an insurable interest in that property, and ownership rights are legally protected. For example, property owners have a legal right to sell, give away, and use their property. The extent of legal ownership determines the extent of insurable interest in the property.

Although the term "property" is commonly used to refer to tangible objects such as buildings and their contents, it also includes intangible items, such as copyrights, patents, trademarks, intellectual property, and stock certificates.

Ownership rights to both tangible and intangible property have economic value and are guaranteed and protected by law.

Contractual Obligations

Insurable interest can arise out of some contractual obligations. Generally, contractual rights and related insurable interests fall into two major categories:

- Contractual rights regarding people—A contract may give one party the right to bring a claim against a second party without entitling the first party to any specific property that belongs to the second party. For example, if Anthony does not pay his credit card debt, the credit card company can bring a claim against Anthony for the outstanding balance on the card. However, the credit card company does not have the right to repossess any of Anthony's property as payment for the debt. In this case, the credit card company is an unsecured creditor. Unsecured creditors do not have an insurable interest in debtors' property.
- Contractual rights regarding property—Some contracts allow one party to bring a claim against specific property held by a second party. For example, if Anthony obtains a mortgage loan in order to buy a house, the mortgage holder can repossess the house if Anthony fails to make his mortgage payments. This type of contract typically creates an insurable interest in the secured property equal to the debt's remaining balance.

Exposure to Legal Liability

Sometimes one party can have legal responsibility for property owned by others. Having this type of legal responsibility creates an insurable interest in that property because the responsible party can suffer a financial loss if the owner's property is damaged. These examples illustrate insurable interests based on exposure to legal liability:

- A hotelier has an insurable interest in guests' property.
- A tenant has an insurable interest in the portion of the premises the tenant occupies.
- A contractor typically has an insurable interest in a building under construction.

In these cases, the responsible party has an insurable interest based on potential legal liability for damage to the owner's property. The extent of that insurable interest is the property's full value, including the owner's use value.

Factual Expectancy

A majority of states have accepted **factual expectancy** as a valid basis for an insurable interest. In these states, a party does not have to establish a specific property right, contractual right, or potential legal liability to prove insurable interest. The party need only demonstrate potential financial harm resulting

Factual expectancy

A situation in which a party experiences an economic advantage if an insured event does not occur or, conversely, economic harm if the event does occur.

from the event to be insured. The focus is on the insured's financial position rather than on a legal interest.

For example, Tina's fiancé gives her a diamond engagement ring that he had stolen from a relative. When Tina's apartment is subsequently burglarized, the ring is one of the items taken. During the investigation of Tina's claim, the origin of the ring is discovered. Because a person cannot legally own property that rightfully belongs to another, Tina was never the legal owner of the ring. Nonetheless, courts would probably find that she would be entitled to recover for the ring under her tenant's policy based on her factual expectancy of loss.

Representation of Another Party

Insurable interest can be based on one party's acting as a representative of another party. In this case, the representative can obtain insurance on property for the benefit of the property's owner. These examples illustrate insurable interests based on representation of another party:

- Agents—An **agent** may insure property in the agent's name for the principal's benefit. Although the insurance proceeds are ultimately payable to the principal, the agent has an insurable interest.

- Trustees—A **trustee** may insure property in the trustee's name for the trust's benefit. The trustee has an insurable interest but must give the insurance proceeds to the trust.

- Bailees—A **bailee** may insure property in the bailee's name for the bailor's benefit. The bailee has an insurable interest, but if the bailor's property becomes damaged or destroyed, the bailee pays any insurance proceeds to the **bailor**.

In these situations, the party obtaining the insurance is not required to have an independent insurable interest in the property. The party derives its interest from its relationship with the party it represents. See the exhibit "Practice Exercise."

Multiple Parties With Insurable Interests

Under some circumstances, more than one party has an insurable interest in the same property and, as a result, the sum of all insurable interests exceeds the property's value. For example, a property owner and the lender holding a mortgage on the property both have an insurable interest in that property. The mortgage holder's interest is the amount of the unpaid loan, and the owner's interest is the property's full value. Combined, the amount of these two interests could greatly exceed the property's value.

For example, Nina purchased a $500,000 home using $100,000 of her savings and a $400,000 mortgage loan. The mortgage holder's interest is $400,000 and Nina's interest is the full $500,000, because she has full use of the property. Their combined interest is $900,000, well above the total value of the

Agent
In the agency relationship, the party that is authorized by the principal to act on the principal's behalf.

Trustee
Someone who has the legal title to a property but is responsible that it be used, handled, and transferred solely for the benefit of the beneficiary.

Bailee
The party temporarily possessing the personal property in a bailment.

Bailor
The owner of the personal property in a bailment.

Practice Exercise

Canston Holdings, Inc. is a property management firm that owns a number of commercial properties. Canston recently sold one of its buildings to Sisterdale & Worthley, an accounting firm. The local Blazek Bank holds Sisterdale & Worthley's mortgage on the building. The two-story building is located at 123 Malvern Street. Sisterdale & Worthley have their offices on the ground floor and lease the second floor to Janasok Communications, a call center. Next door to the building is Courton Eats, a small diner that is popular with staff at both the accounting firm and the call center. Approximately 75 percent of the diner's traffic comes from these two neighboring businesses. Complete the table to show which of the following organizations has an insurable interest in the building at 123 Malvern Street and to describe the basis for that interest.

Organization	Insurable Interest? (Y/N)	Basis of Interest
Canston Holdings		
Sisterdale & Worthley		
Blazek Bank		
Janasok Communications		
Courton Eats		

Answer

The table should be completed as shown here:

Organization	Insurable Interest? (Y/N)	Basis of Interest
Canston Holdings	No	Not applicable
Sisterdale & Worthley	Yes	Ownership
Blazek Bank	Yes	Contractual (secured creditor)
Janasok Communications	Yes	Exposure to liability
Courton Eats	No	Not applicable

[DA06038]

property. However, if the home were completely destroyed, neither Nina nor the mortgage holder could claim more than their actual loss under the homeowners policy. Assuming the dwelling was insured for its full value, the insurer would pay no more than $100,000 to Nina and $400,000 to the mortgage holder.

When more than one person owns the same property, the nature of the ownership affects the extent of each party's insurable interest. Property may be jointly owned according to these interests:

- Joint tenancy
- Tenancy by the entirety

- Tenancy in common
- Tenancy in partnership

Joint Tenancy

In joint tenancy, each owner, referred to as a "tenant," owns the entire property and has a right of survivorship. This is an automatic right of one tenant to the share of the other tenant when that other tenant dies. For example, if Manuel and Gerard are joint tenants of a restaurant building, each owns the entire building. If Manuel died, Gerard would automatically become the sole owner of the building and vice versa.

Because any one joint tenant could become the property's sole owner, each tenant has an insurable interest in the property's full value. If the restaurant were insured for its full value of $1 million, Manuel and Gerard would each have a $1 million interest. Therefore, their combined interest would be $2 million, or twice the value of the property. Nonetheless, if the restaurant were destroyed by fire, their insurance policy would pay no more than the property's value, subject to the $1 million policy limit and any other policy provisions. That payment would probably be made to the first named insured in the declarations.

Tenancy by the Entirety

Tenancy by entirety is a joint tenancy between a husband and wife. As with a joint tenancy, if spouses jointly own a property, each of them owns the entire property. If one of them dies, the other becomes the sole owner; consequently, each spouse has an insurable interest equal to the full value of the property. As a result, the combined interests of both spouses would be twice the property value. However, as with a joint tenancy, in the event of a loss, an insurance policy would pay no more than the property's value.

Tenancy in Common

Tenancy in common is a concurrent ownership of property, in equal or unequal shares, by two or more owners. Unlike joint tenants or tenants in the entirety, tenants in common do not have survivorship rights. For example, Andrew, Colin, and Rita are tenants in common of a factory, each holding a one-third interest. If Andrew died, Colin and Rita would still each own only one-third of the factory. Andrew's third would pass to his heirs.

With tenants in common, each party's insurable interest is limited to that owner's share of the property. In this example, each has an interest worth one-third of the value of the property; therefore, their combined interests are equal to the property value. Any insurance payouts would probably be made to the first named insured, who would then be responsible for distributing the appropriate share of the money to the other tenants in common.

Tenancy in Partnership

Tenancy in partnership is a concurrent ownership by a partnership and its individual partners of personal property used by the partnership. This type of tenancy is similar to a joint tenancy in that the partnership and all partners have rights of survivorship. Therefore, with a tenancy in partnership, both the partnership entity and the individual partners have an insurable interest in property used by the partnership.

Depending on the size of the partnership, the combined interests could be many times the actual property value because each partner, and the partnership, would have an interest worth the entire insurable amount. If a loss occurred, the claim settlement would be paid to the first named insured, which could be the partnership entity or one of the partners. See the exhibit "Practice Exercise."

Practice Exercise

Stone, Rajdev, Lee & Partners is a civil engineering consulting firm. The three original founders, Stone, Rajdev, and Lee, were all major partners in the company, which had several minor partners as well. The company rents space in an office tower, and the insurable value of the office contents is $750,000. The three principal partners chartered a small airplane to attend a meeting with a potential client. The plane crashed, and Stone, Rajdev, and Lee were killed. Who has an insurable interest in the contents of the office, and what is the value of those interests?

Answer

The partnership entity and each of the remaining minor partners has an insurable interest in the office contents. The value of each of those interests is the full $750,000.

[DA06039]

INSURANCE TO VALUE

An important goal of insurers selling property insurance is to motivate each insured to buy a limit of insurance that approximates the full value of the covered property, commonly called "insurance to value."

Insurance to value is beneficial for both the insurer and the insured. If insureds do not purchase adequate coverage limits, the rate that an insurer develops can be adversely affected, resulting in inadequate premiums. Insurers benefit from insurance to value because it ensures that premiums are adequate to cover potential losses and it simplifies underwriting. The insured benefits because sufficient funds are available in the event of a loss. Insurers use a variety of incentives and penalties to encourage insureds to purchase adequate limits of insurance. Although maintaining insurance to value over time can be challenging, various measures are available to assist insureds and insurance professionals with maintaining insurance to value.

Insurance to value

Insurance written for an amount approximating the full value of the asset(s) insured.

Why Insurers Seek Insurance to Value

Insurers seek to achieve insurance to value in the property insurance policies they write. The need for insurance to value can be understood by first examining **loss frequency** and **loss severity**.

During the risk management process, loss exposures are assessed to determine potential loss frequency and loss severity. For property loss exposures, the severity loss distribution is often skewed. That is, most of the losses that occur to property loss exposures, especially real property, are small losses (low severity), with a total loss being a rare occurrence. This point can be illustrated through a hypothetical severity distribution of a typical property valued at $150,000. See the exhibit "Probability Distribution of Loss Severity of Residential Property Losses."

Loss frequency

The number of losses that occur within a specified period.

Loss severity

The amount of loss, typically measured in dollars, for a loss that has occurred.

Probability Distribution of Loss Severity of Residential Property Losses

Size Category of Losses (bins)	Probability of Loss	Cumulative Probability of Loss	Average Bin Value	Expected Value of Loss	Expected Value Truncated	
$0–$1,000	.700	.700	$ 500	$ 350	$ 350	Probability of Loss × Average Bin Value
$1,001–$5,000	.200	.900	3,000	600	600	
$5,001–$10,000	.050	.950	7,500	375	375	
$10,001–$15,000	.020	.970	12,500	250	250	
$15,001–$25,000	.015	.985	20,000	300	300	
$25,001–$50,000	.0075	.993	37,500	281	187.5*	
$50,001–$100,000	.005	.998	75,000	375	125*	Expected Value of Insured Losses: $25,000 Policy Limit
$100,001–$150,000	.0025	1.000	125,000	313	62.5*	
Total	**1.000**			**$2,844**	**$2,250**	Expected Value of Insured Losses: Insured to Value

*For each of these expected values of insured losses, the probability of loss is multiplied by $25,000 (the maximum amount payable) instead of the average bin values.

[DA06036]

The severity distribution shown in the Probability Distribution of Loss Severity of Residential Property Losses exhibit (Probability Distribution table) shows that if a loss occurs, 90 percent of the time, that loss is less than $5,000 (because the cumulative probability is 90 percent). Because the cumulative probability of a loss less than $25,000 is 98.5 percent, then only 1.5 percent of the time is the loss greater than $25,000. The maximum possible loss for the property is $150,000, which would occur only if the property were totally destroyed.

To calculate the insurance rate and premium to insure the property, an insurer could combine the severity distribution shown in the Probability Distribution table with a frequency distribution. For example, the severity distribution in the exhibit has an expected value of approximately $2,844. If an insurer were to assume a simple frequency distribution that has only two possibilities—80 percent of the time no loss would occur, and 20 percent of the time one loss would occur—then the insurer would be able to calculate an expected loss of approximately $569 [(0.8 × $0) + (0.2 × $2,844) = $569]. If the insurer had a 40 percent expense ratio, the premium it would charge would be $948 [$569 ÷ (1 – 0.40) = $948].

The importance to the insurer of insurance to value can be illustrated by showing how the lack of insurance to value affects premium adequacy. For example, suppose that an insurer provides a property insurance policy with a policy limit of $150,000 and that the premium is based on an insurance rate per $100 of coverage. Dividing $150,000 by $100 yields 1,500 units of coverage that the insurer is providing.

The insurer, charging a premium of $948 for a policy with a limit of $150,000 (the value of the property), is using an insurance rate of approximately $0.63 per unit of coverage ($948 ÷ 1,500 = $0.63). Further, suppose that the insured evaluated the severity distribution and chose to retain the 1.5 percent probability that losses would be above $25,000 by buying a policy with a limit of only $25,000.

The insurer would lose money on the $25,000-limit policy (250 units of coverage) if it charged the same rate ($0.63 per unit of coverage) as for the policy with the $150,000 limit; this would result in a premium of only $158 (250 units × $0.63 = $158), and the lower premium would not be sufficient to cover the expected losses under the policy.

If the severity distribution that the insurer faces stops at $25,000, the expected value of that distribution is now $2,250. With the same frequency distribution as used previously, the expected loss is now $450 [(0.8 × $0) + (0.2 × $2,250) = $450], and, assuming the same expense loading, the premium would be $750 [$450 ÷ (1 – 0.4) = $750]. For a policy limit of $25,000, the insurer is offering 250 units of coverage with a rate of $3.00 per unit of coverage. This is substantially higher than the $0.63 per unit rate that was calculated when the property insurance limit was equal to the property's total value.

The insurer is then faced with a decision to either charge a higher rate for property insurance when the policy limit is less than the property's value or require insureds to choose policy limits that are close to the full value of the property. Insurers generally prefer the second choice, referred to as insurance to value.

Insuring to value is typically beneficial for both the insurer and the insured. The insurer benefits in two ways. First, the premium is adequate to cover potential losses. Second, it simplifies the underwriting process by reducing the need to determine exact values during underwriting. The determination of underinsurance (not insuring to value) is made at the time of loss; therefore, the underwriter does not need to determine whether the property is being underinsured.

The insured benefits from insurance to value because sufficient funds are available in the event of a total loss and the uncertainty associated with large retained losses is reduced. See the exhibit "Insurance to Value Liability Policies."

Insurance to Value Liability Policies

Determining the maximum possible loss for most liability loss exposures is impossible because the severity of such exposures, in theory, is limitless. That is, the law generally does not limit the dollar amount of damages that a court can award to an injured party as damages payable by the responsible party. Therefore, insurers do not seek insurance to value for liability policies.

However, liability insurers use insurance rates that are adequate for whatever "layer" of coverage they are insuring. For example, the rate charged for a primary liability policy (which covers the highest frequency of covered claims) is normally higher than the rate charged for an excess liability policy covering claims that exceed the primary policy's limit of insurance.

Although insurance to value does not apply to liability policies, it is still important for insureds to estimate the potential severity of their liability loss exposures and buy appropriate limits of liability insurance to cover those exposures.

[DA06037]

How Insurers Encourage Insurance to Value

Insurance-to-value provision

A provision in property insurance policies that encourages insureds to purchase an amount of insurance that is equal to, or close to, the value of the covered property.

Coinsurance clause

A clause that requires the insured to carry insurance equal to at least a specified percentage of the insured property's value.

As an incentive for insuring to value, many policies include **insurance-to-value provisions** that reduce the amount payable for both partial and total losses if the insured has not purchased adequate limits of coverage. These provisions, which include **coinsurance clauses** and similar provisions, serve a dual purpose: rewarding those who have insured to value and penalizing those who have not.

Many commercial property insurance policies contain coinsurance clauses, which make the insured responsible for retaining part of any loss if the property is underinsured below some specified percentage of the property's insurable value. The most common coinsurance percentages for buildings and business personal property are 80, 90, and 100 percent. The insurable value is the actual cash value (ACV), the replacement cost value, or whatever other valuation basis applies, according to the policy's valuation clause.

The coinsurance formula explains how the amount payable is determined if the coinsurance requirement has not been met, and can be expressed in this manner:

$$\text{Amount payable} = \frac{\text{Limit of insurance}}{\text{Value of covered property} \times \text{Coinsurance}} \times \text{Total amount of covered loss}$$
$$\qquad\qquad\qquad\qquad\text{(at time of loss)} \qquad \text{percentage}$$

Insurance students often remember this formula as "did over should times loss," which can be written as shown:

$$\text{Amount payable} = \frac{\text{Did}}{\text{Should}} \times \text{Loss},$$

where

"Did" = The amount of insurance carried (the policy limit), and

"Should" = The minimum amount that should have been carried to meet the coinsurance requirement based on the insurable value at the time of the loss.

For example, a business owns a building with a replacement cost value of $10 million. It insures the building for $9 million with a property insurance policy providing replacement cost coverage subject to a 100 percent coinsurance clause. If a covered peril causes $5 million of damage to the building, the insured would not receive the full $5 million from its insurer, because the building is underinsured. Instead, the claim settlement would be $4.5 million, calculated by dividing the policy limit by the amount of insurance required and then multiplying that percentage by the amount of the loss ($9,000,000 ÷ $10,000,000 × $5,000,000 = $4,500,000).

Business income and extra expense policies also commonly include coinsurance requirements, but the requirements are based on projected net income and operating expenses for the policy period rather than on property values. The coinsurance percentages available for business income and extra expense insurance are 50, 60, 70, 80, 90, 100, and 125 percent, reflecting the fact that some businesses may be able to resume operations in six months or less (roughly corresponding to 50 percent coinsurance), while others may require a year or more to resume operations (roughly corresponding to 100 percent or 125 percent coinsurance).

Insurance-to-value provisions in homeowners (HO) and businessowners (BOP) policies also encourage insureds to purchase adequate limits, but they do so in a different way than the commercial property coinsurance provision does. With the HO and BOP insurance-to-value provisions, the amount payable by the insurer will never be less than the ACV of the damaged property, subject to policy limits. With coinsurance, the amount payable (depending on the degree of underinsurance) can be less than the property's ACV. Under the HO and BOP insurance-to-value provisions, the amount payable by the insurer will be one of these amounts:

- The replacement cost value of the property—effectively a reward for those insured to at least 80 percent of the replacement cost value of the property
- The actual cash value of the property—effectively a penalty for those not insured to at least 80 percent of replacement cost value of the property
- An amount between the replacement cost value and the ACV of the property, determined by the same "did over should times loss" formula used in the coinsurance penalty, with which the loss amount is on a replacement cost basis

Addressing Insurance-to-Value Problems

Maintaining insurance to value avoids coinsurance penalties and other insurance-to-value provision penalties that might reduce the amount payable in the event of a loss. Underinsurance penalties are not a concern for insureds who maintain property insurance limits that meet or exceed coinsurance requirements or the insurance-to-value requirement. However, maintaining such limits is difficult, for at least these reasons:

- The amount of insurance necessary to meet coinsurance requirements is based on the insured property's value at the time of the loss, but the policy limit is selected when the policy is purchased.
- When selecting insurance limits, an insurance buyer typically estimates property values based on an informed guess.
- The insurable value at the time of the loss often cannot be precisely measured until the property is actually rebuilt or replaced.
- Values change over time.

Insurance professionals can help property insurance buyers minimize problems associated with valuation by recommending that they take these steps:

- Hire a qualified appraiser to establish the property's current replacement cost value and set policy limits accordingly. The property owner should adjust the appraisal using indexes and/or a record of additions and deletions each year and should reappraise the property every few years.
- Review and revise policy limits periodically to ensure that they are adequate to cover potential losses.
- Consider appropriate coverage options—for example, **agreed value optional coverage**, **inflation guard protection**, and the **peak season endorsement**.

Agreed Value optional coverage

Optional coverage that suspends the Coinsurance condition if the insured carries the amount of insurance agreed to by the insurer and insured.

Inflation guard protection

A method of protecting against inflation by increasing the applicable limit for covered property by a specified percentage over the policy period.

Peak season endorsement

Endorsement that covers the fluctuating values of business personal property by providing differing amounts of insurance for certain time periods during the policy period.

PROPERTY VALUATION METHODS

When covered property is lost or damaged, the amount payable under a property insurance policy depends on the property's value. Every property policy states how the insurer and the insured determine that value. The policy's valuation method is contained in its valuation provision.

For some policies, **actual cash value (ACV)** is the standard valuation method, with **replacement cost** available as an option. For other policies, replacement cost is the standard valuation method, with ACV available as an option. Although ACV and replacement cost are the most common valuation methods, property insurance policies may also use other methods.

Actual Cash Value

Actual cash value is one of the most prevalent methods used with property insurance policies to determine the amount payable for a property loss because it supports the principle of indemnity by restoring the insured to its pre-loss condition. ACV is typically calculated as the property's replacement cost at the time of loss minus depreciation.

The term "actual cash value" is rarely defined in insurance policies, and the definition adopted by courts often varies by jurisdiction and the type of property insured. Although the traditional definition of ACV has been limited to replacement cost minus depreciation, other methods of determining ACV have evolved, including the use of market value and the broad evidence rule.

When a property insurance policy specifies that property will be valued on an ACV basis, the insured must choose a policy limit to fully insure the property on that basis. The following is the actual cash value policy provision from the Insurance Services Office (ISO) Building and Personal Property (BPP) Coverage Form (subsections b.–e. change the valuation methods for special items such as glass, outdoor equipment, and tenant's improvements and betterments):[1]

> 7. **Valuation**
>
> We will determine the value of Covered Property in the event of loss or damage as follows:
>
> **a.** At actual cash value as of the time of loss or damage, except as provided in **b., c., d.** and **e.** below.

Replacement Cost Minus Depreciation

Most property has its highest value when new and depreciates at a fairly steady rate as a result of age and use. Depreciation reflects the value of the use that the insured has already received from the property. Although depreciation can be based on physical wear and tear, which usually increases with age, it can be based on age alone. It can also be based on obsolescence caused by fashion, technological changes, or other factors that occur rapidly and

Actual cash value (ACV)
Cost to replace property with new property of like kind and quality less depreciation.

Replacement cost
The cost to repair or replace property using new materials of like kind and quality with no deduction for depreciation.

suddenly. Disagreements regularly develop about how to determine the appropriate amount of depreciation to deduct.

The important distinction about depreciation in calculating ACV is that the ACV calculation is based on economic depreciation, not accounting depreciation. See the exhibit "Accounting Depreciation and Economic Depreciation."

Accounting Depreciation and Economic Depreciation

In accounting, if property is expected to have a useful life greater than one year, organizations can depreciate the property over its useful life rather than expensing it in the year of the purchase. This accounting depreciation expense is the allocation of the property's value, as reflected in an organization's accounting and tax records, over the property's useful life (usually a schedule set by tax codes).

Accounting depreciation is distinct from the economic depreciation of property. Economic depreciation is the difference between the replacement cost of the property and its current market value. Economic depreciation is typically the result of physical or functional depreciation. Physical depreciation is the wear and tear on the property and is usually reflected in a reduction in the property's ability to perform its intended function, regardless of use.

Functional depreciation is usually the result of technological advances because the function performed by the capital expenditure is no longer needed or can be performed better by other methods. For example, personal computers that an organization purchased three years ago would have a greatly reduced current value even if they had never been taken out of their original cartons.

[DA03232]

Market Value

Market value

The price at which a particular piece of property could be sold on the open market by an unrelated buyer and seller.

Many courts have ruled that ACV means **market value** (also referred to as fair market value). Market value is easily established for autos, personal computers, and other property that has many buyers and sellers and for which information is available about recent sales. However, it can be difficult to establish market value if there have been few recent transactions involving comparable property. For example, it may be difficult to determine a market value using recent sales of unique manufacturing machinery and equipment.

Market valuation is also useful when property of like kind and quality is unavailable for purchase, such as with antiques, works of art, and other collectibles. These types of property may be irreplaceable, making replacement cost calculations impossible. Although these types of property may not fit the standard of having many comparable sales, examining the sales history of a piece of art and recent transactions involving other pieces of similar quality may be the only method of determining its value. Market valuation can also be the most accurate way to determine the value of some older or historic buildings built with obsolete construction methods and materials.

The market value of real property reflects the value of the land and its location, as well as the value of any buildings or structures on the land. Because most insurance policies cover buildings and structures but not land, the land's value must be eliminated in establishing insurable values of property.

Broad Evidence Rule

The **broad evidence rule** arose when courts stipulated that insurers had to consider more than just depreciation or market value when determining ACV. The exhibit contains a sample of some of the elements that various courts have used in applying the broad evidence rule to determine a building's ACV. See the exhibit "Factors Considered in Determining a Building's ACV."

Broad evidence rule
A court ruling explicitly requiring that all relevant factors be considered in determining actual cash value.

Factors Considered in Determining a Building's ACV

- Obsolescence
- Building's present use and profitability
- Alternate building uses
- Present neighborhood characteristics
- Long-term community plans for the area where the building is located, including urban renewal prospects and new roadway plans
- Inflationary or deflationary trends
- Any other relevant factors

[DA03234]

Replacement Cost

The second valuation method in property insurance policies is replacement cost. Replacement cost is commonly used in insurance policies covering buildings and in many policies covering personal property. The exhibit contains the replacement cost valuation provision from the ISO HO-3 policy. See the exhibit "Replacement Cost Valuation Provision in the ISO HO-3 Policy."

According to the terms set out in the exhibit, if property covered on a replacement cost basis is damaged or destroyed, the insured is entitled to the current cost of repairing damaged property or of buying or building new property of like kind and quality, even if the destroyed property is several years old, and even if its replacement cost exceeds the original purchase price. If the cost of new property has decreased, as often happens with computers or other electronic equipment, replacement cost coverage pays the current lower cost.

Often, a particular model or style of electronic equipment is no longer made. Although the equipment is technically irreplaceable, the replacement cost

Replacement Cost Valuation Provision in the ISO HO-3 Policy

C. **Loss Settlement**

2. Buildings covered under Coverage **A** or **B** at replacement cost without deduction for depreciation, subject to the following:

   a. If, at the time of loss, the amount of insurance in this policy on the damaged building is 80% or more of the full replacement cost of the building immediately before the loss, we will pay the cost to repair or replace, after application of any deductible and without deduction for depreciation, but not more than the least of the following amounts:

      (1) The limit of liability under this policy that applies to the building;

      (2) The replacement cost of that part of the building damaged with material of like kind and quality and for like use; or

      (3) The necessary amount actually spent to repair or replace the damaged building.

      If the building is rebuilt at a new premises, the cost described in (2) above is limited to the cost which would have been incurred if the building had been built at the original premises.

   b. If, at the time of loss, the amount of insurance in this policy on the damaged building is less than 80% of the full replacement cost of the building immediately before the loss, we will pay the greater of the following amounts, but not more than the limit of liability under this policy that applies to the building:

      (1) The actual cash value of that part of the building damaged; or

      (2) That proportion of the cost to repair or replace, after application of any deductible and without deduction for depreciation, that part of the building damaged, which the total amount of insurance in this policy on the damaged building bears to 80% of the replacement cost of the building.

   d. We will pay no more than the actual cash value of the damage until actual repair or replacement is complete. Once actual repair or replacement is complete, we will settle the loss as noted in **2.a.** and **b.** above.

      However, if the cost to repair or replace the damage is both:

      (1) Less than 5% of the amount of insurance in this policy on the building; and

      (2) Less than $2,500;

      we will settle the loss as noted in 2.a. and b. above whether or not actual repair or replacement is complete.

   e. You may disregard the replacement cost loss settlement provisions and make claim under this policy for loss to buildings on an actual cash value basis. You may then make claim for any additional liability according to the provisions of this Condition C. Loss Settlement, provided you notify us of your intent to do so within 180 days after the date of loss.

for property of comparable material and quality can still be determined. For example, a manufacturer might have discontinued a particular television model. However, a comparable television can be purchased, often from the same manufacturer. The insured is usually willing to settle a claim based on the existing model's cost, provided the replacement item is not inferior.

Even when the replacement cost method of valuation is specified by the property insurance policy, certain types of property are not valued using that method. For example, replacement cost coverage often does not apply to property such as antiques or artwork, primarily because there is no adequate replacement for such property. These types of property are typically valued at their ACV as determined by market value.

Technically, replacement cost coverage violates the principle of indemnity. An insured who sustains a loss to old, used property and receives insurance payment for new property has profited from the loss. To reduce the moral hazard, most replacement cost policies pay out only after the insured has actually replaced the damaged or destroyed property or, in some cases, only if the loss is a relatively low value.

In many policies with replacement cost provisions, the insured has the option of settling the claim based on ACV and then has 180 days to refile the claim on the replacement cost basis. This gives the insured the opportunity to obtain funds from the insurer at the time of loss, use those funds to help pay for the rebuilding, and then collect the full replacement cost value on completion.

If the policy specifies that property is covered on a replacement cost basis, the insured must select a policy limit to fully insure the replacement cost property value. For buildings, the replacement cost value is usually higher than the property's depreciated ACV. Property insurance rates per $100 of insurance are usually the same whether the property is insured for replacement cost or ACV. However, replacement cost insurance is more costly because higher limits are required to insure to value because replacement cost is generally higher than ACV.

Other Valuation Methods

Although insurers usually settle losses by paying the replacement cost or ACV of lost or damaged property, many other valuation provisions are used for special classes of property, sometimes within policies that value most property on a replacement cost or ACV basis.

These are two of the more common other valuation methods:

- Agreed value method
- Functional valuation method

Agreed Value Method

Agreed value method
A method of valuing property in which the insurer and the insured agree, at the time the policy is written, on the maximum amount that will be paid in the event of a total loss.

Some property insurance policies are valued policies, not contracts of indemnity. These policies typically cover commercial watercraft, antiques, paintings, and other objects whose value can be difficult to determine. The valuation provision in such policies uses the **agreed value method**. If a total loss occurs, the insurer will pay the agreed value specified in the policy. Partial losses are paid based on actual cash value, repair cost, replacement cost, or whatever other valuation method the policy specifies. Although the agreed value method is not a specific formula as are some of the other valuation methods, it is nonetheless useful when it would otherwise be difficult to calculate a precise value. The agreed value method does not stipulate what the agreed value has to be relative to the true value of the property. The only stipulation is that both parties have to agree to the value in the policy.

The agreed value method should not be confused with the agreed value optional coverage, which is an arrangement for suspending the coinsurance clause in commercial property insurance coverages such as the Building and Personal Property Coverage Form or the Business Income Coverage Form.

Functional Valuation Method

Functional valuation method
A valuation method in which the insurer is required to pay no more than the cost to repair or replace the damaged or destroyed property with property that is its functional equivalent.

The **functional valuation method** is sometimes used when replacing buildings or personal property with property of like kind and quality is not practical and when the ACV method does not match insurance needs.

For example, suppose an organization that has been using a former schoolhouse as an office suffered a fire that destroyed the building. The functional valuation method would value the building at the cost to rebuild an office, not a schoolhouse. In the functional valuation method, the insurer is required to pay no more than the cost to repair or to replace the damaged or destroyed property with property that is its functional equivalent. This method is available by an endorsement to a commercial property policy. It is also used for residential buildings covered by the ISO Homeowners Modified Coverage Form, sometimes called Form HO-8.

When applied to personal property, the functional valuation method requires the insurer to pay no more than the cost to replace with equivalent but less expensive property. This method is commonly used with electronics and computers—for example, when new computers may be more functional but less expensive than the models that have to be replaced. The insurer might also pay the actual repair cost or the applicable policy limit, if either is less than the cost of functionally equivalent property.

When applied to real property, the functional valuation method permits the insurer to use common construction methods and materials. For example, a three-coat plaster wall might be replaced with wallboard, restoring its function but not using the same material.

VALUATION OF LIABILITY CLAIMS

A crucially important issue in post-loss analysis of liability insurance policies is the valuation of covered claims.

Unlike property insurance policies, liability insurance policies (or the liability coverage provisions within a multiline policy) usually do not specify how the amount of a covered claim is determined. Under most circumstances, the maximum amount the insurer pays is the lesser of two amounts:

• The compensable amount of the claim
• The applicable policy limit(s)

Compensable Amount of the Claim

The compensable amount of the claim depends mainly on the variables involved in how the claim is settled and the extent of **damages** ultimately awarded to the claimant.

Damages
Money claimed by, or a monetary award to, a party who has suffered bodily injury or property damage for which another party is legally responsible.

Settlement of the Claim

Most liability claims do not go to a formal trial, and the compensable amount of the claim is determined by negotiations between the liability insurer (or its attorney) and the claimant (or the claimant's attorney). During these negotiations, the parties try to anticipate what a court or jury would do if presented with the same facts. Both parties have an incentive to reach an out-of-court settlement because of the uncertainty, time, and expense involved in a formal trial.

Most liability insurance policies give the insured/defendant no right to prohibit the insurer and the claimant from reaching a settlement within policy limits. Often, an insured wants its insurer to mount a vigorous defense and vindicate the insured. However, the insurer's goal is usually to minimize its total costs for defense or damages. Sometimes the insurer pays a claim that might successfully have been defended because defending the claim would cost more than paying damages. In other cases, the insurer does not want to risk losing a lawsuit that would set a dangerous precedent for other, similar claims.

If a settlement cannot be reached by the parties involved, the liability claim will go to trial, and the extent of the insured's liability to the claimant is then based on legal principles. The compensable amount of the claim is the amount the jurors decide to award to the plaintiff as damages. Subject to policy conditions and limits, the insurer pays that amount on the insured's behalf. In some situations, the judge exercises the power to reduce or set aside an award or reduce or overturn an award on appeal. This may be done if the judge believes the jury award was excessive or not based on legal principles. Although policy limits restrict the insurer's liability, neither the jury nor the judge is bound to confine an award to policy limits. If the court awards a judgment that exceeds policy limits, the insured/defendant is responsible for paying the excess award.

For claims exceeding policy limits, the insured has a right to legal counsel, usually at the insured's expense, to protect the insured's interests. Otherwise, the liability insurer usually has control over defense costs and the amount it wants to offer as a settlement.

Extent of Damages

When the insured is liable for damages, the key issue affecting the valuation of a liability claim is the amount of monetary compensation that will reasonably indemnify the party who incurred the loss. Although a judge or jury may ultimately determine this amount, the insurer, the insured, and the claimant try to estimate this amount during any settlement negotiations.

The United States common-law system requires the amount of damages awarded to compensate the claimant for loss incurred as of the trial date. This presents a problem if not all damage has been repaired by the trial date or settlement date. In some cases, such as those involving permanent disability, damages must be partly based on an estimate of future expenses.

The claimant usually has the burden of proof regarding bodily injury and property damage. The claimant must establish what losses were proximately caused by the insured. However, even though the insured caused the loss, the claimant has a duty to mitigate loss. Consequently, the claimant may not recover for damages that result from the claimant's lack of care after the accident.

When property is damaged, the owner may recover the reasonable cost to repair the property or to replace it if it cannot economically be repaired. When property must be replaced, the owner is entitled to its reasonable market value before damage or destruction. Generally, the owner may also recover damages to compensate for the loss of use of the property for a reasonable period. For example, a claimant could recover the cost of renting a substitute car while a damaged car is being repaired.

Under certain circumstances, a claimant may also recover for profits lost from the inability to use the damaged or destroyed property. For example, the owner of a damaged truck or tractor-trailer might lose revenue while the vehicle is being repaired, especially if the owner cannot rent a substitute vehicle. Similarly, the owner of a damaged building might lose rent from tenants or sales from customers while a building is out of use. A few jurisdictions also permit third-party damages for the reduction in value of property that has been damaged and repaired.

Unlike property damage claims, evaluation of bodily injury claims considers a much broader range of damage elements for the claimant, such as these:

- Reasonable and necessary medical expenses incurred and those expected to be incurred in the future
- Type of bodily injury
- Wage loss or loss of earning capacity because of the bodily injury
- Other out-of-pocket expenses, such as household assistance
- Current and future pain and suffering resulting from the bodily injury
- Extent and permanency of disability and impairment
- Disfigurement resulting from the bodily injury
- Preexisting conditions that could have contributed to the bodily injury

When bodily injury results in a claimant's death, the claim is generally categorized as either a survival action (how much would have been recovered if the claimant had lived) or a wrongful death action (monetary loss to the survivors). The category into which the claim falls affects its valuation.

Policy Limits

The insurer's payment of the claimant's compensable damages for which the insured is liable is capped by the policy's applicable limit(s).

A liability policy (or the liability provisions within a multiline policy) may be subject to only one policy limit or to several. For example, the only limit applicable to liability coverage in many commercial auto policies is a dollar amount, such as $1 million, which is the most the insurer will pay for all damages because of bodily injury or property damage in any one auto accident. In contrast, commercial general liability (CGL) policies typically contain multiple policy limits, such as those shown in the exhibit. See the exhibit "Examples of Multiple Policy Limits in a CGL Policy."

Examples of Multiple Policy Limits in a CGL Policy

EACH OCCURRENCE LIMIT	$1,000,000	
DAMAGE TO PREMISES		
RENTED TO YOU LIMIT	$ 100,000	Any one premises
MEDICAL EXPENSE LIMIT	$ 5,000	Any one person
PERSONAL & ADVERTISING INJURY LIMIT	$1,000,000	Any one person or organization
GENERAL AGGREGATE LIMIT		$2,000,000
PRODUCTS/COMPLETED OPERATIONS AGGREGATE LIMIT		$2,000,000

When a liability policy contains multiple limits, the maximum amount payable for a covered claim depends on a complete analysis of the interactions among the various limits. For example, a covered CGL claim for $600,000 in damages may be within the $1 million each occurrence limit, but if prior claims paid during the same policy period have reduced the applicable aggregate limit (the most the insurer will pay during the policy period) to $200,000, the insurer's payment will not exceed $200,000. If the same claim is subject to the policy's $100,000 Damage to Premises Rented to You limit, then the insurer's payment will not exceed $100,000.

In addition to covering the claimant's damages, insurers also agree to pay defense costs and various supplementary payments, such as the cost of surety bonds required in connection with claims, court costs taxed against the insured, and interest on judgments. In many common policies (such as homeowners policies, personal and commercial auto policies, businessowners policies, and CGL policies), defense costs and supplementary payments typically do not reduce the policy limits. However, once the insurer has paid out the applicable limit(s) for a claim, the insurer's duty to defend and pay supplementary payments ends.

In other policies (such as directors and officers liability policies, pollution liability policies, and other specialty liability policies), the insurer's payments for defense costs and supplementary payments are typically applied to reduce the policy limits. In such policies, defense costs can consume a significant part of the applicable limit(s).For example, if an insured with a $1 million policy limit were held liable for a $950,000 judgment and defense costs were $100,000, the insurer would pay only $900,000 of the judgment after having paid the defense costs. If instead the insured had a liability policy that covered defense costs in addition to the limit, the insurer would pay both the $100,000 in defense costs and the $950,000 judgment in full.

REASONS FOR PROPERTY INSURANCE DEDUCTIBLES

Deductibles are a risk financing technique that requires the insured to retain a portion of the loss that is being transferred to an insurer. Knowing how deductibles in property insurance can benefit insureds assists insurance and risk management professionals in selecting or recommending deductibles.

By requiring the insured to retain some part of each loss covered by property insurance, deductibles reduce the premium cost to the insured through these effects:

- Encourage risk control by the insured
- Eliminate the need for the insurer to process small losses, thereby reducing the insurer's loss costs and loss adjustment expenses

Encourage Risk Control

Having some of the insured's own funds at stake theoretically gives the insured the risk control incentive to prevent or reduce losses. A deductible serves this purpose most effectively when it is large enough to have a noticeable financial effect on the insured. Deductibles that are too small do not offer enough financial incentive, and deductibles that are too large defeat the purpose of transferring the loss exposure to the insurer.

Deductibles are not particularly effective when used with large property exposures, especially those that are not likely to incur a partial loss. For example, consider the costs involved in launching a satellite. With hundreds of millions of dollars at stake, even a $100,000 deductible on satellite launch insurance would neither encourage additional risk control nor substantially reduce the insurer's costs.

Reduce Insurer's Costs

A typical property deductible eliminates the insurer's involvement in low-value losses. It is not cost-efficient for an insurer to deal with low-value losses because the insurer's loss adjustment expenses often exceed the amount of indemnity payable to the insured.

The expensive and inefficient process of insuring small claims is sometimes called **dollar trading** (or trading dollars).

Dollar trading

An insurance premium and loss exchange in which the insured pays the insurer premiums for low value losses, and the insurer pays the same dollars back to the insured, after subtracting expenses.

Risk transfer mechanisms in general—and insurance in particular—are not designed to cope with these types of low-severity losses. Sizable property insurance deductibles help to eliminate dollar trading. The insured retains small losses as normal, out-of-pocket expenses and uses insurance to protect against major, unpredictable losses. Deductibles are most effective in reducing insurers' expenses for coverages such as auto collision, in which small, partial losses are common.

Deductibles reduce the premiums insurers must charge and ultimately benefit the insured because they (1) reduce insurers' overall loss costs and loss adjustment expenses, (2) provide insureds with risk control incentives, and (3) reduce the morale and moral hazard incentives. For most property insurance policies, insureds can choose from a variety of deductible levels. In making this choice, the insured must balance the benefits of the premium reduction with the need for insurance protection for large losses.

For most property insurance policies, the premium reduction is not directly proportional to the size of the deductible. Because small losses are more frequent than large losses, the premium reduction is on a sliding scale—that is, the premium credit increases much more slowly than the size of the deductible, as illustrated in the exhibit. See the exhibit "Hypothetical Premium Credits for Various Deductibles."

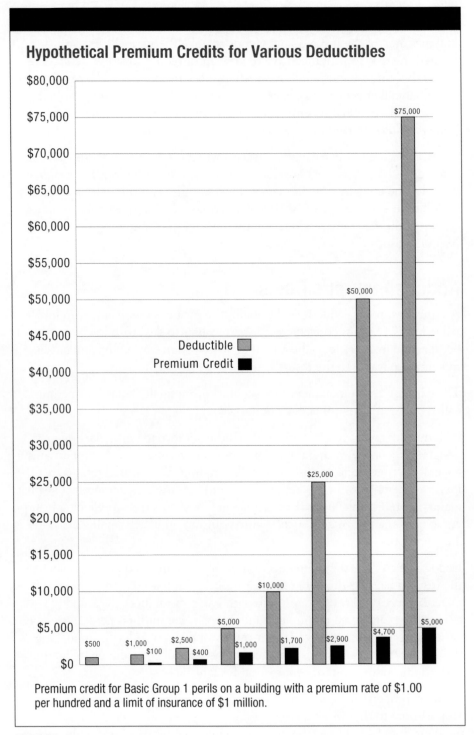

Hypothetical Premium Credits for Various Deductibles

Premium credit for Basic Group 1 perils on a building with a premium rate of $1.00 per hundred and a limit of insurance of $1 million.

[DA03248]

As shown in the exhibit, shifting from a $500 deductible to a $2,500 deductible reduces the policy premium by $400 while increasing retained loss exposures by $2,000. The premium reduction for shifting from a $50,000 deductible to a $75,000 deductible is only $300, and retained losses are increased by $25,000. Given these figures, shifting from a $500 deductible to a $2,500 deductible would be attractive in many cases.

However, shifting from a $50,000 deductible to a $75,000 deductible is not as attractive. Even if the pricing is actuarially sound and the organization could absorb the extra $25,000 loss, few organizations would choose to retain an extra $25,000 in property losses to save $300 in premium unless other factors were involved, such as the insurer offering much broader coverage when the high deductible applies.

When premium costs are considered, premium credits tend to encourage the use of medium-sized deductibles that eliminate dollar trading for small losses but that provide a reliable source of recovery for large losses. What constitutes "medium-sized" varies substantially among both families and organizations that purchase property insurance.

LIABILITY DEDUCTIBLES AND SELF-INSURED RETENTIONS

Knowing when and why a deductible or a self-insured retention (SIR) is appropriate for a particular liability policy helps insurance and risk management professionals to arrange coverage competently.

Although deductibles are commonly used with most types of property insurance policies, deductibles are seldom used for some types of liability insurance but are commonly used for other types. In some cases, a **self-insured retention (SIR)** is used instead of a deductible in liability policies.

Self-insured retention (SIR)
A dollar amount specified in an insurance policy that the insured must pay before the insurer will make any payment for a claim.

Reasons for Limited Use

Insurers have multiple reasons for restricting the use of deductibles in liability policies.

If a liability insurance policy has a deductible, the insured may not report seemingly minor incidents until the situation has escalated. However, because insurers want to control liability claims from the outset, they want to be involved in even small liability claims. Liability claim investigation involves determining not only the nature and extent of damages, but also who is legally responsible for paying those damages.

In addition, for most liability insurance policies, deductibles would not noticeably reduce premiums. One reason for this is that relatively few liability claims involve small amounts. Although most property losses are small enough for the insurer to avoid them by using a moderate deductible, liability losses tend to be larger. More important, as mentioned, the liability insurer wants to be involved in all claims, including small ones. Even with a deductible, the liability insurer usually pays all costs without contribution from the insured, for investigation and defense coverage, just as it does for policies without deductibles. Usually the deductible applies only to the damages paid to the claimant, not to defense costs.

With property insurance, the insurer simply subtracts the deductible from the covered loss amount to determine the amount payable to the insured. However, in liability insurance, the insurer must recover the deductible from the insured. The insurer usually must pay the third-party claimant the agreed-upon settlement in full, without reduction for any deductible. The insurer then has the right to recover the amount of the deductible from the insured. Sometimes, the insured may be financially unable or unwilling to pay the deductible. So, the insurer may ultimately have to bear the deductible cost.

Consequently, insurers are selective in choosing the insureds for which they will consider a liability deductible because the deductible, while providing a premium discount to the insured, can present problems for the insurer.

Deductibles are not usually included in commercial general liability, personal liability, or auto liability policies. However, significant deductibles are common with some specialty liability policies, such as those covering professional liability or directors and officers liability. By involving the insured in each loss, these deductibles are used primarily to encourage risk control. Deductibles are also common in bailee legal liability coverages, such as those for warehouses and auto service businesses. These coverages protect the insured against loss to a specified category of property, and the deductibles function similarly to those used with property insurance.

Self-Insured Retentions

Some liability insurance policies include an SIR. The differences between a deductible and an SIR are these:

- With a liability insurance deductible, the insurer defends on a first-dollar basis, pays all covered losses, and then bills the insured for the amount of losses up to the deductible.

- With an SIR, the insurer pays only losses that exceed the SIR amount. The insurer does not defend claims below the SIR amount. Consequently, the organization is responsible for adjusting and paying its own losses up to the SIR amount.

- With an SIR, the full policy limit is payable on top of the SIR, while a liability policy deductible may reduce the policy limit. (Individual policies can vary on this point of comparison.)

To compensate for the insurer's lack of control over self-insured claims, a policy with an SIR usually requires strict reporting to the insurer of any claims that have the potential of exceeding the SIR amount.

SIRs are common in professional liability insurance policies and some other specialty policies. SIRs are also commonly found in the "drop-down" coverage of umbrella liability policies. The drop-down coverage of an umbrella policy provides primary coverage, subject to the SIR, on claims that are not covered by an underlying primary insurance policy and not excluded by the umbrella policy.

OTHER SOURCES OF RECOVERY

In many cases, an insured will have one or more other sources of recovery for a loss covered by the insured's policy. In post-loss coverage analysis, insurance and risk management professionals seek to ascertain all other sources of recovery so that the appropriate policy provisions can be applied.

Additional sources of recovery may violate the principle of indemnity because the insured could be indemnified more than once for the amount of loss. Various insurance policy provisions, such as other-insurance provisions and subrogation provisions, have been developed to manage situations in which multiple recoveries may be possible. Before applying these policy provisions, one must identify the other sources of recovery, which can include these:

- Noninsurance agreements
- Negligent third parties
- Other insurance in the same policy
- Other insurance in a similar policy
- Other insurance in dissimilar policies

Noninsurance Agreements

Individuals and organizations often have a contractually enforceable source of recovery that does not involve insurance. Examples of noninsurance agreements that may overlap with insurance coverage of the loss include these:

- A lease agreement might make a tenant responsible for damage to leased property that is also covered by insurance.

- A credit card protection plan might protect the cardholder against claims for damage to a rented car, partially duplicating auto physical damage coverage in the renter's personal auto policy.

- A credit card protection plan might protect property purchased with the card against theft or accidental damage. The same property could be covered under a homeowners policy.

- An extended auto warranty, home warranty, appliance service agreement, or other plan can provide a contractually enforceable source of recovery that may overlap with an auto or a homeowners policy, depending on the cause of loss.

Although credit card benefits are often underwritten by an insurer, the benefit itself is provided through a contract between the credit card company and the cardholder. The cardholder is contractually entitled to the benefits promised by the credit card company, which often duplicate insurance benefits. Even if the property is also insured, a cardholder might find it desirable to claim benefits from the credit card company. Unlike property insurance, the credit card benefit generally is on a first-dollar basis with no deductible.

To respond to the overlap in coverage provided by noninsurance agreements, many homeowners policies include a provision addressing noninsurance (service) agreements. This provision indicates that the coverage provided by the homeowners policy is excess over any recovery that the insured may be able to get from a service agreement provider.

Negligent Third Parties

As a matter of law, a party who is injured or whose property is damaged by a negligent third party generally has a right to recover damages from the third party—regardless of whether the third party has liability insurance. The recovery from a third party (or the third party's liability insurance) could overlap with any first-party property insurance coverage (the insured's own property insurance policy). Most first-party insurance policies have policy provisions that address these situations. Although two types of policies might be involved (the third party's liability insurer and the insured's property insurer), the relevant policy language is captioned "subrogation" rather than "other insurance."

For example, Tara and David are both drivers in a state that does not have no-fault insurance (the example may not apply in no-fault states). Tara's car is struck and damaged by David, a negligent driver. David has liability insurance; that is, an insurer has agreed to pay liability claims on his behalf. Tara has a right under tort law to seek recovery from David, who will file a claim with his insurer. Tara also has a contractual right to recover under her own insurer's collision coverage. Tara's first-party right of recovery from her insurer does not reduce or eliminate David's obligation to pay damages to Tara. Nor can Tara's insurer deny her claim because David has liability insurance.

Regardless of whether a careless driver like David has liability insurance, his legal obligation to pay damages does not affect the contractual obligations of the insurer providing first-party property coverage—unless the insurance contract specifies otherwise. David is legally obligated, and Tara's insurer is contractually obligated, to pay for the damage to her car. However, that does not mean Tara will recover twice the amount of loss she incurred. According to the subrogation provision in Tara's personal auto policy, if she recovers from her own insurer, that insurer can attempt to recover from David or his insurer. If David's insurer pays Tara directly, she is required to reimburse her insurer.

Other Insurance in the Same Policy

A third other source of recovery is other insurance in the same policy. Property and/or liability insurance policies may provide two or more coverages under the same policy. When these package policies are used, a given loss may be covered by more than one of the coverages offered. Therefore, an insurance professional needs to analyze the policy to determine whether it contains a policy provision that limits the number of coverages that apply.

These are examples of losses for which insurance is provided by more than one coverage:

- A scheduled personal property endorsement attached to a homeowners policy provides coverage for scheduled (specifically listed) items, many of which are also covered under the unscheduled personal property coverage of the homeowners policy.

- Personal property used to maintain or service a building—such as fire extinguishing equipment, outdoor furniture, or refrigerators—is specifically covered under the building coverage of many commercial property insurance forms. The same items may also qualify for coverage as personal property under another insuring agreement of the same form.

- A passenger injured while riding in a car may have medical payments coverage for medical expenses regardless of who was at fault. The passenger may also bring a bodily injury liability claim against the driver of the car (if the driver was partly at fault for the accident) and may have a right of action against any other drivers involved. Coverage might apply under the liability, medical payments, and uninsured motorists coverages of the car owner's personal auto policy, depending on the facts of the case.

Because the insured's loss is covered, it might not seem important to know which coverage applies. However, although each of these examples may appear to involve a distinction that does not have a material effect on the claim, the distinction may be material to the amounts payable. Consequently, it is important to be aware of the applicability of more than one coverage in an insurance policy and to be able to determine which coverage applies in a given situation.

If the multiple coverages involved have different valuation provisions or deductibles, the insured may be able to recover more by filing under one coverage instead of another. The second example shows that under certain commercial property insurance policies, personal property used to maintain the building may be considered part of the building as well as personal property. For example, if the insured suffers a fire that destroys a storage shed and all the landscaping equipment that was stored in it, the insured may claim the equipment as a personal property loss or a building loss. If the building is insured on a replacement cost basis and personal property is insured on an actual cash value basis, the insured may be better off claiming the loss as a building loss.

Alternatively, the insured may have the option of combining (stacking) the limits of coverage of all the coverages that apply. That is, the insured can combine the various limits to cover losses that are larger than any one individual limit.

To illustrate, suppose Rick and Ann have two cars insured under their personal auto policy, and each vehicle has $50,000 in uninsured motorists coverage. Rick suffers a $75,000 loss resulting from bodily injury caused by an auto accident with an uninsured motorist. Based on the statutory regulations of the state in which they live, if the uninsured motorists limits are stackable, Rick and Ann have a total of $100,000 in uninsured motorists coverage that will pay for the entire $75,000 in bodily injury losses.

Other Insurance in a Similar Policy

A fourth other source of recovery is other insurance in a similar policy. In some cases, coverage overlaps because the same party is protected by two or more policies usually issued by different insurers.

For example, suppose Fred moves to a new home and buys a homeowners policy to cover it, but does not cancel the homeowners policy on his old home, which is still for sale. Both policies simultaneously cover some of Fred's loss exposures, such as personal property at other locations. Other-insurance situations like this usually involve more than one insurer as well as more than one policy. The question is therefore not simply which coverage applies to a loss, but which insurer will pay and how much. These situations are often resolved with each insurer sharing some portion of the loss, in accordance with the policies' other-insurance provisions.

Other Insurance in Dissimilar Policies

A fifth other source of recovery that affects amounts payable in liability insurance is other insurance in dissimilar policies. A loss is sometimes covered by more than one type of insurance, often from two or more insurers. Some examples of losses that may be covered by dissimilar policies include these:

- Bill owns a utility trailer. Under some circumstances, liability claims involving the trailer might be covered by both Bill's homeowners policy and his personal auto policy.
- A restaurant offers valet parking on its premises. The valet parking activity might be covered under both the restaurant's commercial general liability policy and its commercial auto policy.
- Janice is injured in an auto accident while performing work-related activities. Janice may be able to recover under her personal auto insurance, her individual or group medical expense or disability insurance, or her employer's workers compensation insurance.

Dissimilar insurance policies do not necessarily include provisions that clearly coordinate coverage with other types of policies. Because of the typical lack of provisions governing coordination of coverage for dissimilar policies, these types of overlaps in coverage are often the most difficult to resolve. In some cases, the relationship between policies when more than one policy is in place is governed by the policies' other-insurance provisions.

SUMMARY

Legal bases for insurable interest include an ownership interest, contractual obligations, exposure to legal liability, factual expectancy, and representation of another party. In some situations, multiple parties can have an insurable interest in the same property. In joint tenancy, tenancy by the entirety, and tenancy in partnership, all owners have survivorship rights. In tenancy in common, when an owner dies, that owner's share passes to his or her heirs.

Insuring to value benefits insurers because it ensures that premiums are adequate to cover potential losses and it simplifies underwriting. The insured benefits by having sufficient coverage in the event of a loss. Insurers use coinsurance clauses and other insurance-to-value provisions to encourage insureds to purchase adequate coverage limits. Determining and maintaining insurance to value may involve having a qualified appraiser value the property, revising policy limits periodically, and exploring coverage options such as the agreed value optional coverage.

Insurance policies that provide property coverage use various methods for valuing covered property. The two most common property valuation methods are actual cash value and replacement cost. Examples of other valuation methods include agreed value and functional valuation.

The valuation of liability claims is based on the amount of damages for which the insured is legally liable, not to exceed the applicable limit(s) in the policy. Liability claims can also include defense costs and other supplementary payments, which, depending on the particular policy, may be payable in addition to limits or included within limits.

Reasonable deductibles can reduce property insurance premiums by encouraging the insured to practice risk control and by reducing insurer costs.

When arranging liability coverage, an insurance or a risk management professional needs to know when and why deductibles and SIRs are appropriate and how an SIR differs from a deductible.

Five other sources of recovery that can affect amounts payable under an insurance policy are noninsurance agreements, negligent third parties, other insurance in the same policy, other insurance in a similar policy, and other insurance in dissimilar policies. After other sources of recovery have been identified, the insured's policy or policies can be reviewed to find any provisions addressing the other sources.

ASSIGNMENT NOTE

1. Copyrighted material of Insurance Services Office, Inc., with its permission.
    Copyright, ISO Properties, 2007.

Index

Page numbers in boldface refer to pages where the word or phrase is defined.